Achieving Total
Quality Management

Achieving Total
Quality Management
A Program for Action

MICHEL PÉRIGORD

Publisher's Message by
Norman Bodek
President, Productivity, Inc.

Productivity Press
Cambridge, Massachusetts and Norwalk, Connecticut

Originally published as *Réussir la Qualité Totale* by Les Éditions d'Organisation, Paris, France. © 1987.

Productivity Press, Inc.
P.O. Box 3007
Cambridge, MA 02140
(617) 497-5146

Cover design: Hannus Design Associates
Typeset by Rudra Press, Cambridge, MA
Printed and bound by Maple-Vail Book Manufacturing Group
Printed in the United States of America

Library of Congress Cataloging-in-Publication Data

Périgord, Michel.
   [Réussir la qualite total. English.]
   Achieving total quality management : a program for action / Michel Perigord.
      p.   cm.
   Translation of: Réussir la qualite total.
   Includes bibliographical references and index.
   ISBN 0-915299-60-7 (alk. paper)
   1. Production management — Quality control.   I. Title.
TS156.P38413 1990   90-48163
658.5'62—dc20   CIP

92 93 10 9 8 7 6 5 4 3 2

Contents

Contents   vii

Publisher's Foreword

Quality control methods were never meant to be seen as tools alone. The Japanese, for example, when they first began to implement quality tools, recognized the strategic company-wide implications of their use. When they embraced Deming and Drucker's ideas they did so totally — throughout their organizations and as the basis for all strategic decision-making. In Western companies, however, we have often misunderstood the company-wide implications of total quality control tools. We have seen the tools being applied in one area of a company, on the factory line for example, but not supported in accounting procedures or in upper management policy.

Consequently, Productivity Press has sought to provide our readers with books on the applications of quality control tools and methods in all departments of an organization. We also recognize the need for upper managers to understand how to put all of these applications together. Total quality management (TQM) refers to the all-important methods related to managing a company-wide strategy based on the principles as well as the tools of quality improvement.

Achieving Total Quality Management: A Program for Action, by Michel Périgord, pulls the quality message together. It is by a Western manager for Western managers and includes cases and implementation details to help a company reap the full range of benefits of a quality strategy. In the current highly competitive global environment it hardly seems possible to consider doing business without such a strategy.

Of particular value in Périgord's approach are the clear and detailed explanations of the quality/price ratio (Part 1) and cost of quality (COQ) issues (Part 3). Périgord also describes the tools and methods of designing quality into products at the development stage, discussing value analysis and quality function deployment (QFD) among other approaches (Part 3). Part 2 melds the two important wings of a total quality approach: increasing productivity and enhancing employee involvement. The philosophy that brings these two ideas together is at the heart of TQM, and Perigord provides us with some insights into why it works. The cases and implementation strategies in Part 4 offer valuable descriptions of how to make TQM happen in Western companies.

We are happy to be able to offer our readers this comprehensive guide to TQM and are grateful to Michel Périgord and his publishers, Les Editions d'Organisations, for the opportunity to translate this book from the French. Our thanks go also to Joseph P. Manley (Cambridge, Massachusetts) for his translation; to Diane Asay and Marie Cantlon for their editorial input; to David Lennon for production management; to Gayle Joyce, Susan Cobb and Jane Donovan at Rudra press for composition and interior design; and to Dick Hannus for the cover design.

Norman Bodek
President

Preface

Today there are at least seven good reasons to wake up and move toward total quality management (TQM); it is important to review these as a prologue to this important book by Michel Périgord.

The first reason, which by itself transforms TQM from a possible option to an inevitable and absolute necessity, is the advent of an internationalized economy. The sudden invasion of new competitors on the world economic scene renders obsolete those companies that are not technologically innovative and those that are self-absorbed. It obliges all those that wish to survive to build their future efforts upon painstaking, attentive, and permanent monitoring of the market in order to achieve consistent improvement in the quality of their response to it.

The second reason that establishes the inevitability of TQM is the sudden inversion in industrialized countries of the ratio between demand – which is increasing at a slower rate than during the "thirty glorious years" (1945-75) – and supply, which has multiplied since the mid-1970s because of the economic explosion in Japan and the newly industrialized countries (NIC).

Now consumers and clients are faced with an excessive array of choices, and they have consequently become exacting, constantly demanding greater quality for ever-cheaper prices.

The third ineluctable reason, as Alvin Toffler has so aptly described, is the end of the trend toward mass production. With new production technologies, diversity is now becoming as inexpensive as uniformity. Moreover, those who manage these new production processes must be capable of exploiting all their advantages by becoming experts in "Just-In-Time" techniques and strict control of product flow, and by systematic monitoring of work-in-progress (WIP) inventory, useless padding, and excess fat in the company. Here too, TQM makes a difference.

The fourth reason is unexpected: we have changed. Although the rush into a job in the face of the growing menace of unemployment mobilizes one's energies, enthusiasm is considerably diminished if the job, once obtained, does not provide opportunities for self-actualization — if it is, in short, boring. At the very moment that business competition is becoming keener than ever, today's salaried employees tend to indicate that they become personally involved only if they as individuals can profit by the competitive process. In the absence of anything better, people allow themselves to be recruited for uninteresting jobs, yet they make no personal investment in their jobs; they assume low profiles. TQM offers an organizational response to this attitude, to prevent it from producing suicidal consequences.

The fifth reason for TQM is the inability of a company modeled on Taylor's principles to reduce the costs of quality deficiencies. Taylorist companies are organized into large, self-centered, functional areas that are concerned more with "doing more" than with "doing it better," more with checking and correcting than with anticipating. Overloaded with unnecessary costs, with their resources dedicated to "producing nothing," such companies quickly lose ground in business competition and condemn themselves to extinction. TQM represents their only path to health.

The sixth reason also applies to the Taylorist company, which had the luxury of tolerating intellectual stagnancy so long as the ratio between supply and demand was the inverse of what it is today. It is no longer possible to leave fallow the intelligence found at all levels and, in particular, that of blue and white-collar workers at the implementation level. The battle for quality is too arduous. TQM offers a method for mobilizing this intelligence.

The seventh reason is certainly the most convincing. Now that a program for TQM exists and has been adopted by several national economies, economies that do not make use of the concept will find themselves moving full speed in the opposite direction of competitiveness. What is true for economies is also true for companies. It is useful to recall the statistics reported by

Philip Crosby, who compared the cost of the quality deficiencies in Western economies (20 percent of sales volume) with that of the Japanese economy (12 percent of sales volume). Such a gap, if not quickly reduced, is a harbinger of inevitable defeats.

Michel Périgord's book takes these seven reasons as its point of departure for an urgent awakening. Pragmatic, intelligent, and practical, it shows us the path by which total quality, the only answer appropriate to the challenges of tomorrow, can be attained as promptly as possible. This is one book that must be read without delay by managers who wish their companies to remain in the running.

Dr. Georges Archier
President of AFCERQ
Member of the Academy of
Business Sciences

Hervé Serieyx
Chairman of EUREQUIP
Vice President of AFCERQ
Director of the Public Service
Innovation Project

Part 1

The Background

There is no prescription against the truth.

– P. Bayle
News of the Literary Republic

1
Historical Overview

Seducing history is allowed, provided you give her a child.

– A. Dumas

The history of quality is inseparable from the development of the companies that operate in the primary (raw materials), secondary (manufactured products), and tertiary (service firms) sectors. The secondary sector is considered to have been of great relative significance in the past as a result of its technical and technological developments, history, constraints, procedures, and processes.

In the early 1950s, quality was discussed primarily in terms of the characteristics of manufactured products. Among the great industrialized nations, at least two had to totally rebuild their economies: Germany and Japan. Each would develop a school of economic thought. But the German school, surrounded by the Western bloc, would in the 1960s be surpassed by the Japanese school, which was isolated in the Orient. The experiences of these two countries represent, in essence, the evolution of two strategies for the development of quality: one rather Western, the other totally Eastern. They appeared immediately after the birth of another method for viewing quality: value analysis (VA) in 1948. The following is an outline of the principal phases and major figures in these two approaches.

A Systematic Professional Approach to Quality

Around 1950, the United States, faced with safety and availability problems in aerospace and nuclear facilities and equipment, extended military standards (the famous "Military Standard" or "Mil.Std.") to the field of quality. The practical difficulty that it encountered was the recruitment of a large corps of testers and inspectors who had flawless training. Military standards had proven themselves during the Second World War. The important consideration was not only to preserve their strategic potential, but also to extend their field of application to the civilian sector. The latter had to be done, furthermore, in a manner consistent with the specific characteristics of contemporary national economic development, and, in fact, with the international development occasioned by the Marshall Plan signed by Harry Truman in April 1948. It was therefore important to ensure compliance with manufacturing procedures and to inspect parts, components, and subsystems intended for aerospace and nuclear equipment and facilities. Faced with this twofold problem of recruiting and training, the Americans initiated in 1952 a concept they called "quality assurance."

The principle is simple: instead of inspecting parts (to check their consistency with predetermined data so as to evaluate whether they meet established requirements), it is sufficient to ensure that the company that produces them is optimally organized. The postulate is the following: if a company's procedures (production and inspection methods) are well defined, if the systems for parts and documents are fully and explicitly detailed, and if a number of other conditions are met, then it is evident that if item number N meets specifications, so too will item number $N + P$.

Therefore, before actual production, and on the basis of an examination of written and verifiable documents, the client could have confidence in obtaining quality with item $N + P$ once he or she is satisfied with item N. Even better, this level of confidence is equally valid for items that are physically impossible to inspect. That is the quality assurance concept.

Among the leading theoreticians of the 1950s, A. V. Feigenbaum deserves mention. In 1951, he introduced the concept of total quality control (TQC). It was also he who revealed to industry the famous *ghost factory*, attempted to popularize the notion of the *cost of quality* (COQ), and perceived and described the need for a strong and well-structured operational entity with veto rights. This organization was to have total responsibility for managing quality. Departments assigned responsibility for product quality therefore sprang up in large numbers. Quality was seen, therefore, as the result of controlling not only products, but also procedures. Standards become indispensable.

At the beginning of the 1970s, the customer bought goods on the basis of the reputation of the supplier. The supplier was required to provide the customer with goods of appropriate quality that had been carefully inspected by the supplier itself, often in the absence of any legal or commercial obligation. Also during this period, with the Club of Rome, the expression *quality of life* appeared.

Quality: A Management Tool

In the Japan of 1950, at the initiative of vice-consul General Douglas MacArthur, the development of the trend toward quality changed form. The Japanese Union of Scientists and Engineers (JUSE) was founded in 1946. The United States wanted Japan, rather than brood over its defeat, to reconstruct itself by applying its military impetus to the economy and, in particular, to industry. JUSE employed the services of an eminent American specialist, Dr. W. E. Deming, who not only conveyed the quality message, but demonstrated the absolute need for the use of statistics, which was his specialty. He refused to have any audience that was below the rank of general manager. He made his "students" aware that statistics, rather than being the province of specialists, should be simple, basic, and stripped of formulas. To accomplish this, statistics must be used by everyone, from the CEO to the machine operator. He summed up his comments with a prediction: "You now produce cheap goods, but if you listen to me, you will see that, in less than 15 years, other nations will fight you with customs barriers." If only he had not said that!

It is appropriate to clarify that the use of statistical controls in industry, which began in the early 1930s, is due to Dr. W. A. Shewhart of the Bell Institute in the United States. In 1935, Great Britain adopted such controls at the initiative of K. Pearson.

In 1951 the famous Deming Prize was established to reward the organization in Japan that best implemented the principles Deming previously enunciated.

The year 1954 saw the arrival in Japan of Dr. J. M. Juran, the second great American specialist, who was also only interested in Japanese CEOs. He confirmed what W. E. Deming had stated but introduced another dimension: quality management is the concern of the entire company, including the personnel department. According to this management principle, *the human dimension should be omnipresent.* There is no product quality unless the processes are appropriate and personnel are comfortable with their work.

In 1956, the Japanese media, in view of the bad international reputation of their products, made quality a national slogan.

In 1957, the first quality control circles (QCC) appeared in Japan. Between 1951 and 1970, K. Ishikawa, an excellent student of the two American specialists, made it his mission to develop JUSE as a training organization for managers, engineers, higher-level technicians, and foremen. This association continued to pursue its purpose by reinstituting TQC, but in a manner different from that recommended by Feigenbaum. Beginning in the 1960s, this approach was termed companywide quality control (CWQC). In fact, the Japanese used the acronym TQC because, they said, "you Westerners understand what that means, but we are doing something completely different." CWQC (the control of quality throughout a company) involves not only the entire company, but also its clients, suppliers, subcontractors, subsidiaries, cooperating firms, and so on. It is a national undertaking.

The founding of the 10,000th quality control circle was celebrated in 1966, and the 100,000th in 1977, on the basis of those that had been officially counted.

In 1970, the quality control circle concept returned to the United States where, in 1974, the first circles were organized, often with differences that would be disastrous for them.

In France, the first quality control circles appeared in 1979, and nationwide introduction of them occurred in 1980.

The Association Française pour les Cercles et de la Qualité Totale, French Association of Quality Control Circles (AFCERQ) was founded in 1981 on the basis of initial plans that dated from mid-1980.

Summary

The foregoing is a rough description of two approaches: one focused on inspection and procedures, the other oriented toward total quality. The first is principally concerned with products, whereas the second involves the entire company and its environment. *Total quality* means that all participants in a company are involved regardless of their position in the hierarchy. All participants must share the same vision and the goal of consistent, ongoing improvement, and each must feel responsible for the entire product cycle, from initial design until the end of the product's service life.

Does this mean that the existence of two approaches was not recognized? No, the Japanese completely understood and integrated the first but were of the opinion that it was only a part of the second. This integration was accomplished to such a degree that, when Western managers crowded into airplanes to discover what was happening in that Asian nation that no longer produced cheap goods, at the outset they saw only quality control circles, which were simply the result of extensive quality training and implementation, particularly by managers. What tales have been told about differences in culture! That subject shall be addressed further on. In the course of this brief account, one great person should not be forgotten: Philip Crosby, who, after having studied Feigenbaum's ideas, attempted, in an American fashion, to integrate the messages of Deming and Juran. At the beginning of 1979, in his famous "Elevator Speech," he became known for a 14-phase program which he implemented at ITT, where he was the vice-president in charge of quality.

Figure 1-1 illustrates Feigenbaum's interpretation of TQC and quality assurance programs, which do not involve all the participants in a company and which focus on products.

By contrast, CWQC involves all the participants in a company, as well as the company's environment. A new acronym appears in Figure 1-1: CWQI (companywide quality improvement), which, with its final letter, refers to a permanent process for improvement. CWQI is oriented toward both the total market as well as all the individuals and firms associated with a company. It is interesting to note that the majority of companies are also part of the market itself, which is to say many colleagues and cooperating firms must also be privileged clients. CWQI assigns importance not only to monitoring markets, but also to cooperation with other companies. Quality is a national undertaking. The prospects for quality control circles can therefore only expand.

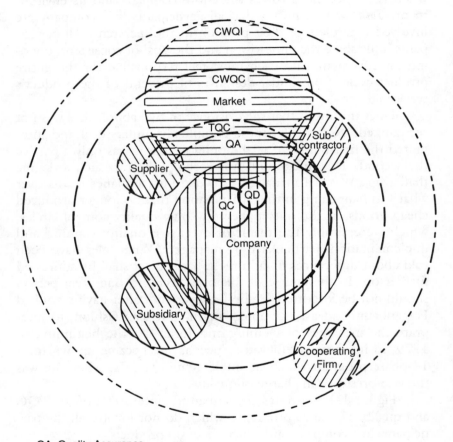

QA   Quality Assurance
QC   Quality Control
QD   Quality Department
TQC   Total Quality Control
CWQC   Companywide Quality Control
CWQI   Companywide Quality Improvement

Figure 1-1. A Company's "Quality" Territory

2
A Status Report

Quality is more important than quantity.

– Seneca

We are witnessing an acceleration in the technology for both manufactured goods and services as a result of scientific progress and transfers of technology. This has led to a considerable increase in complexity. Figure 2-1 illustrates this complexity, using the memory location as an example. A memory location is a transistor, which is not designed by humans. With machines, processes and procedures evolve exponentially.

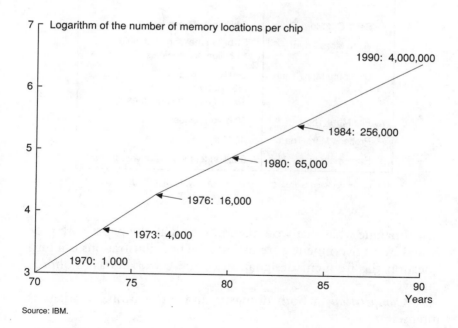

Source: IBM.

Figure 2-1. Complexity: Monolithic Memory

9

Another example of this complexity concerns paperwork (Table 2-1). This is illustrated by the fact that each worker in the tertiary sector of industry:

- Processes a stack of paper 3.20 meters in height each year
- Carries nearly 3 times his or her weight in paper each year
- Could paper the walls of a 4-5-room apartment 10 times a year

Table 2-1. Paperwork in Business Firms (1983)

Active Population	24 million
Tertiary	9 million, consisting of • 3,600,000 professionals • 2,700,000 secretaries • 2,700,000 clerical workers
Who	
Send Out More Than	5 billion business letters
Write More Than	51 billion messages of which 11 billion are originals
Distribute More Than	250 billion pages (33% internally), of which 15 billion are photocopies
File More Than	50 billion pages
Process More Than	400 billion pages
Participate In	5 billion telephone conversations

Sources: Institut Remy Genton (CPE bulletin no. 16, May, 1985)

Imagine what that would amount to if all the paperwork processed by a government were included! These illustrations call into question the frequent designation of these workers as "nonproductive."

Competition in both domestic and international markets is intense.

Tables 2-2 and 2-3 illustrate the following two observations. First: the highest penetration rate for manufactured goods pertains to the least complex goods – consumer goods. Second: although rapidly developing countries constitute a small portion of the entire picture, their total production, when added to that of Japan, indicates rapid progress that is significant in relation to European production.

Table 2-2. Rate of Penetration by Manufactured Goods in France

Share of French Market (%)	1970	1981	Change (%)
Semifinished Goods	25.8	34.0	+ 31
Major Household Appliances	28.5	46.4	+ 63
Professional Equipment	26.1	47.7	+ 83
Automobiles, Land Transportation	17.9	32.2	+ 80
Naval Construction, Aircraft, Armaments	15.7	31.0	+ 97
Consumer Goods	11.2	26.0	+ 134

Source: I.N.S.E.E

Table 2-3. Distribution of World Production (% GNP)

	1960	1981	% Change
World	100.0	100.0	
Europe	27.6	23.4	- 15
Japan	4.6	8.0	+ 74
Rapidly developing countries Brazil Mexico South Korea Singapore Hong Kong Taiwan	4.1	6.9	+ 68

Source: CEPI

Awareness of this global competition dates from March 1980, when the Hewlett-Packard Company reached the conclusions shown in Figure 2-2 after inspection of computer memories supplied by six manufacturers (three Japanese and three American). One would think that the Japanese had selected only their best components for testing. However, once the defects detected during initial inspection had been removed, the items supplied by the competitors were subjected to an operational testing, the results of which are shown in Figure 2-3. What a revelation!

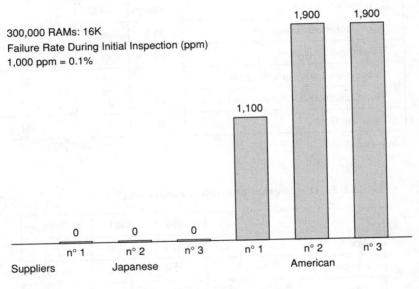

Figure 2-2. Measurement Results: Hewlett-Packard

On the *sociological* plane, Juran explained that, given the parallel relationship between knowledge *required by* the job and knowledge *acquired on* the job, all company employees must be trained each year so that they will be able to keep pace with increasing complexity (Figures 2-4 and 2-5).

In conclusion, it is appropriate to assign the proper value to Figure 2-6, which is well known, by replacing the term *Japan* with

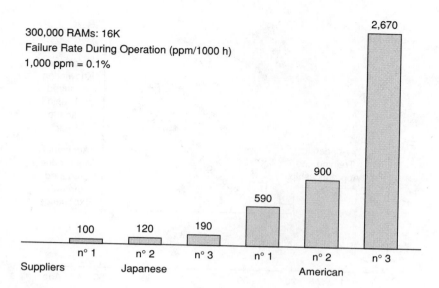

300,000 RAMs: 16K
Failure Rate During Operation (ppm/1000 h)
1,000 ppm = 0.1%

Figure 2-3. Measurement Results: Hewlett-Packard

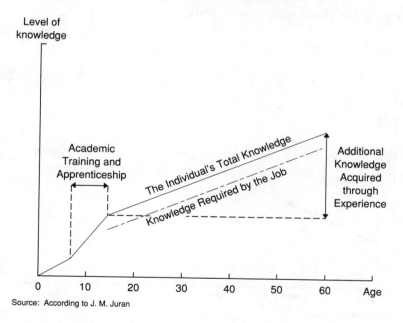

Source: According to J. M. Juran

Figure 2-4. Sociological Impact in the Past

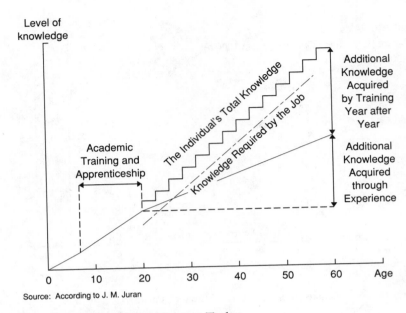

Figure 2-5. Sociological Impact Today

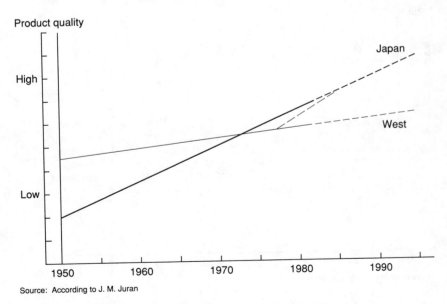

Figure 2-6. The West's Need for Improvement in Quality

Japan plus developing nations. It is imperative that the West revitalize itself by altering the slope of its product quality curve. As
Figure 2-7 makes evident, it is no longer possible to tolerate a system in which corrective action is taken after the fact. Improvement
in quality realized by means of a loss in market share may lead to
excellent product quality, but it also means the loss of customers
over time.

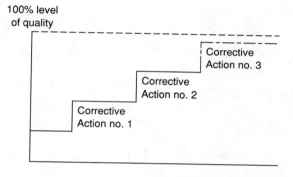

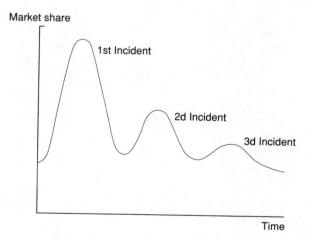

Figure 2-7. A Posteriori Corrective Action and Market Share

3
The Quality/Price Ratio

Price is soon forgotten, but quality endures.

– Commercial slogan

Terminology

The Product

The dictionary indicates that a *product* is a substance, an action, or a living thing that is the result of either a natural process or a human activity. A product may therefore be a fruit, vegetable, meat, fish, or tangible good. This definition differs significantly from that of a *service.*

For the purposes of this work, a service is considered as the personal decision to provide, and the act of providing, one of the following:

- Assistance (as a courtesy or favor)
- A benefit (free of charge)
- An action (for payment or other remuneration)

Thus, the term *service* denotes activities that have economic value but do not pertain to the production of goods. Therefore, the term *product* encompasses the term *service.* So that a tautology may be avoided, it is preferable to refer simply to *products*, rather than to *products and services.* A product may be succinctly defined as the result of a natural process or a human activity.

In such terms, an assembly, a system, a subsystem, a plan, an estimate, a telephone call, a statement, a receipt, an invoice, a word of advice, a greeting, a smile – all may be considered products.

The Market

The *market* is the interaction of supply and demand with respect to a given product. The market represents the volume of a given product that has been exchanged. This definition emphasizes that a company has a share of the market for a given product, whether it is a tangible good (an automobile) or an intangible good (leisure activities). The volume exchanged depends upon the parties participating in the exchange, that is, upon the companies and clients. These parties are influenced by the overall environment (Figure 3-1).

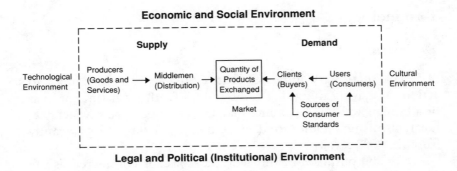

Figure 3-1. The Market: An Exchange Process

The environment is:

- Cultural
- Political and legal (institutional)
- Technological
- Economic and social

On the supply side, there are competitors and middlemen who market the products.

On the demand side, there are direct participants – the clients – and indirect participants – the users other than the clients themselves – and sources of consumer standards, who are the clients' advisers. (These include, for example, consumer groups, consulting engineers, technical centers, physicians, pharmacists, buyers, veterinarians, teachers, and school headmasters.)

The Client

In ancient Rome, a client was a plebeian (commoner) who placed himself under the protection of a patrician, who was called a "patron." By analogy, a client is someone who places himself under the protection of another person. Isn't that a wonderful idea?

Later in history, a client was someone who solicited services in exchange for remuneration. It was not until the 19th century that a client became (in economic terms) a purchaser, and subsequently, a consumer.

The User

The user is the person who actually uses a product. For example, a delivery person is the *user* of the vehicle purchased by his employer. The latter is a *client* of the manufacturer. In the case of a vehicle that is personally owned, the children riding in the back are users in terms of their safety, while the mechanic is a user in terms of his access to mechanical parts.

The user can therefore be described as the last link in a chain that includes the client, seller, manufacturer, designer, and suppliers.

The Company

In economic terms, a company is an organization providing goods or services of a commercial nature.

The Cost

The cost of a product is the total amount of the expenses incurred by the manufacturer in order to obtain the product and subsequently sell it to clients.

Etymologically, an enterprise is the act of taking, seizing, or attacking something as a whole. For an entrepreneur, it is also his commitment to undertake work, which often pertains to a given project under given circumstances.

The Price

Price is the ratio of the *value* of one good to the value of another; it is the *exchange* ratio between goods and money.

The Value

This term indicates the quality of a given item based on its objective or subjective usefulness (use value), the relationship between supply and demand (exchange value), and a product's particular properties and characteristics that make it attractive and desirable to own (perceived value).

Quality

See Table 3-1.

Table 3-1. Attribute of Quality

Quality: The Ability of a Product or Service to Meet Users' Needs
Users: individuals, companies, government agencies Needs: expressed or potential Ability = the sum of its attributes: Known in advance of purchase { Product or service features / Packaging, aesthetics / Performance / Market response Discovered after purchase or upon use but reflected in the brand name's image { Adherence to time frames / Reliability / Maintainability / Availability / Durability / Safety during use / Environmental safety / Total cost of ownership

Quality Assurance

See Table 3-2.

Quality Management

See Table 3-2.

Table 3-2. Quality Management and Quality Assurance

Quality Management

The portion of overall company management that is devoted to quality is a function of the company's quality policy and specifically includes:

- the setting of goals*
- organizational design and determination of methods
- personnel training and motivation
- implementation of methods and coordination of the various segments involved in implementation
- evaluation of results
- corrective action

* The setting of goals includes defining the technical parameters used in determining the total cost of ownership.

Quality Assurance

Implementation of an appropriate system of predetermined and systematic requirements designed to create confidence that the quality required shall be achieved.

- The creation of confidence is an objective and implies a motivational process that involves the various activities carried out both inside the company and inside the client's firm, both on the individual and the collective level.
- "Appropriate" means that the system of predetermined requirements is suitable for the intended purpose and use of the product or service.

A Survey of Standard Approaches

The Boston Consulting Group (BCG) asserts that, if the effects of inflation are eliminated by dividing costs by the price index (constant currency), added value costs decrease by approximately 20 to 30 percent each time that cumulative production (or experience) doubles. The interrelationship of costs and experience is clearly illustrated in Figure 3-2.

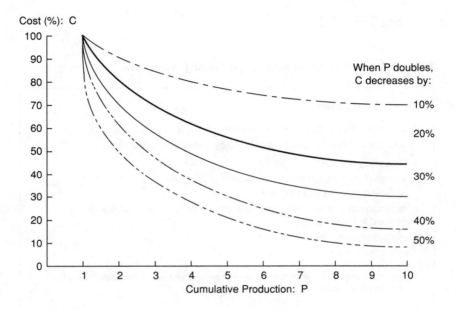

Figure 3-2. The Impact of Experience on Costs

Therefore:

- Costs are inversely related to market share and an increase in the latter should lead to lower prices.
- If the company grows at a more rapid rate than its competitors, its costs should improve in comparison to their costs.
- The choice between manufacturing and subcontracting should be guided by a comparison of the company's relative amount of experience, if it is a manufacturer, with that of the potential supplier.
- An estimate of market potential can be made by comparing the elasticity of demand with the rate of cost reduction.

BCG therefore rejects the price umbrella strategy in favor of a parallel relationship between prices and costs (Figure 3-3).

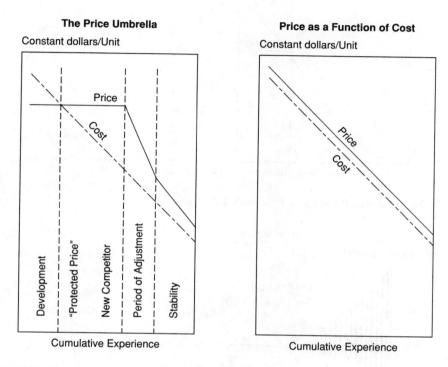

The Price Umbrella

Constant dollars/Unit

Price as a Function of Cost

Constant dollars/Unit

Figure 3-3. Two Possible Price Strategies

Figure 3-4a is a typical representation of the phases in a product's life cycle.

Figure 3-4b is an example from the photography industry, which survives and grows by regularly launching new products. The figure's purpose is to highlight the cost price and sales price of two products as a function of their relative age.

Figure 3-5 shows two well-known graphs. The graph on the left shows that if quality increases, the demand at the same price increases, as might be generally assumed. The one on the right shows that demand curves (*vn*) do not in fact follow quality/price ratios, which are represented by broken lines.

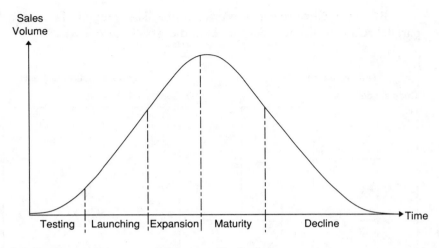

Figure 3-4a. Phases in a Product's Life Cycle

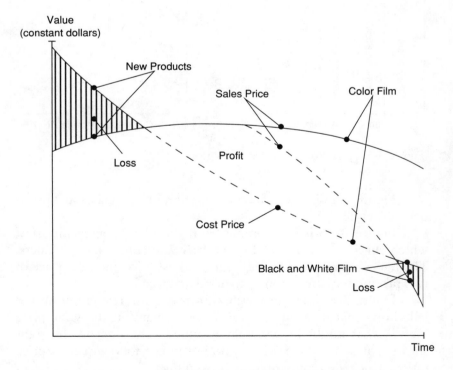

Figure 3-4b. Price and Life Cycle Length Using Film as an Example

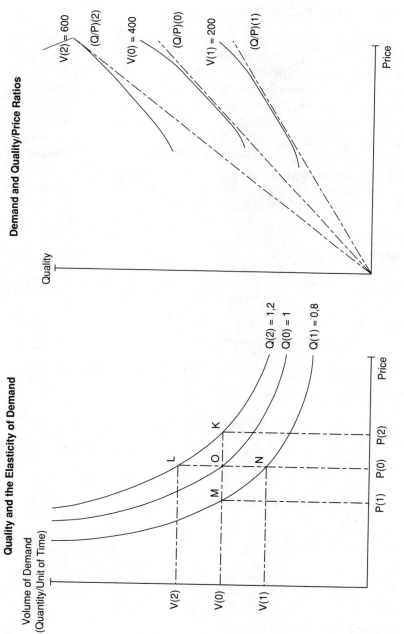

Figure 3-5. Demand, Quality, and Price Relationships

Acceptable Quality Level (AQL)

When there are a large number of products to be inspected (one lot out of a total population), statistics show that sampling is desirable. The procedures to be followed are called *sampling plans.* If all units in a population are inspected, the precise percentage of defects (p) is obtained and measurement efficiency is 100 percent. The curve is then a rectangle. If inspection follows a designated testing plan, the theoretical efficiency curve obtained is no longer a rectangle. This curve therefore indicates the probability of accepting a lot that contains a proportion of defective items, which is a function of what has been determined to be the average percentage of defective items (Figure 3-6).

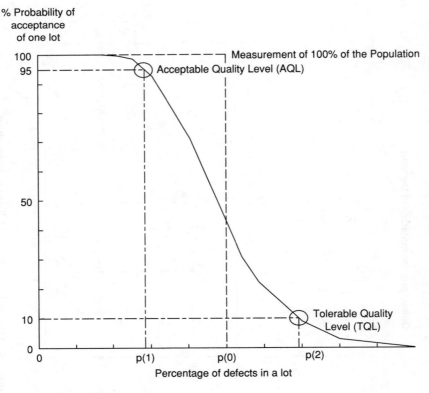

Figure 3-6. **Efficiency Curve**
(N,n = **Population size, sample;** p = **% of defects)**

The point marked $p(1)$ shows an *acceptable quality level* (AQL). Rejection of lots that have *acceptable* quality constitutes the *supplier's risk*, in that he may reject lots that are of *good* quality. This risk is generally set at 5 percent.

Point $p(2)$ indicates the probability of accepting lots of marginally acceptable quality. This is the client's risk, since the client might in this instance accept lots that should normally be rejected. This risk is often considered to be 10 percent and is termed the *tolerable quality level* (TQL). A 50 percent rate of efficiency, which is, one chance in two of being accepted, is called a *neutral percentage* $p(0)$.

Figure 3-7 indicates the average quality of the defective items in the lot, after the defective parts found in the samples have been replaced with parts of sound quality.

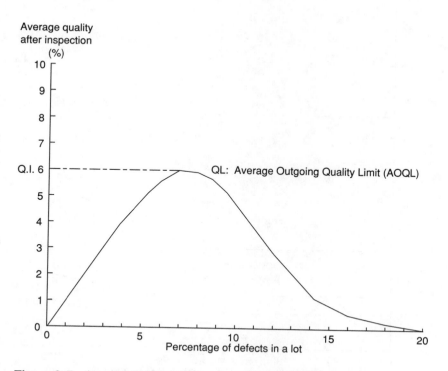

Figure 3-7. **Average Quality After Inspection and Screening of Rejected Lots**

This level of efficiency also applies to acceptance trials, which can be performed at the minimal cost by conceding that the lot contains defects. The average quality would be written into a contractual agreement between the client and the supplier – as would a specification of the testing system used.

A specific example is given in Figure 3-8, which indicates, for printed circuits on which integrated circuits (chips) have been mounted, the percentage of corrective repairs necessary as a function of the number of integrated circuits installed on each printed circuit.

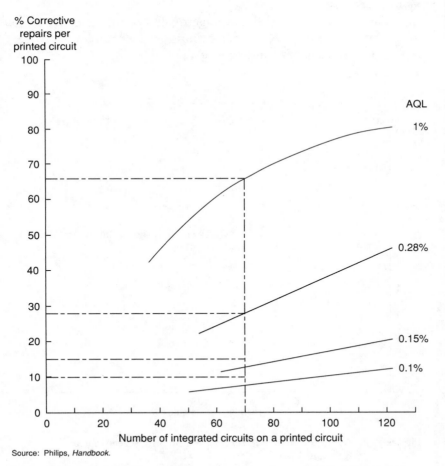

Source: Philips, *Handbook.*

Figure 3-8. The Impact on a Subsystem of Defects in Individual Units

Conclusion

More examples of standard economic theories could be given, but the important question is, *Who is the client?*

The Client in Terms of the Quality/Price Ratio

The discussion in this section, which is in no way an exhaustive exposition of the quality/price ratio, is influenced by the ideas of Claude Zarouk, of Cabinet Energy. Zarouk developed a method called OXEAMME, which is an analytical matrix, a tool. This term, which may sound strange, is derived from the following terms: *O* for objective, *X* for matrix, *E* for external environment, *A* for aptitudes, *M* for means, *M* for methods, and *E* for internal environment.

While this author does not accept Zarouk's approach to internal marketing, his reasoning remains valid.

External Clients

A company's clients are *always* actual persons who have two characteristics:

- *Needs*, which may be urgent and require immediate response, or dormant and in need of awakening.
- *Purchasing power*, both current and future. The latter presents a potential risk for the company.

To avoid errors in dealing with clients, a company must identify their characteristics at the outset.

The optimal method of handling clients is not only to satisfy their needs and tap their purchasing power, but to make a profit for the company in the process.

Since no organization, association, institution, or company can exist without clients, it must be a rule that "the client is always right." It is important to bear in mind that their level of satisfaction involves what they were told by users and sources of consumer standards. Moreover, 80 to 90 percent of product improvements come from users, and therefore, from clients.

Determining Client Satisfaction

The level of client satisfaction can be determined by answering the following questions:

What? The product, as defined above, with all of its characteristics and advantages, is considered in relation to the client's wishes. This involves taking into account the competition and, therefore, the array of choice as it relates to client preferences.

Where? A company must define the product's *location* – not only its niche within the market, but also the accessibility of both the product and after-sales service.

How? What is the effect of *marketing* – in other words, the company's advertising, its public relations, the reception it gives the client, the sales presentation, the sales transaction, and so on? Consistency between what is advertised and what is delivered is one of the fundamental elements of client satisfaction.

How much? What is the *price*? In other words, what is the exchange ratio between product and money.

At this point, it is appropriate to make two observations, which are based on the ideas of Daniel Adam.

The demand curve responds to decreases in price in the standard manner found in manuals on the subject. However, this phenomenon holds true for only one portion of the curve. Below a certain minimum pricing threshold (Q'), psychological factors make clients suspect inferior quality. This finding is valid not only for top of the line products, but also for mass market goods. The zone within which a company may operate is defined by $Q'Q$, since below Q' there is the risk that demand will fall as the price decreases. Pricing psychology is illustrated in Figure 3-9.

Price acceptability is shown in Figure 3-10. Curve A indicates the percentage $P(1)$ of potential clients who state that they have no intention of buying *below* a certain price. Curve B represents the percentage $P(3)$ of potential clients who have no intention of buying *above* a certain price. $P(2)$, which indicates the percentage of clients who consider the price acceptable, is located between curves A and B. It is apparent that if the price X changes, the optimal level (maximum percentage of potential clients) is $P(0)$. Certain companies and certain brands fall below the optimal price $X(0)$, sometimes without being aware of it.

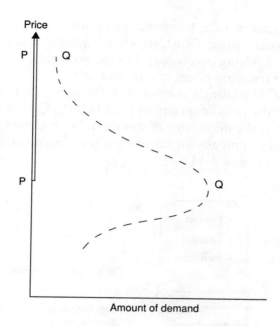

Figure 3-9. Demand and Pricing Psychology

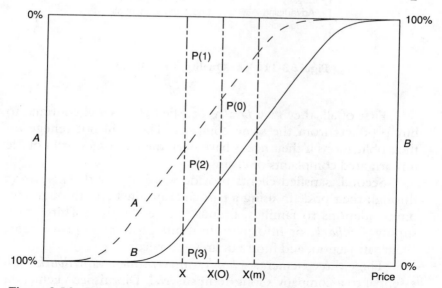

Figure 3-10. Price Acceptability (S-Curves)

As a general rule, however, the optimal price is less than the average market price *(Xm)*, which adequately explains the phenomenon of pricing psychology. On the average, it is reasonable to expect that reducing prices will increase sales.

Why? The client's *opinion* of the company and its product is defined by the ratio of quality to price (Q/P). Quality is traditionally shown as the numerator of this ratio, but if clients are satisfied, they give the company far more than mere payment of the product's price. (Figure 3-11)

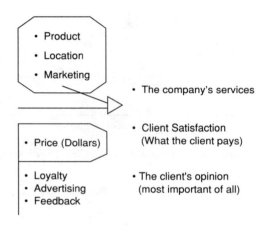

Figure 3-11. The Quality/Price Ratio

First of all, they give *loyalty*. Satisfied clients will continue to buy products from the same company. They will not renege on their obligations if their needs have been met, and they will not file unwarranted complaints or claims.

Second, satisfied clients provide word-of-mouth *advertising* through their pride in using a particular product and through recommendations to families, friends, and colleagues. Third, they supply *feedback*, or information about product improvement, client satisfaction, and future desires and needs.

These three elements – *loyalty, advertising*, and *feedback* – are essential to a company's long-term survival. Dissatisfied clients, on the other hand, can bring a company to ruin.

The Q/P ratio is therefore determined also by the *service* that accompanies the product. Product and service are inseparable and support the company's progress toward total quality.

A final question about client satisfaction illustrates this last point.

When? The *time* when clients want products depends upon circumstances, but as soon as clients make the decision to buy, they will tolerate no failure to meet deadlines. For them, a deadline represents a commitment on the part of the company; it is included in the price paid. Besides, everyone knows how slowly time passes when someone is waiting.

It is quite clear that four factors – *product*, *location*, *marketing*, and *price* – all have relative weight.

The company in relation to its competitors

Evidence shows that it is in the interest of a company to enhance its Q/P ratio in order to increase its market share and make a profit. The ideal is to reach a one-to-one ratio, both in the client's perception and from the perspective of the company's interests.

Competitors will obviously take the same approach, which is to increase their own Q/P ratios. Clients therefore face the following hypothetical situations in choosing between two companies:

1. Usual supplier's Q/P > potential supplier's Q/P
2. Usual supplier's Q/P = potential supplier's Q/P
3. Usual supplier's Q/P < potential supplier's Q/P

In the first two instances, which discourage change, clients would maintain ties to their usual suppliers, with whom they have valued relationships. In the third instance, they would likely give the competitors an opportunity to prove the worth of their products.

All else being equal, therefore, it is in the interest of the company to increase its Q/P ratio in relating to its clients and its environment. Competitors will attempt to do likewise.

When confronting the same external constraints, the only recourse for each supplier is improvement in service, with maximum efficiency being drawn from inside the company. Such efficiency must be improved not only by use of customary quality criteria, but above all through the company's greatest resource: personnel. Employees vary from company to company, but it is they who will make the difference, not only in innovation, but also in design, development, production, sales, and after-sales service. In this context, the external image of a brand name can only improve as a function of the internal image of the brand name. If marketing is considered to be a process affecting the market, it is necessary to think of this process as including *internal marketing*.

Internal Clients

Every employee should be considered an *entrepreneur* and, in which capacity to have clients within the company. Any company without clients is doomed to extinction. To be competitive, a company must improve its Q/P ratio, which implies increasing the Q/P ratio of each employee. What is the employee's ratio?

It is exactly the same as the Q/P ratio for the company and consists of the same four factors. For pedagogical reasons, price shall be discussed first.

Each employee has the expectation of receiving a salary in exchange for his or her work. The components of price are:

- Salary
- Interest in the job
- Prospects for advancement
- Possibilities for personal growth:
  - Leave time
  - Nature of the work
  - Responsibility

The relative importance of these components varies from one individual to another.

Location as a factor in the employee's *Q/P* ratio can be broken down into:

- Distance from the employee's residence
- The firm's prestige and reputation
- Job security
- Mobility (one work location or frequent reassignment)
- Hours of work
- Working conditions (ergonomics of the job)

Marketing includes:

- Internal publicity and dissemination of information
- Internal public relations
- Relations with superiors
- Individual communication
- Recognition
- Formal and informal contacts

Employees make five contributions to the product, which are identical in every company. These might be described in the following terms, from the employee's perspective.

- What we are actually paid for: our work products represent our *normal contribution*. Only our clients can prove to us that our work is satisfactory. Our goal is to satisfy our clients, and our efficiency is measured in terms of that goal.
- Since everyone is an innovator, we all can contribute to the improvement of our work products. And since we are innovators, our colleagues are also innovators; thus, we should consider any suggested improvements to our work before rejecting them (in one form or another). Of course, our clients are the judges of what constitutes an innovation. That is our *contribution to innovation*.
- We know that the company must be profitable if our jobs are to be secure. One of our *contributions to profits* is cost reduction.
- Our *contribution to the internal image of the brand name* depends upon how our clients present the quality and quantity of my product to others.
- Our contacts with our superiors are an occasion to provide them with feedback. This is our *contribution to information*. It includes all of our interactions with the clients. We are intensely aware of the competition, and we monitor the market environment. We make a quantitative and qualitative assessment of our resources. These contributions constitute our performance and our output.

This entire set of contributions is our *responsibility*.

As is shown in Figure 3-11, *opinion* should be added to these definitions.

A company in which employees feel comfortable and that recognizes their contributions will have their *loyalty*.

Satisfied employees convey their pride in the company to those around them, at home, and socially. That is a form of *advertising*.

Employees may have valuable ideas to contribute. To do so, they must have the opportunity to give *feedback* to their superiors.

If the opinions of employees are negative and remain unvented, they could begin to lose interest in their work products (the five contributions). They may be looking for another job, spreading negative information, and growing increasingly disenchanted for lack of meaningful feedback. If there are several demoralized employees in the company, conditions may gradually deteriorate until a conflict occurs. Although *opinion* is the result of a person's own judgment and will, the opinion of employees about their company is also a function of their perception about the company's quality.

Summary

The quality/price relationship can be summarized in the following points:

- The quality/price ratio makes product and service inseparable.
- Any organization exists only by virtue of its clients. The client is always right.
- Any increase in the Q/P ratio is obtained by mobilizing the company's internal forces: its personnel.
- Every employee is an entrepreneur.
- Every employee is an internal client, a supplier, and exists solely by virtue of his or her clients.
- Each employee has a Q/P ratio that he or she can manage by setting and negotiating individual and company goals.
- Profits are made when the company's Q/P ratio is optimized. For that to occur, each employee's Q/P ratio must also be optimized.

4

Total Quality

It all adds up.

– French Proverb

As of 1986, there were approximately:

- 1.5 million QCCs (Quality Control Circles) in Japan, with 15 million persons directly involved
- 500,000 QCCs in China, with 5 million persons directly involved
- 400,000 QCCs in the United States, with 4 million persons directly involved
- 40,000 QCCs in Europe, with 400,000 persons directly involved
- 20,000 QCCs in France, with 200,000 persons directly involved

Today, Quality Control Circles are expanding rapidly in 50 other countries.

Japan (with 120 million inhabitants) began to experiment with QCCs 30 years ago. France (with 50 million inhabitants) began 5 years ago with the creation of AFCERQ, which has been the driving force of the total quality movement. All things being equal, annual growth has been greater in France than in the Orient. This is an indication of significant motivation, considering that it took Japan 10 years to establish 10,000 QCCs.

QCCs are an extraordinary training tool that should be maintained and further developed. Many have already been started: large, medium-sized, and even several small ones. France's government has some concerns about these developments, but there seems to be an overall desire for further development and progress.

Quality is neither a fad nor a gimmick (Figure 4-1). Consulting firms have been overwhelmed by requests for diagnosis and training.

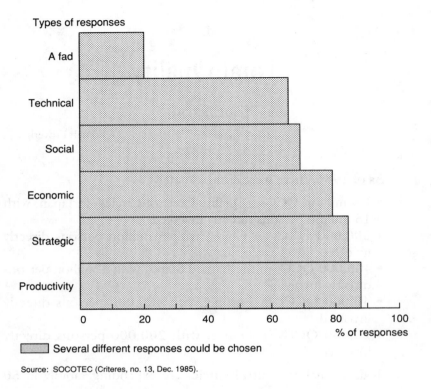

Source: SOCOTEC (Criteres, no. 13, Dec. 1985).

Figure 4-1. For You, Quality Is:

References to total quality and even to QCCs appear on radio and television. In short, a movement is in progress and it is up to each country to successfully rise to this challenge in the 1990s.

Companies, profits, employers: these words are no longer taboo; they are spoken, written, read, and seen. France is changing and wants progress.

Networking

A *network* is a group of companies of all sizes in which members share the conviction that problems can be overcome and goals achieved more effectively if tackled by a group than if worked on alone. This type of group has no legal or financial ties, but operates by means of periodic exchanges among managers, both vertically and horizontally. It has given rise to clubs in which top managers exchange all types of information.

Of course, such networking is extensive in Japan and the United States. In France it can be seen in *industrial reconversion zones*, where large industrial companies design programs of action for the creation of new companies and for assisting small and medium-sized companies. Such activity is concentrated in zones that have lost their industrial or economic base.

There has also been progress in France on other fronts: the birth of *venture capital* in the banking industry; investment in small *capital-risk* companies, or the creation of stock portfolios with shares of companies that are regarded as capital risks; *rapid expansion*, whose principal feature is assistance to small and medium sized subcontractors or suppliers in their respective fields; *prolifer-ation*, by which certain companies attempt to help staff members found small companies; *business takeovers*, which enable the profes-sionals in a firm to make a new start with all or part of a company; *network associations*, such as AFCERQ, which provide training in progressive management based on techniques that have been proven successful.

No, it can no longer be said that France is behind. The country is advancing at a good pace while it is still learning to walk. Quality is a national issue that must be pursued with strength and vigor.

An Economic Necessity

The economic *crisis* has now been discussed for twelve years. What crisis? In 1789, France created a revolution; in 1793, it cut off the head of its king; in 1802, it crowned an emperor! *Change, evolution,* and *transformation*: these are more appropriate terms than *crisis*. However the change is termed, it has been engendered by three principal developments.

First, *geopolitical transformation* has meant a new perception of the planet Earth. Before 1974, there were two power centers –

the United States and Europe – that were concerned exclusively with themselves. Then the oil crisis struck, triggering a transformation in the relations of these power centers with their trading partners, who were undergoing economic development. The most visible of the trading partners was Japan, which attracted attention because of the quality of its products, but it was not the only one.

Second, *internationalization*, because of the complexity it entails, has made every client and every user better informed at an increasing rate of speed. It is now possible to find out what is being produced on the other side of the world on that very day.

Third, under the influence of the Club of Rome, business firms discarded the idea of undifferentiated growth (moderate income housing projects, large high schools, an automobile and television for everyone) in favor of organic growth. The principal feature of undifferentiated growth is quantity: production for the sake of production. There had even been talk of the *growth of growth*. Organic growth in companies is similar to the growth of the human body. Every organ in the body (liver, brain, kidneys, and so on) grows by means of its own cells; growth is differentiated, qualitative. When the same process occurs in companies, clients demand fewer defects, become more exacting, create consumerism, defend themselves, attack, and seek quality in every area. This trend leads to increasingly stiff *competition*, not only in France, but on an international scale.

The Western nations initially perceived these three phenomena as monstrous. After a period of retrenchment, however, they began to examine the changes more closely.

It was then that PIMS (Profit Impact of Market Strategies), an American data bank, furnished evidence of the fundamental role of the client's perception of quality in achieving profitability. Three parameters were key to this conclusion: relative market share, the relative quality index, and return on investment (Table 4-1).

In Figures 4-2 and 4-3, the horizontal axis, which indicates relative quality, is divided into three sections: less than -1 percent (it can, by definition, be negative), between -1 and 40 percent, and more than 40 percent. The different types of cross-hatching indicate more specific breakouts within each graph.

Table 4-1. PIMS Survey

> **PIMS: Profit Impact of Market Strategies**
> (Strategic Planning Institute)
>
> **Relative Market Share:**
> Your market share
> divided by the
> total market shares of your three largest competitors
>
> **Relative Quality index:**
> % of your sales volume
> (achieved by products that are considered
> superior to those of your competitors)
> Minus % of your sales volume
> (achieved by products that are considered
> inferior to those of your competitors)
>
> **ROI**
> (Return on Investment)
> Profits (before taxes)/Investment (average)

Quality thus appears in Figure 4-2 as a significant factor in market share. Market share does not account for all sales income, but it increases in tandem with quality if it was already significant at a lower level of quality. It should be added that relative market share may result in a significant return on investment if quality increases.

The second graph in the same figure shows that marketing efforts, measured by marketing expenses (sales force, advertising, promotion), cause a deterioration in sales income if quality is inadequate or decreases. In other words, if quality is not good, it is not in a company's best interest to attract attention.

Research and development activities (Figure 4-3) reduce the consequences of a perception of poor quality. If quality has not first been corrected, efforts to prepare new products are impaired.

**Relative
Market Share**

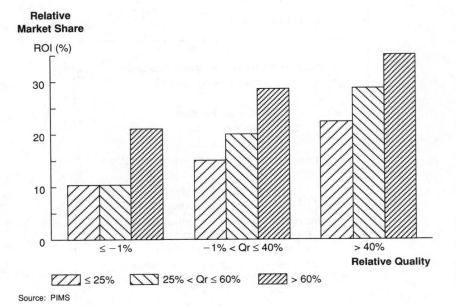

Source: PIMS

**Marketing/Sales
Expenditures**

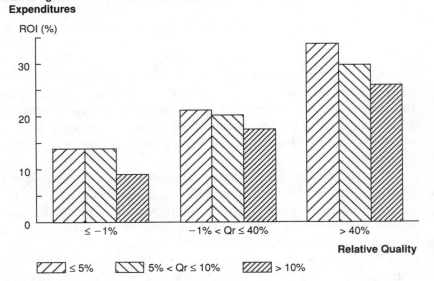

Source: PIMS

Figure 4-2.

R & D / Sales Expenditures

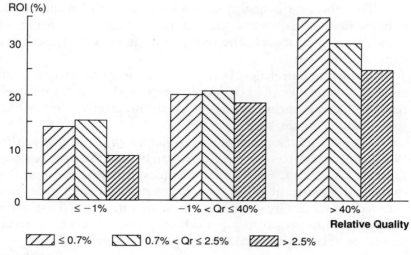

Source: PIMS

New Products
(As a % of Total Sales)

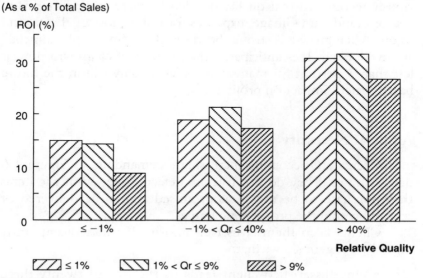

Source: PIMS

Figure 4-3.

The greater the expenditures are for this purpose, the greater the impairment becomes.

Therefore, if the quality of products currently on the market is inadequate, it is useless to attempt to escape that reality by launching new products. The thing to do is to correct the brand name's quality image.

As for the correlation between the phases of a product's life cycle and its relative market share, it is quite clear that a relatively new product's chances for success are all the greater when market share is high (Figure 4-4).

Products are therefore consistently judged on the basis of quality. With the current economic downturn, and on the basis of Japanese, American, and French examples, it has been found that there is a significant difference between companies that have adopted a total quality system and those that have not. That difference is accentuated during periods of recession, even if market shares are stable during periods of expansion (Figure 4-5).

The economic situation over the past 12 years has caused companies to sense empirically that quality deficiencies are more damaging to profitability when market growth is slow. It was previously recognized that quality deficiencies were costly in terms of loss of brand name image, expenses for claims, loss of clients, and so on. When growth is strong, however, these "minor phenomena" are overlooked. It is anticipated that, with market growth now at less than 3 percent for many companies, quality will in the future have a crucial impact on profitability.

A Social Necessity

Clients are becoming increasingly demanding, as Figure 4-6 demonstrates. They do not tolerate defects. They want the items they purchase to be usable as promised and to be delivered or repaired within the proper time frames.

Clients keep themselves well informed, and a recent study made by Peugeot shows that:

- One dissatisfied client leads to the loss of twenty-three potential clients
- One satisfied client leads to seven potential clients

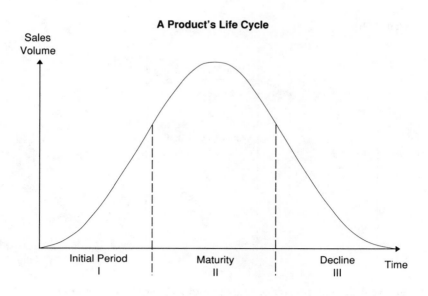

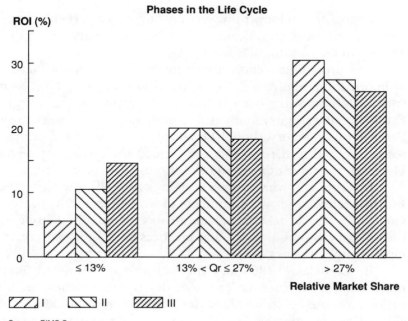

Source: PIMS Survey

Figure 4-4.

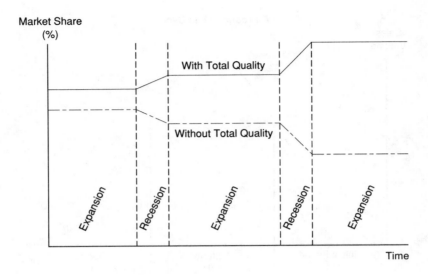

Figure 4-5. The Impact of Quality and Delivery Delays on Sales

Clients are no longer unswervingly loyal to a particular brand name. Even more significantly, they inform others about their changes in brand name allegiance.

The preceding section underscored the internationalization of information. Figure 4-7 shows that data processing professions (not only computer occupations) now represent the largest employment category both inside and outside business firms. Perhaps this category should be added to the standard primary, secondary, and tertiary sectors and termed the quaternary sector. However, the three other categories also use data processing.

In Table 4-2, which shows sociological trends, the term *feminization* refers to growing numbers of women in the work force. Companies should take this phenomenon seriously in considering their social customs, policies, and practices because it may create a rapid change in values.

B. Cathelat (1985) and the Center for Advanced Communication have given an excellent description of these trends, including those involving "lifestyles." Such trends should be considered as an objective sociological fact, without reference to good and evil. Hedonism, for example, the pursuit of pleasure

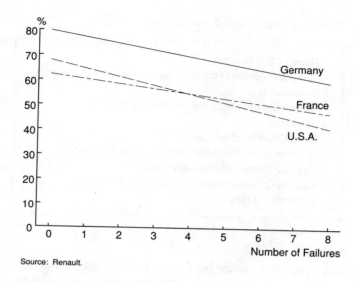

Source: Renault.

Figure 4-6. Client Loyalty

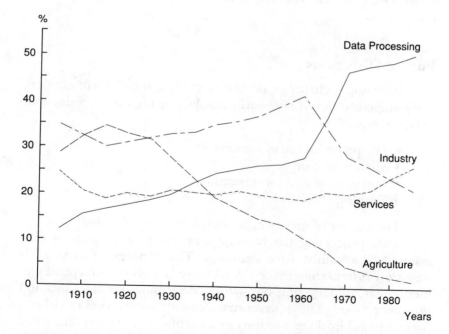

Figure 4-7. Distribution of Employment in the United States

Table 4-2. Sociological Trends

- Need for Self-Realization
- Growing Rejection of Bureaucracy and Institutional Hierarchy
- Feminization
- A Decrease In Individuality and Distrust of Others
- Hedonism
- Being Effective rather than Being Right
- A Tendency to View Business Firms More Favorably
- Aggressiveness and Combativeness
- Seeking Consensus rather than Confrontation
- Enjoyment of Risk

Source: COFREMCA.

and satisfaction, has today become another fact to be taken into account. So have aggressiveness and combativeness, which can be appreciated for the energy, dynamism, discussion, and conflict they create.

Future Directions

Initiating a challenge on the economic, social, technological, and competitive levels necessarily involves taking into account four major trends:

- The preeminence of information
- Miniaturization
- Automation and robotization
- Training

The impact of these trends is explained in Table 4-3.

Data processing has become a necessity in all areas of economic and administrative endeavor. The concept of message is based on *information* theory. A message is a set of perceptual elements that, by targeting our senses, determine our reactions and our inner mood. These perceptual elements are symbols of either a natural (wind evoking a storm) or an artificial (the print characters for this book) character. Information theory is concerned with

describes a company/subcontractor relationship involving negotiations and discussions toward a common end. It is not a relationship in which a particular supplier competes with others essentially on the basis of price. The company has several preferred suppliers it deals with. The criteria include not only price, but also quality, time frames, and uniformity. There is a reciprocal exchange of information in which contractual agreements are made in principle rather than formalized in writing. The client may see first-hand how the product is manufactured, and the supplier may see how it is used. In this manner, the supplier receives all pertinent information – not only from the client but from all other sources. This body of information assists the supplier in making improvements. The supplier has the technical support of its preferred client and together they attempt to improve product quality in progressive stages – for example, on an annual basis.

Table 4-4. Total Quality

TQC: Total quality control
CWQC: Companywide quality control
CWQI: Companywide quality improvement
Quality management
Integrated quality
Overall quality

Total Quality

The same goal:

- To constantly improve the quality of products, services, and use of human and material resources
- In short, to take the path towards perfection for the benefit of the company and the satisfaction of individuals

---

The term *monitoring* means that each professional and each employee is also an observer for the company. In the past, colleagues traveling through France collected information in every city, and their findings represented a mass of information collected throughout the provinces. Today, the international nature of competition

Table 4-5. Total Quality: A Definition

**Total Quality is a Set of Principles
and Methods Organized as a Comprehensive Strategy
with the Goal of Mobilizing the Entire Company in Order to
Achieve the Greatest Client Satisfaction
at the Lowest Cost**

It involves

- all company functions
- all the company activities
- all employees, regardless of their rank in the organization
- all relationships: client-supplier as well as inside the company
- all improvements in quality:
  resolution of existing problems and subsequent prevention
- the entire life cycle of the product: from its design until its elimination
- all relationships with suppliers, subcontractors, partnerships, networks
- monitoring of all markets, current and potential

The Same Philosophy for Everyone: "Zero Defects"

---

means that such information is gathered through international travel. Professionals and technicians must therefore be asked to open their eyes and observe everything, even if it is not directly within their field of competence. The Japanese do so by requiring not only a standard field trip report, but a "report of first-hand impressions." The purpose of this permanent surveillance is to detect the slightest background noise that could be indicative of the appearance of a new signal, a new need, or a new market. Monitoring could be highly useful to a marketing department in spotting new developments.

Table 4-6 summarizes the essential differences between quality control and total quality. The last line of each column indicates the mindset fostered by each approach. For example, in the case of quality control, improved quality requires additional inspection, which entails costs. These costs are not lessened by the declaration that "quality is everybody's business." In the case of total quality,

Table 4-6. Quality Control or Total Quality?

Controlled Quality	Total Quality
• A Posteriori inspection	• A Priori design
• Action oriented toward effects rather than causes	• Identification and elimination of cause
• Field of action: "Product"	• Field of Action: The entire company
• The client is the purchaser	• The client is the user
• Static	• Vital and evolving
• Quality without a price, at any price	• Fiscal evaluation: Cost management
• Standard, tolerance, customary practice AQL: Defects are "normal"	• Rejection of quality deficiencies • Zero defects, excellence • Personal initiative, ambition • Developmental specifications
• Quality control is assigned to someone	• Quality control is everyone's business
• Distrust (external, internal)	• Confidence (external, internal)
• The client is made to pay	• Quality is included
• Quality on a "differential" basis	
• Quality generates costs	• Quality pays

inspection is everybody's business and quality is each individual's responsibility. Under these circumstances, "quality pays."

Philip Crosby (1980) wrote: "Quality is free! But it is not a gift." It is in fact apparent that quality requires not only an effort by everyone from the CEO to the machine operator, but also a reexamination of all our mental attitudes and points of view.

Quality control produces mistrust in employees because it classifies as separate groups those who think, those who organize, those who produce, and those who inspect. What counts is quantity: dollars, products, market share. Quality is a technique that is important only to specialists. It is a measurement whose goal is reached by inspecting the product's characteristics. Defects are allowed: "Nothing is perfect." Quality is defeated. For decades, specialists have searched for and sometimes found permanent improvement in manufacturing processes and inspection techniques. There has been sales promotion and advertising.

Nevertheless, we have witnessed a significant decline in relative competitiveness in many fields. This is a policy and strategy failure caused by overly directive management, the cost of quality (even though most of the time it is unknown), and the idea of quantity as a vector for expansion.

Total quality involves all the properties of products, processes, and work life. It is based on trust, and responsibility is shared by everyone. Each person is called upon to seek perfection, with the goal being a very high degree of competitiveness at the national and international levels. The satisfaction of users not only with the product itself, but also with the service given by the company, will be reflected in client loyalty.

What does the user want? Important criteria include:

- Technical characteristics
- Compliance with performance data
- Reliability
- Aesthetic qualities
- Technological progress
- Ease of operation
- The lowest purchase price
- The lowest cost of ownership
- Authorized service

Quality in companies is a higher priority than the product, and each employee has the right to create progress, knowing that inspection, as it is still perceived today, is destined to disappear. Total quality has become a vector for economic expansion. It is therefore a priority for every company manager.

Figure 4-9, a spiral created by Juran, is in fact a helicoid and therefore three-dimensional. The axis around which it revolves represents the evolution of needs and has no scale, because needs are variable over time and cannot be considered to be either linear or logarithmic. The stages in the development of a product are located all along the helicoid, beginning with the detection of needs, and ending with the product's use, which encompasses after-sales service. Before beginning another cycle, market studies should measure the discrepancy between the need detected and user satisfaction. This discrepancy is of fundamental significance.

In the case of products that have a long cycle, it should become standard procedure to check at each stage the correlation between the evolution of needs and the development of the product.

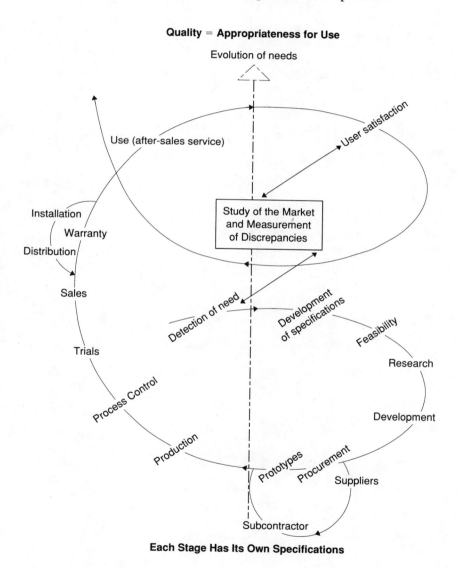

Figure 4-9. Juran Spiral

Part 2

The Five Requirements
for Quality

*A person who is learning should believe,
one who knows should question.*

– Roger Bacon

5

Conformance

The worst of all defects is to be unaware of them.

— Publius Syrus, *Sententiae*

Conformance must be defined in terms of users' needs. Users, who may not be customers but act as the sources of standards and requirements for the client, have the intrinsic universal characteristic of being human. They have attitudes, behaviors, perceptions, and motivations. Their needs form the basis for defining quality in product.

In a broad psychological sense, *attitude* denotes a stable and systematic set of ideas, beliefs, principles, or opinions which function as an enduring frame of reference for everything a person thinks, says, or does with respect to perceived reality. An attitude is a personality structure: a means of organizing experience and behavior at an unconscious level. This last definition implies that an individual is predisposed to act in a positive, negative, or neutral fashion when faced with a given situation.

Behavior. In the general sense, *behavior* refers to all of an individual's actions and reactions. In the strict sense, it denotes an objectivistic frame of reference that defines psychology as the study of everything that is observable about an individual, without concern for consciousness. It can therefore be said that attitude precedes behavior (which is action) and that behavior is that which is observable. Thus, the act of purchasing is a behavior, and it is the role of advertising to trigger that behavior based on consumer attitudes toward this or that product.

Habit. Habit is an acquired behavior (series of actions) that ultimately becomes routine, established, and permanent. Habits are predictable. They lead to familiarity and thus to action (doing by habit) and an enhanced ability to perform the action (the habit of doing creates skill).

Mentality. Mentality derives from the Latin *mens, mentis,* which means "mind." In current usage, mentality is often associated with the moral values observable in behavior: to deplore someone's mentality is to condemn a type of conduct and the moral standards on which it appears to be based. Perceived mentality, or state of mind, influences how we define social groups and individuals. We discover a mentality different from our own when we are taken aback by the behavior of others (or by the group to which they belong) in connection with an event or a situation that we had interpreted differently than they had.

Perception. Perception is a mental process that results in cognition. This awareness may occur by experiencing a particular sensation or intuition. We can have a perception not only of our immediate environment, but also of our company or of our government.

Need. A need is a requirement that has its origin in nature or society. It is also a strong yearning for something.

Motivation. Motivation has its etymological origin in the word *motive*: "that which initiates movement," from the Latin *motivus*: "mover." Motivation refers to all the internal conscious and unconscious factors that determine behavior. Motivations include instincts and impulses, needs, habits and conditioning, complexes, emotions and interest, fantasies, archetypes and imaginary perceptions, attitudes, personal or social standards, and values. The principal component of motivation is self-esteem, which gives meaning to every action a person undertakes.

Needs. A discussion of needs, then, involves a set of human characteristics. These should be recapitulated, since they are often overlooked.

- Behavior is observable.
- Attitudes precede behavior.
- Habits are acquired behavior.
- Mentalities are perceptions of the world that define the moral values observable in behavior.
- Motivation is inner-directed.
- The principal component of motivation is self-esteem.
- Motivation without a vector (direction) may result in confusion. A client's perception of his supplier determines his

motivation. An employee's perception of his company creates his motivation.

At the individual level, needs can be broken down into three developmental stages:

1. *The affective aspect*: a need is an emotional state; the individual is aware that he or she lacks something.
2. *The perceptual aspect*: a need appears as an understanding and anticipatory image of the proper means to quiet the disturbance experienced by the emotions.
3. *The functional aspect*: the need is translated into an impulse to act. M. H. Joannis indicates that motivations are "positive psychological forces that lead to buying." These forces are:

   - hedonistic: involving the need to experience pleasure.
   - altruistic: involving the need to do good.
   - self-expressive: involving the need to express individual identity

At the social level, Thorstein Veblen identified five influences on the behavior of clients:

- *Cultural influences*: Culture is "social heritage."
- *Social classes*
- *Reference groups*: groups with which clients identify but to which they do not belong.
- *Peer groups*: part of the client's immediate environment (friends, neighbors, colleagues at work, and so on).
- *Family*

From Experiencing a Need to Defining Product Specifications

A need is first *experienced* and then *expressed* as *demand*. For example, one can "need" a high-fidelity system. This individual need, which originated in a social group and an existing market, will be translated into a demand or request formulated in the client's own terminology. The client might say, for example: "For speakers, I want the works, but with *lows* that are not *round* and highs that are not *grating*. I need a turntable, a cassette deck, an amplifier, and two loudspeaker enclosures." The producer and the specialist who hear these words are able to understand them and will transform them into specifications such as the following, for a turntable:

- Turntable speed 33 $\frac{1}{3}$ and 45 rpm
- Wow and flutter less than 0.09%
- Hum less than -45 dB
- Angle error less than $\pm$ 0.2°
- Stylus tracking pressure 2 grams
- Maximum electrical consumption 9 W
- Dimensions: 320 × 90 × 325 mm
- Weight: approx. 2.7 kg

Specifications for the cassette deck, the amplifier, and the loudspeaker enclosures might be written similarly.

We can assume that the client will purchase the product on the basis of listening to it and judging its aesthetic qualities in the store. There is no certainty that the client who was satisfied in the store will be satisfied in the home. To prepare for a possible discrepancy and to justify the product's advertising, the manufacturer establishes *alternative specifications*.

Demand is transformed into *specification*, formulated in a different terminology: that of the specialist. This is a necessity.

It is essential to know whether the client is *satisfied* with the acquisition. If the client is not satisfied, he or she may not say so but will never again purchase that brand of equipment. *A client who says nothing is not necessarily a satisfied client*. It is calculated that only 1 in 1,000 dissatisfied clients actually tells the manufacturer.

Specifications

Specifications are a product's quantifiable and verifiable characteristics. Table 5-1, which recapitulates the definition of a product, shows that it is possible to set specifications for all products that are the result of human activities.

Table 5-1. The Product

The product is a result of a natural process or a human activity

In addition to fruits, vegetables, fish, and the like, it may be

- the transformation of raw materials (steel, or a mechanical part, for example)
- assembled products (cars, televisions, furniture)
- subassemblies (printed circuits, car seat, dashboard)
- components (screws, nuts, integrated circuits, paint, flour, salt, pepper)
- plans (estimates, designs, photographs, models)
- telephone calls (greetings, information, sales, purchase, meeting)
- transactions (statements, checks, receipts, invoices, purchase orders delivery orders)
- consulting services (advice, expertise, arbitration) etc...
- correspondence (letters, telexes, reports, memoranda)

Any result of any human activity is a product

In a strict sense, *specifications* are a document that prescribes the *requirements* that the product must meet. The pertinent file should include designs, models, and other documents, or else make reference to them. It should also indicate the means and criteria by which conformance with specifications may be established. The term *requirement* is closer in meaning to the term *need* and represents the supplier's understanding of the demand or request.

Figure 5-1 demonstrates the discrepancy between need, demand, and specifications, as seen by the client. Two observations are relevant to this situation:

- To clients, specifications are their demands or requests, in other words, what they expect. These requests are expressed in the clients' own vocabulary.
- Suppliers need *an alternative set of specifications* that cover not only the users' demands or requests, but also all the other constraints that are indispensable if suppliers are to be sure of being responsive to requests. These specifications are formulated in the suppliers' vocabulary.

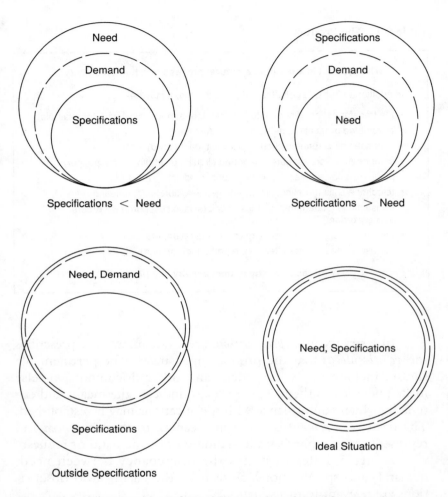

Figure 5-1. The Matching of Need, Demand, and Specifications from the User's Point of View

To implement the specifications, the producer (in a larger sense, the manufacturer of the product) needs facilities, materials, personnel, operational parameters, and processes, among other things. The production plan will specify time frames as well as other constraints with which the manufacturer and the staff are familiar.

Matching Needs, Specifications, and Implementation

Figure 5-2 illustrates the correlation between need, specifications, and implementation. For instance, the intersection of the three circles represents *perfect quality management*. When specifications have been made for the need but have not been implemented, *defects* exist. *Excess quality* is the result of the implementation of specifications for which the user has no need. Implementation without specifications or demand is *waste*.

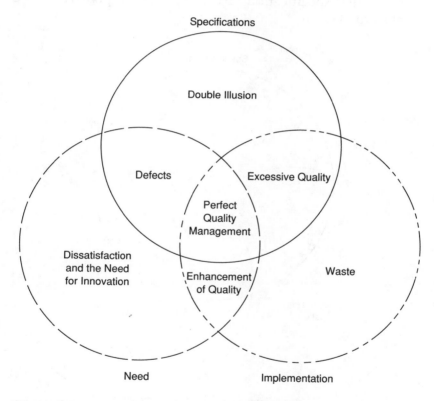

Figure 5-2. Quality Action Zones: An Analysis of the Intersections

The implementation of something for which there were no specifications but that meets the client's need is an *enhancement of quality*. For example, a client who buys an automobile that has all the options for a given model considers each option to be an enhancement of quality.

Now look at Figure 5-3. Zones 1 and 2 represent *demand*, or rather *explicit need*. Zone 7 represents dissatisfaction and *unconscious need*. Zone 5 is *excessive specifications*. Defining these zones assists the company in discerning the client's need and ensuring that specifications are completely responsive to the client's expectations.

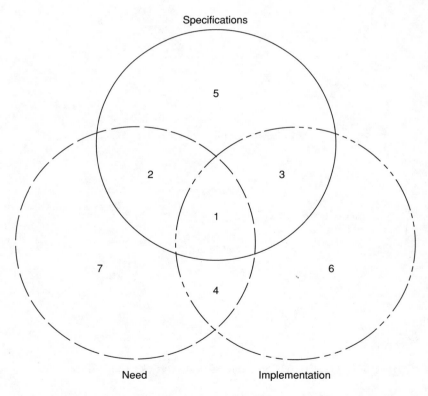

Figure 5-3. Quality Action Zones: An Analysis of the Convergences

Zones 1 and 3 represent the conformance of implementation with specifications. Zones 2 and 5 show implementation not in conformity with specifications. Zone 6 is *potential for improvement*, from which the company may benefit by including it in the implementation process.

Zones 1 and 4 represent *true quality*.

The goal of total quality is to develop this true quality convergence and to increase market share by using areas of waste as sources of innovation (J. Chove).

Conformance Outside the Company

Conformance can only mean meeting the needs of the client and therefore those of the user. This implies that it is necessary to assist clients in articulating their needs in order to clarify their demands. Specifications must subsequently be established, and repeated efforts must be made to confirm that they can be adequately met. This involves a process of negotiation that attempts to match the client's demand with the company's capabilities.

Finally, it is necessary to ensure that the product meets these specifications exactly by means of one or more very clear procedures established jointly by the negotiator, the designer, and the producer.

Confirmation of product conformance can be accomplished only through an in-depth analysis of client satisfaction, since market studies are concerned solely with the nature of the clients and their needs.

Conformance Inside the Company

As indicated above, market studies are reinforced and enhanced by surveys of client satisfaction. Moreover, it has been shown that a company must have clients to survive. An extended sequence therefore comes into play: client → producer → client → user.

The Client-Supplier Relationship

Figure 5-4 is the model for the following discussion. A company, a department, a division, a person – all are *actors*. An actor has special experience and training – in other words, knowledge. Likewise, a company has its area of specialization and expertise. It also has a means of production in terms of equipment, materials, and personnel.

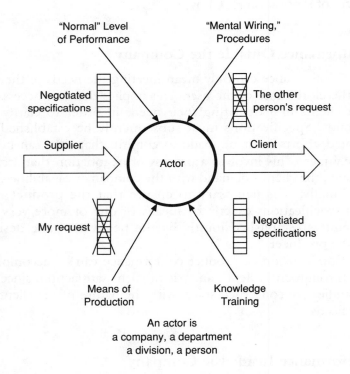

Figure 5-4. The Client-supplier Relationship

Each actor's method of reasoning, "logic," and mental processes cause him or her to act one way rather than another. Each actor would proceed differently in order to achieve the same result. In addition to this personal and specific "mental wiring," there are procedures and constraints that a given actor is aware of or that are imposed by others. The equivalent for a company is its niche in the market.

Finally, an actor does everything with "personality." He or she knows how to do so without making an extraordinary effort or display, making the performance seem natural, a reflection of particular attitudes, behaviors, habits, mentality, perception, and motivation. The equivalent of a personality for a company is its corporate culture.

The supplier receives a request from the client, expressed in the client's language. The supplier and client then jointly negotiate specifications that define the product the client wants. The supplier's role is to explain its own capabilities, based on its available resources – that it can do this, but not that. A discussion is initiated regarding the quantifiable aspects of the client's specifications so as to reach a negotiated set of specifications. This is the client-supplier relationship.

The supplier then itself becomes a client, negotiating with *its* supplier in order to obtain a negotiated set of specifications. In this regard, specifications are considered to be anything that is quantifiable, verifiable, and subject to a joint agreement. They do not involve vague terms, but precise factual data such as quantities, time frames, money, product characteristics, and so on.

Specifications must be complied with once they are negotiated: they constitute a mutual obligation. Within a company, the term *requirements* is used in preference to *specifications*, but the rationale remains the same: requirements that represent the needs of the internal client must be established. If the results of the negotiation are not complied with, or if the negotiation is not successfully completed, an internal client may find another supplier. Competition is intense.

Such specifications are often only implicit within our companies, and this lack of precise articulation leads to useless discussion, misunderstanding, errors, and repetitious efforts. It also allows people to hide behind words or to waste precious time in defending their positions.

Determining specifications means listening to the other person's request in his or her own language and then translating that request into one's own language.

The Client-supplier Sequence

The company is a *sequence* of clients and suppliers, ending with the user (Figure 5-5). Specifications and process management continue throughout this extended sequence, and each participant is linked to the other by mutually respected obligations (Figure 5-6).

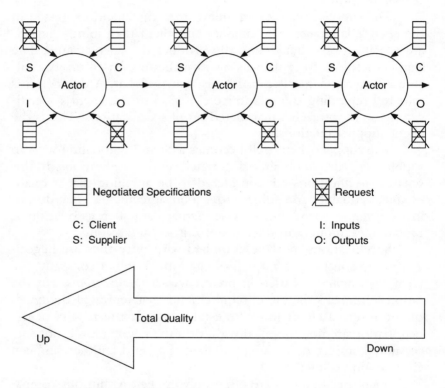

Figure 5-5. The Client-supplier Sequence

The tools of total quality furnish superior information regarding methods for implementation of this concept. Henceforth, be aware that *all of us, both inside and outside the company, are clients and suppliers.*

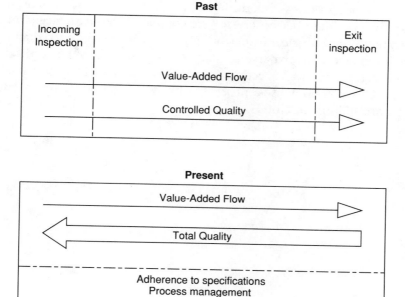

Figure 5-6. Value Added and Quality

Many couples are expert in providing themselves with specifications for things that make their lives more enjoyable: a house or apartment, a car, a vacation, a family, a wardrobe, and so on.

The same process of fulfilling needs through specifications takes place in a company. Conformance, defined as the fitness of products to the satisfaction of client needs, is a fundamental factor both inside and outside the company.

Thus, the client-supplier relationship is valid both inside and outside the company.

Conformance and Additional Needs

The principal purpose of specifications is to eliminate dissatisfaction by eradicating defects, reducing the time required for delivery, cutting costs (which is discussed in Chapter 6), and improving respect for the client's wishes and requirements.

If specifications include fitness for use, they increase satisfaction by providing better service (the company's service), facilitating product use (with clear instructions), increasing reliability, reducing maintenance and ownership costs, taking into account aesthetic considerations, and respecting a number of other client concerns.

This comprehensive process is likely to unearth many needs that are still unconscious.

6

Prevention and the Cost of Quality

It is better to prevent than to be prevented.

– Walloon proverb

The cost of quality (COQ) consists of four parameters:

Prevention. Prevention costs include the cost of all measures taken to *avoid* errors, defects, and failures at all levels and for all activities. Prevention involves company policy, preparatory meetings, client satisfaction studies, the implementation of plans of action, safety, analyses of potential failures, study of crucial points for all services, operational procedures for trials, design of testing facilities, reliability studies, maintainability, product specification documentation, appropriateness for production, the suppliers' capabilities, testing and inspection procedures to be implemented before and after procurements and subcontracting, quality training, professional training – in short, everything that can be done before a defect, error, failure, or dissatisfaction, occurs.

Evaluation. Evaluation costs include the cost of all actions taken to *confirm* that the product or service conforms to the user's expectations. In contrast to the preceding cost, this cost item concerns the finished product, before and after its sale. It is also often termed *verification, detection, checking* or even *inspection*.

Internal failures. Costs are documented *within the company* for all products, materials, and equipment that do not meet the client's requirements, even *before* their use. It is during this phase that rejections and corrective alterations occur.

External failures. Costs are also documented *by the user* for products and equipment that do not meet its requirements. Returned merchandise, reimbursements, and claims may occur during this phase.

These four parameters can be categorized more broadly as *conformance* and *nonconformance*.

Conformance is the sum of the costs for *prevention* + *evaluation*. It involves *all* costs incurred in the effort to ensure that products *conform* with the client's requirements.

Nonconformance is the sum of the costs for *internal failures* + *external failures*. It involves all costs incurred *before* or *during* use due to rejections, corrective alterations, refusals of merchandise, claims, returns, and reimbursements.

The *cost of quality* is therefore the sum of the costs for conformance + nonconformance. It includes *all* expenditures incurred to make the product *satisfy* the *client*.

Table 6-1 summarizes these definitions.

Table 6-1.

(COQ)
The Cost of Quality
Cost of conformance = cost of prevention + cost of evaluation
Cost of nonconformance = cost of internal failures + cost of external failures
COQ = cost of conformance + cost of nonconformance

Juran's Model

A model that illustrates cost trends and is frequently found in literature on the subject is shown in Figure 6-1. The term *failure* denotes both internal and external failures.

In his book, *Quality Control Handbook*, Dr. Juran presents a more realistic and more complete model in which costs are shown on the y-axis and conformance is shown on the x-axis expressed as a percentage (Figure 6-2). It should be noted that the quality improvement zone is to the left of the optimum zone, and the zone of perfectionism is to the right.

Since the $Y1$ and $Y2$ functions are not straight line functions, there is no reason why the minimum value for $Y3$ would be located to the right of the axis for the point $Y1 = Y2$.

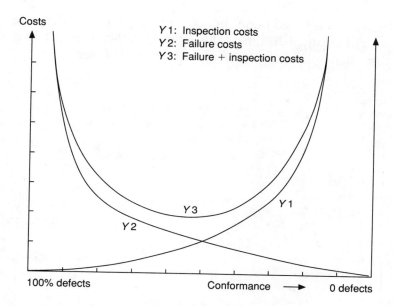

Figure 6-1. The Model Frequently Found in Quality Control Literature

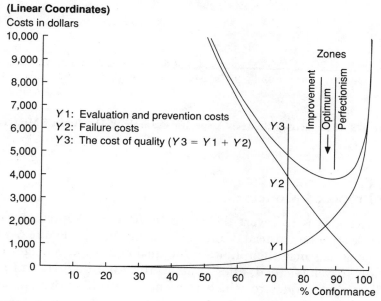

Figure 6-2. Dr. Juran's Model

Figure 6-3 is based upon the same model and, with the scale for the *x*-axis enlarged 10 times, illustrates the difficulty in defining these three zones when approaching an asymptotic value.

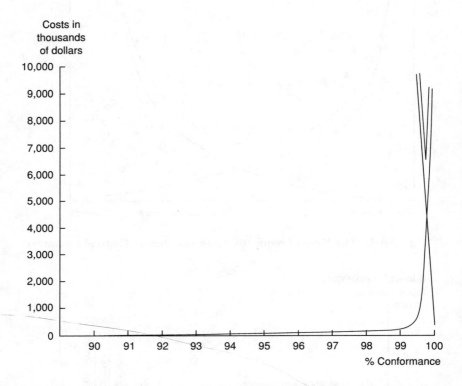

Figure 6-3. Linear coordinates: A specific example of Dr. Juran's Model

The Proposed Model

The idea is to invert the *x*-axis by having it represent the defect or error rate instead of the rate of conformance (Figure 6-4). This same axis may then indicate the quality cost percentages in relation to value-added, sales volume, the total budget, and so on. The three zones to which reference is made above appear with the position of the outside zones reversed in relation to the optimum zone.

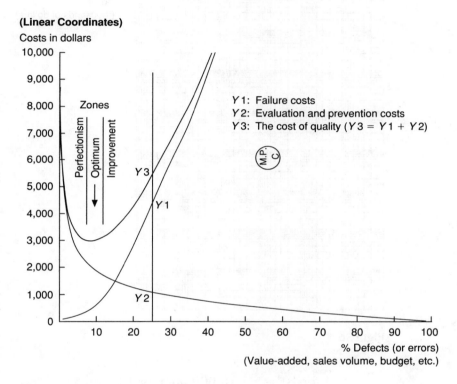

(Linear Coordinates)

Costs in dollars

Y1: Failure costs
Y2: Evaluation and prevention costs
Y3: The cost of quality (Y3 = Y1 + Y2)

% Defects (or errors)
(Value-added, sales volume, budget, etc.)

Figure 6-4. Proposed Model

Figure 6-5 is presented on logarithmic graph paper composed of blocks that are arranged six across and eight down. It is used to show an enlarged view of one portion of Figure 6-4. On the horizontal axis, it shows p.p.m. (or percentages) and uses exponents of 10 instead of numbers.

$$0 \text{ for } 10^0 = \quad 1 \text{ ppm}$$
$$1 \text{ for } 10^1 = \quad 10 \text{ ppm}$$
$$2 \text{ for } 10^2 = \quad 100 \text{ ppm}$$
$$3 \text{ for } 10^3 = \quad 1,000 \text{ ppm}$$

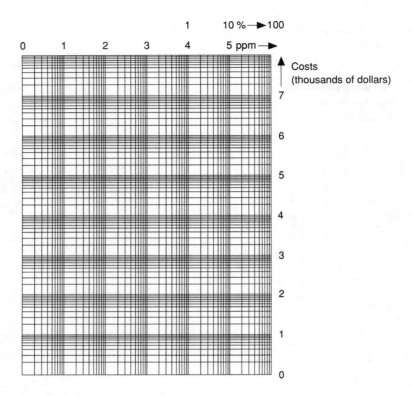

Figure 6-5.

$$4 \text{ for } 10^4 = 10{,}000 \text{ ppm, or } 1\%$$
$$5 \text{ for } 10^5 = 100{,}000 \text{ ppm, or } 10\%$$
$$6 \text{ for } 10^6 = 1{,}000{,}000 \text{ ppm, or } 100\%$$

The concept of ppm will also appear in the following chapter.

The vertical axis shows the costs in thousands of dollars with the same notation as above: exponents instead of numbers. In other words, the y axis values encompass the zones from 1,000 dollars to 100 million dollars.

The range covered is therefore from 1 ppm to 100% on the x-axis and from 1000 dollars to 100 million dollars on the y-axis.

It is quite clear that the number of modules or units may be adapted to fit the problem being addressed.

X is the % of defects or errors

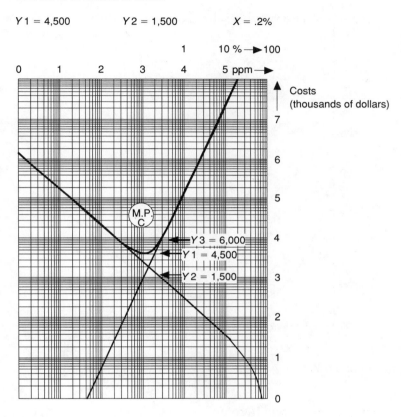

Figure 6-6.

As a first example, the asymptotic curve from Figure 6-3 is shown on graph paper in Figure 6-6 with kF as the unit of measurement.

The same curve can be shown with linear coordinates, as illustrated in Figure 6-7.

The AFCIQ Grid.

On the basis of Feigenbaum's work and British standards, the AFCIQ established a *Guide to the Costs of Quality* for small and

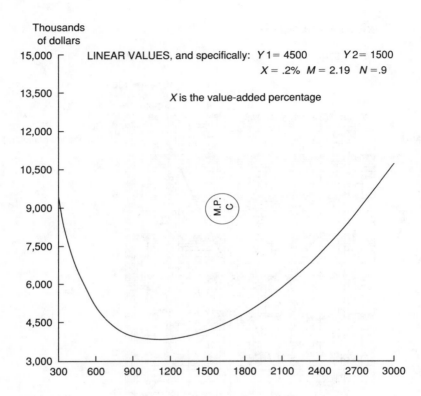

Figure 6-7.

medium-sized French companies and industries, which was published in 1981 by AFCIQ and AFNOR.

Currently in the process of revision, this book contains not only the grid presented in Table 6-2, but also the most complete and precise set of definitions for terminology in this field that is applicable to private firms.

This grid is only a model and may be modified and adapted for use in a particular company, department, or division. For example, quality management during production may be added under the heading of evaluation; equipment failures and their consequences could be added under internal failures; and delivery errors could be included under external failures. In other words, it is an *outline* that should be adapted to each specific use. An administrative group such as a department or a division may construct its

Table 6-2. Presentation of the AFCIQ Grid

Cost of Prevention	Cost of Evaluation
A.1 Quality Management	**B.1 Industrial Evaluation of the Product**
A.1.1 • Administration	
A.1.2 • Quality Engineering	**B.2 Acceptance Inspections of Products Purchased Externally**
A.1.2.1 • Quality research	
A.1.2.2 • Inspection methods	B.2.1 • Evaluation of products purchased externally
A.1.2.3 • Quality audit	
	B.2.2 • Inspection at the supplier's premises
A.2 Preparation and Implementation of Reviews	B.2.3 • Inspection of incoming goods
	B.2.4 • Cost of materials expended
A.2.1 • Design review	B.2.5 • Data processing and analysis
A.2.2 • Review of product specifications documentation	
	B.3 Inspection of Production
A.2.3 • Review of production documentation	B.3.1 • Inspection of the process
	B.3.2 • Inspection of production start-up
A.2.4 • Review of inspection documentation	B.3.3 • Inspection of production in progress
	B.3.4 • "Super-inspection"
A.3 Quality System for Procurements	B.3.5 • Inspection of the packaging process
A.3.1 • Evaluation of suppliers	B.3.6 • Final inspection
A.3.2 • Inspection specifications	B.3.7 • Certification by official agencies
A.3.3 • Verification of purchase orders	B.3.8 • Evaluation of inventory
	B.3.9 • Materials expended during testing
A.4 Quality Training Programs	B.3.10 • Processing of inspection data
	B.3.11 • Product quality audit
A.5 Other prevention expenditures	
	B.4 Metrology
	B.4.1 • Materials used for inspection
	B.4.2 • Materials used for production

Cost of Internal Defects	Rejections
C.1 Production Failures	**D.1 Claims and Complaints**
C.1.1 • Production failures	D.1.1 • After-sales service
C.1.2 • Design failures	D.1.2 • Products rejected and returned
C.1.3 • Failures in external procurements	D.1.3 • Technical assistance/repair of rejected products
C.2 Corrective Alterations	D.1.4 • Replacement under warranty
C.2.1 • Production failures	D.1.5 • Installation defects
C.2.2 • Design failures	D.1.6 • Error in product application research
C.2.3 • Failures in external procurements	D.1.7 • Design error
	D.1.8 • Civil and criminal liability
C.3 Locating of Defects	
	D.2 Loss of Known Clientele
C.4 The Rejection Process	
C.5 Reinspection of Products that Have Been Corrected	
C.6 Downgrading or Termination of the Product	

own grid by having a brainstorming session based on the following questions:

- What is prevention in our particular case?
- What is evaluation in our particular case?
- What are internal errors, in our particular case?
- What are external errors, in our particular case?

Once this initial phase is completed, the resulting ideas should be organized under the existing *codes* in the AFCIQ grid, and kept as a permanent reference for any other such study in which divisions of the company or corporation participate.

A Sample Implementation of the Proposed Model

Let us assume that the Empe Company uses the AFCIQ grid to make a rough initial estimate of its quality costs. The results obtained are expressed in Pareto analyses, shown in the following figures:

- Figure 6-8: prevention
- Figure 6-9: evaluation
- Figure 6-10: conformance (which is the sum of the two preceding items)
- Figure 6-11: internal failures
- Figure 6-12: external failures
- Figure 6-13: nonconformance (which is the sum of the two preceding items)

The "model" quality costs curve for this company is expressed in linear values in Figure 6-14 and logarithmic values in Figure 6-15.

Simulations carried out on the basis of this model illustrate that it is *dynamic*, as shown by Figures 6-16 and 6-17.

In fact, as a result of a series of measures taken with respect to failures and prevention, the minimum moves toward the left and its value decreases. Figure 6-17, which summarizes this simulation, shows that the CQR changes from 42 million francs to approximately 20.6 million francs. The difference between the company's position and the minimum is the broken curve marked "Ideal." The cost of conformance shows practically no change,

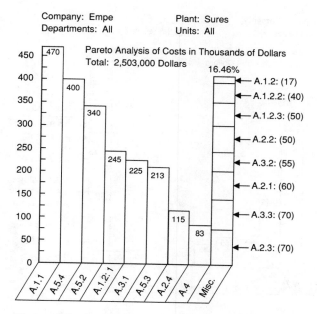

Figure 6-8. Prevention

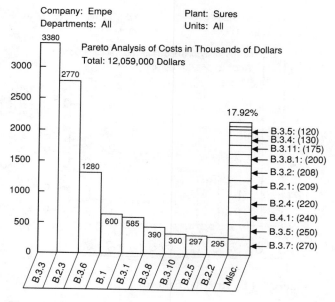

Figure 6-9. Evaluation

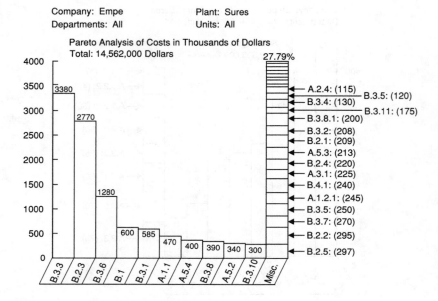

Figure 6-10. Conformance

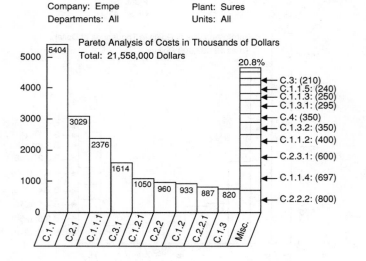

Figure 6-11. Internal Failures

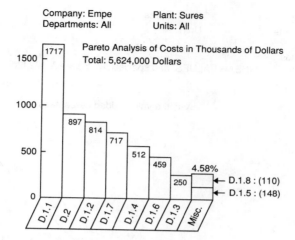

Figure 6-12. External Failures

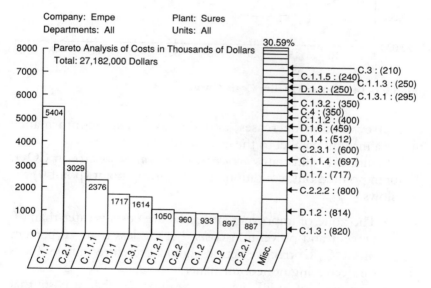

Figure 6-13. Nonconformance

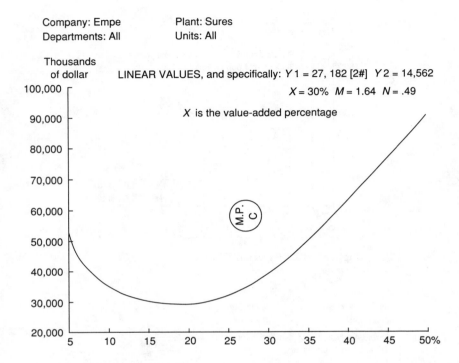

Figure 6-14. Linear Quality Costs Curve

cost of evaluation decreases, and the cost of nonconformance moves almost in parallel to the cost of quality.

Figure 6-17 illustrates *prevention's leveraged impact* on COQ. As Juran pointed out, conditions at the starting point (point 0) are as follows:

- The zone of improvement has failure costs greater than 70 percent and prevention costs that are less than 10 percent of COQ. Corrective action should therefore initially focus on decreasing nonconformance.
- The zone of indifference (optimum) has failure costs that are 50 percent and prevention costs that are nearly 10 percent of COQ. Corrective action should therefore initially focus on evaluation and prevention.

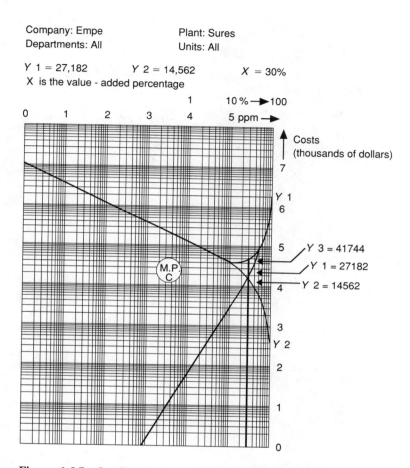

Company: Empe   Plant: Sures
Departments: All   Units: All

Y 1 = 27,182   Y 2 = 14,562   X = 30%
X is the value - added percentage

Figure 6-15. Quality Costs in Logarithmic Values

- The zone of perfectionism has failure costs that are less than 40 percent and evaluation costs that are greater than 50 percent of COQ. Corrective action should therefore consist of studying all defects, easing tolerances, reducing inspection controls, and rooting out perfectionists.

Bear in mind that the above is true only for the first curve, since the system is dynamic.

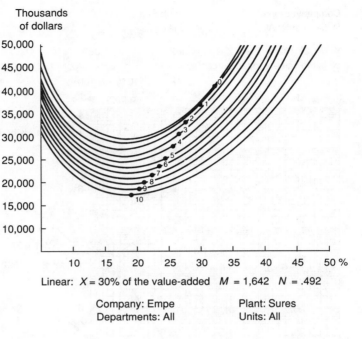

Linear: *X* = 30% of the value-added   *M* = 1,642   *N* = .492

Company: Empe   Plant: Sures
Departments: All   Units: All

Figure 6-16.

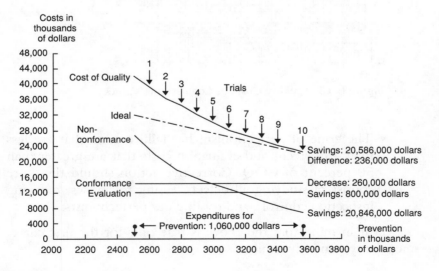

Figure 6-17.

The fact that these effects, which have their principal impact in the area of prevention, are dynamic in nature serves to reconcile the ideas of Juran and Crosby. It should be noted that the horizontal axis pertains to prevention, and its scale permits the following observation: an investment of 1 million dollars in prevention leads to a savings of 22 million dollars in the CQR.

This model has several advantages. First, it calculates the order of magnitude of the four elements of COQ; second, it indicates the status of the company with respect to a minimum, and thereby shows the size of its *potential for improvement*; third, it is a decision-making aid (a point that will be further discussed in Section 3); fourth, it is broken down unit by unit, department by department, and even division by division.

The Relative Size of COQ

A majority of experts concede that companies that have not yet introduced total quality have a total COQ of from 10 to 30 percent of total sales volume. Service companies have figures that are from 20 to 40 percent of their value-added activities. COQ may be expressed in dollars or in percentage of sales volume, value-added, the value of production, budget, and so on.

A reasonable assessment led the same experts to believe that COQ could be reduced to about 5 to 15 percent of sales volume. Such a *potential for improvement* could increase margins by proportions far greater than is possible with any other methods. Such improvement in profit margins would very likely stimulate investment as well.

Some companies focus their efforts on evaluation and inspection. Figure 6-18 shows that this strategy indeed brings about a decrease in external failures, or those failures perceived by the client. In contrast, however, internal failures increase, although they have no impact on the client. Average savings in COQ are estimated at practically zero and product quality expenditures are constant or on the increase.

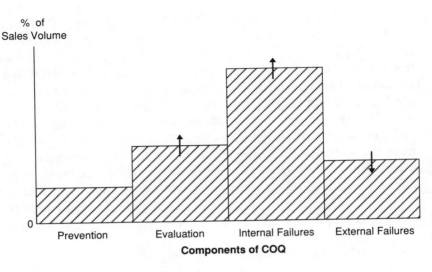

Figure 6-18. COQ Trends in Using the Quality Control Philosophy

Prevention

The ABC Company, an actual case often cited by Juran, has the following characteristics:

Millions of $

- Sales volume
  — 1,000

- Investments
  — 500

- Profits
  — 100

- Cost of nonconformance
  — 200

- Investment necessary in order to divide the cost of nonconformance in half
  — 12.5

In summary, 12.5 million dollars must be invested in order to earn 100 million dollars through improved quality. Figure 6-19 compares the results before and after implementation of a quality improvement strategy. Before an investment in defect prevention, it took a $500 million investment to result in $100 million of profit. Without understanding the profit potential of defect prevention it would have seemed necessary to double sales volume and therefore double investment in order to earn a second 100 million dollars. That would be a gamble like playing poker: would the market accept that amount of production? Such self-limiting thinking has been sustained for years by many companies who also sought economies of scale.

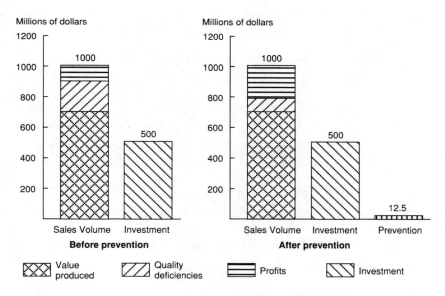

Figure 6-19. The Leveraged Effect of Prevention (Juran's Example of the ABC Company)

The second example cited involves the results of a survey of 500 American and Japanese companies (Figure 6-20). The graph on the left shows that, with less evaluation than in the West, but with triple the amount of prevention, the Japanese wound up with half as many internal and external failures as were found in Western companies. The summary graph on the right illustrates a second observation: for the same sales volume, the Japanese achieved an additional 8 percent margin as a result of their prevention efforts. In this same regard, several statistics on personnel assigned to inspection should be mentioned: in the West, they represent as much as 15 percent of personnel, while in Japan they amount to no more than 1 percent of the work force.

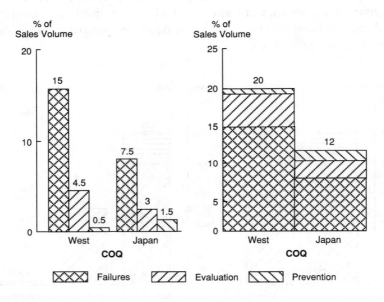

Figure 6-20. Comparison of 500 American and Japanese Companies

The Principles of Prevention

Our schools have always taught us foresight, but not prevention. *Foresight* is asking, "What does my client need from me?" followed by, "What can I do to satisfy the client's needs?" Foresight therefore means imagining the future – considering probabilities and possibilities – and then organizing and making decisions based on such contemplation. Despite the constancy of human passions and pastimes, there are no reliable systems for predicting the future in terms of client satisfaction, since clients' needs are constantly evolving. This is all the more so when the cycle between demand and delivery is prolonged.

Prevention is a set of measures undertaken to prevent undesirable occurrences. Prevention is asking, "What could happen to
make my client dissatisfied?" and then "What can I do to prevent
this from happening?" Note that the first question is not the
opposite of "What can I do to satisfy the client?" The following
example underscores the difference between the two questions.
With the first remote control televisions, technicians had designed
the small self-contained control box to change channels, adjust
volume, color, and contrast, and to be hand held. All these fea-
tures, translated into specifications, occasioned the marketing of
the first remote control televisions. The medium used to replace
the wire that had connected the television to the control box was
ultrasonic signals. No one foresaw that, unless the walls were
made of thick concrete, the ultrasonic signals could remotely control the neighbor's television (if it were the same type). No one
foresaw that at 8:00 P.M. during the evening news, the unit could
also bring on the barking of every dog in the neighborhood. This
was a lack of prevention. Prevention, then, is to foresee the
"unforeseeable."

Let's think for a moment about the remote control device, a
wonderful gadget that has great potential for the future and that
already has many other applications in the home: the stereo system, microwave oven, alarms, exhaust hood, electric range, and
so on.

Sometimes it is left on an armchair and forgotten. The user
or a guest may set off an alarm by sitting down. It is often placed
on a coffee table in the living room, since it can most easily be
found there. Drinks and refreshments are often placed on the same
living room coffee table. Children play, glasses get knocked over,
and corrosive liquids spill into the box and make it unable to function. All this is lack of prevention, to which the client's reaction
can be imagined easily.

As a safety measure, an automobile manufacturer designed the
doors of a vehicle to lock as soon as it began moving (at a low
speed). The clients, even though they had been advised of this fact,
took their car to the carwash, where they left the keys in the igni-
tion. The vehicle then moved through the carwash, but when it
exited the washing equipment, there was great surprise at finding
the car locked with the keys inside.

Obviously, it is impossible to foresee, and therefore to prevent, every undesirable circumstance. However, that realization does not diminish the validity of drawing up a list of "unforeseeable" factors and for each entry asking: "What can I do to prevent this from happening?" The four questions are therefore the basis not only for foresight, but also for prevention. To restate, they are:

1. What does my client need from me?
2. What can I do to satisfy the client?
3. What could happen to make my client dissatisfied?
4. What can I do to prevent that from happening?

How might these questions have prevented problems with the remote control system?

1. What does my client need?
   - a self-contained control box that gives a person remote control of his or her television set
2. What can I do to satisfy the client?
   - design a control box that allows the client not only to switch channels, but also to adjust the volume, contrast, and color
3. What could happen to make my client dissatisfied?
   - dogs barking when the client uses the remote control
   - damage to the control box caused by household wear and tear
4. What I do to prevent that from happening?
   - change from an ultrasonic to an infrared transmitting system

This is truly a novel kind of reasoning.

If any possibilities listed under question 3 cannot be resolved, there is a risk that they may occur. If, for example, resolving a certain risk would be too costly, its seriousness can at least be assessed and, if necessary, it can be covered by insurance: that is foresight. We do likewise in our private lives: we want our insurance to cover the unforeseeable. For example, we often have several types of insurance both for life and death. We know that we have to die, but uncertainty about the date of our death makes us feel uncomfortable. Foresight and precautions allay this discomfort.

The answers to questions 2 and 4 are specifications when expressed in figures.

There are in fact two types of prevention:

- *Anticipatory prevention*, that is, prevention implemented during design, research, or even development. Although it obviously pertains to products, it also involves processes and procedures. It is carried out by means of group efforts, and also by simulation on models. Prevention may also make use of redundancy, that is, parallel use of crucial components. If one component fails, the "parallel" component ensures that the device operates properly. Prevention also encompasses preventive maintenance and the diagnostic aids provided with the product.
- *Active prevention*, or the elimination of errors or failures at the earliest possible point in the production process, which requires detection of defects as early as possible.

One example pertains to the cost of correcting an error in a software program. If the error is detected:

- During the program design phase, it costs
  —————————————————————— $100
- During the delivery notification phase, it costs
  —————————————————————— $2,000
- After the first delivery, it costs
  —————————————————————— $8,000
  or the initial cost multiplied by 80

A second example, which is well known to television manufacturers, concerns the detection of a defect in an integrated circuit (chip):

- During procurement, it costs
  —————————————————————— $0.50
- During production, it costs
  —————————————————————— $5.00
- During inspection, it costs
  —————————————————————— $50.00
- Once the client has the product, it costs
  —————————————————————— $500.00

If the client is lost, he will cause other potential clients to be lost. The cost is then exorbitant.

The ideal is for the defect to be detected at the supplier level using the data or the expertise of the client. The reason for this is apparent in Figure 5-5. Each actor, each stage in the process obviously contributes added value to the defective product. As the product moves farther through the process, however, it becomes more and more difficult to locate the point at which the defect occurred. Determining the defect's point of origin as expeditiously as possible is fundamental to quality control since other defects may be generated at the same point. That is true active prevention.

Table 6-3, which is based on the ideas of Professor Shigeo Shingo, employs a medical analogy to illustrate the relationship of prevention to both judgmental inspection (good-bad) and to informational inspection. Prevention is like a vaccination in that it has a double purpose: to prevent an illness and to prevent an epidemic.

The Japanese use two terms, *baka-yoke* and *poka-yoke* to indicate the final phases of "mistake-proofing," that is, any simple and obvious test that serves to ensure successful production even by a rank beginner.

Baka-yoke can be illustrated by some recent events involving the French national railway system. In 1986, after many incidents and accidents had occurred, it was discovered that most automobile drivers did not understand what the flashing red signals on the train track meant. Some defied them and maneuvered around the two half-gates, some broke them down, and some even stayed with their vehicles when blocked between the two gates. Flashing red signals and half-gates are designed to prevent an automobile driver from passing when a train is coming. True baka-yoke in this instance would be to have set the road either above or below the rail line.

Likewise, if a press is quite dangerous to operate, safety systems are installed that shut off power in the event that someone violates safety procedures. Why not apply this idea universally?

An example of poke-yoke is placing in a product mechanisms that ensure that a part or component is always installed in the proper manner. Some machines stop if the part is not in the correct position.

Table 6-3. Inspection Techniques

Judgmental Inspection: Death certificate
Informational Inspection: Medical consultation
Preventive Control: Vaccination

No defective products should be transferred to the downstream actor

100% Inspection

Consecutive Inspection

Self-Inspection

• Risk/ Allowing oneself to compromise
  Errors due to distraction
• Concrete Methods for Prevention
  Baka-yoke: fool-proofing
  Poka-yoke: mistake-proofing

Process Control:
• Vertical, from the outside, elimination of causes
• Horizontal, from the inside, inspection of parameters

Goal: "Zero Defects"

Source: Shigeo Shingo

Management of prevention entails two types of data collection. The first type involves data that is physically extracted from the production process in order to be checked or recorded. The use of such data facilitates the pinpointing of causes and is termed *vertical external* control. The other type of data collection is internal to the process, and the purpose of the parameters recorded is to regulate the process. Since these parameters are internal to the sequence shown in Figure 5-5 (see pg. 72), the applicable term is *horizontal internal* control. The recording of extreme variations in these internal parameters may enhance vertical external control.

The following list is far from exhaustive and gives only a few examples of preventive measures:

• Company policy
• Preparatory meetings for design, research, and audit activities
• Project reviews
• User satisfaction studies
• Safety
• Research into causes of failures

- The study of potentially crucial points in the overall production process
- Operating methods for tests and trials (processes and products)
- Design of testing equipment
- Reliability and maintainability studies
- Supplier capabilities
- Testing and inspection procedures
- Subcontracting procedures
- Quality training
- Professional (skills) training
- Quality control circles
- Analysis of failure modes and criticality (FMEA, Failure Mode and Effects Analysis, and FMCEA, Failure Mode and Critical Effects Analysis)
- Value analysis

Quality Improvement

The sole purpose of the model proposed at the beginning of this chapter is to set a goal for nonconformance that, when the total cost of quality is in the zone of improvement, would entail action in this sequence:

1. Prevention
2. Evaluation

If the total cost is in the optimum zone or in the zone of perfectionism, the nonconformance goal should be achieved by action in this sequence:

1. Evaluation
2. Prevention

Of course, it remains possible during each phase to use the true cost of nonconformance to maintain contact with reality. The management tool permits this.

The leveraged effect of prevention in the zone of improvement may be observed in Figure 6-17. A slight effort with respect to the cost of conformance ($200,000) leads to an improvement in nonconformance that is a great deal larger (often 10 times as large).

This type of tool is available in order to encourage and promote – but above all, to provide standards for – both goals and results.

It is quite evident that the "model" curve may change during the course of trials that, by taking into account actual values, make it possible to calculate numerous parameters. The most important thing is to begin the process and stay on track by knowing what can and should be expected from it. Each plant, department, and division has its inputs, outputs, and goals and can visualize its outcomes in relation to the goals that have been set.

Figure 6-17 proves Crosby's assertion that prevention leads to an almost permanent reduction in quality costs. It is in fact apparent that, beyond the optimum zone defined by Juran, in the so-called zone of perfectionism, the COQ continues to decrease with an increase in prevention, which also affects the cost of evaluation. The COQ curve then tends to move toward the cost-of-conformance curve. Nonconformance tends toward zero. The asymptote is reached when quality costs become equal to the costs of prevention. To continue to that point would be to achieve *veritable perfection* since evaluation would be eliminated, a situation not likely to occur in the near future.

An increase in prevention therefore causes nonconformance to decrease almost to zero, and the COQ then tends to be equal to the cost of prevention.

Perfectionism, as defined by Juran, would exist only if the model kept the same parameters. Throughout this quality improvement process

- the parameters for nonconformance decrease, and
- the parameters for conformance increase.

Before beginning any quality improvement program, the company's status should be established using the format shown in Figure 6-21.

The characteristics of this situation are the same for every organization, department, or division, with variations of scale only.

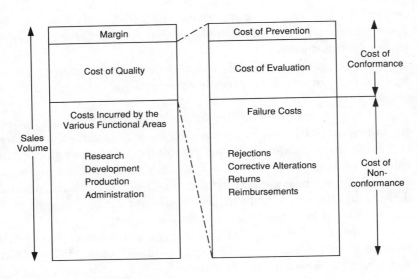

Figure 6-21. Cost Analysis

The leveraged effect of prevention, as evidenced by the simulation carried out for the Empe Company, produces the results shown in Figure 6-22.

There is an increase in the costs of prevention, a slight decrease in the costs of evaluation, and a very great reduction in the cost of failures. This method shall be discussed further at a later point.

In addition to Juran's example of the ABC Company there is the example of ITT (Figure 6-23) cited by Crosby in his book *Quality is Free* (1980). Among other assertions, he wrote that "quality is not only desirable but it is free . . . and not only is it free but it is the most profitable product that we have."

In June 1985, at the National Quality Control Circles Convention organized by the AFCERQ, the Hewlett-Packard Company issued results obtained during an 18-month study (Figure 6-24).

Another example illustrates Solmer Company's determination to tap the *potential for improvement*. In 1984, Solmer was

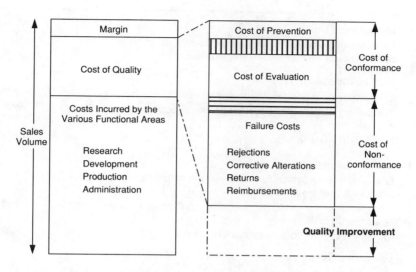

Figure 6-22. Quality Improvement

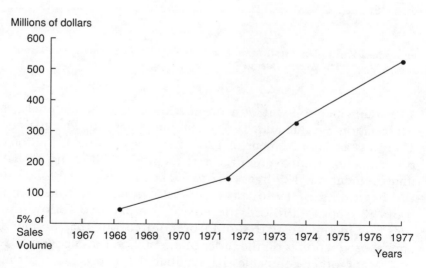

Figure 6-23. P. Crosby's Example (ITT) — Earnings in Relation to the Cost of Quality (COQ)

ent Quality	
in the delays for annual interviews in which the goals and performance of each employee are reviewed	↑ 10
Product Reliability	
The failure rate during production was reduced by one-half	↑ 2
The defect rate during final post-production inspection was reduced by one-half	↑ 2
A twofold increase in production linearity	↑ 2
Client Satisfaction	
Despite a noticeable increase in the number of options, the number of errors is 25% of the previous level	↑ 4
Compliance with our obligations regarding promptness and shipment dates has doubled	↑ 2
The length of time required for deliveries is 3 times less	↓ 3
Internal Performance	
Warranty costs have been reduced by 30%	↓ 30%
The accuracy of sales forecasts, which was on the order of +/- 60%, is currently less than +/- 20%	↑ 3

Source: Hewlett-Packard, May 1985

Figure 6-24. Implementation of Total Quality: Improvement over an 18-Month Period

440 francs per ton out of a production cost (raw materials + depreciation + value-added) of 1,600 francs per ton. The goal for 1985 was an improvement of 125 francs per ton out of the total potential for improvement. At the end of 1985, the actual improvement was 129 francs per ton. The new goal established at the beginning of 1986 was again 125 francs per ton, and a monthly report allowed the entire company to follow the progress in this area. It should be pointed out that Solmer's annual production is on the order of 3.5 million tons per year.

Many other companies have initiated this process and can therefore produce numerous examples of improvements. The movement has now spread to service firms, banks, insurance companies, hotels, and even the government.

7

Excellence:
The Zero Philosophy

If you wish to advance toward the infinite,
explore the finite in every direction.

— *Goethe*

In school we learned that *zero* means the purely arithmetical figure above which values are positive and below which they are negative. This abstraction is nothing but an artifice that is useful for calculations. The history of its invention is quite instructive, however.

In the fourth century A.D. a Hindu conceived of a special character that symbolized nothingness, now called zero, in order to mark the absence of a figure with a specific value. During the seventh century, the Arabs understood the significance of the principle of position that is so familiar to us. Today it is said that zero is an operator because any zero, when placed to the right of a number, instantly multiplies it tenfold. A monk from Auvergne named Gerbert introduced the zero to the French upon returning from his journey to Cordoba in A.D. 980 – he was later to become Pope Sylvester II. The zero appeared in France for the first time in the eleventh century in a treatise on astronomy.

Incidentally, the designation *A.D.* (after the birth of Christ) carries the implication that Christ was born in the year "zero." The beginning of the Christian era is therefore only a conventional reference point.

The Celsius temperature scale has zero ($0°$ C) corresponding to the fusion point of pure water (the melting point of ice) and $100°$ C for the point at which water evaporates into the atmosphere (to put it simply). Fahrenheit, a German physicist, proposed a scale in which zero is the temperature of a coolant mixture (crushed ice and sal ammoniac), and, at the other extreme, the temperature of the human body; this range is divided into 96 degrees. Here too, zero is only a reference point.

The entity that aspires to be zero does not exist in nature. Nothing is not null because references can be found to "less than nothing" and even "nothing at all." Everyday language also contains many expressions that reflect this fact, such as "less than nothing" and "the nth degree of nothingness" (which assumes the existence of something before and after nothingness.

In fact, zero is only a reference point. Physicists know very well that, with regard to temperatures, absolute zero ($0° K = -273.15° C$) is never reached. Even if it is approached every day, it remains inaccessible. Another example: an absolute vacuum, which is a theoretical concept, could only exist in an enclosure in which all the walls stretched out to infinity. A perfect vacuum (zero molecules) can be approached to any degree that is desired, but it can never be achieved.

Therefore, zero defects, zero failures, zero delays, zero inventory, zero paper, zero accidents, zero loss of reputation: what does it all mean? As in physics, these are theoretic values that everyone knows can never be attained. Why then should these concepts be discussed at such length?

Physicists spend their lives conducting research into such topics while fully aware of what is involved. It is part of their long quest for perfect knowledge of nature. They continually progress toward the absolute. It is a never-ending quest that they are unwilling to abandon. They know very well that zero is the inverse of the infinite and that, since the infinite cannot be attained, they will never reach zero.

When any such temperature or vacuum value is reached, the results are considered a reference for future experiments. In other words, they become acquired knowledge that defines what can now be done. The next phase builds on those results and aims to reach even farther. It is the same way in sports, where records must continually be broken.

In the same way, to say *zero defects* is to say, "This is what we are capable of today and from this point forward, we shall not only not remain at this same level of capability, but we will make the commitment to do better." Like sports players and physicists, the men and women of our private firms and public entities are issuing a challenge and adventurously setting out to break records. Zero is not what counts, but rather the challenge of doing better. We will never achieve zero, but there will be no retreat from what we know how to do well today and what we will learn to do better tomorrow.

Doing It Right the First Time

Doing it right the first time means meeting the commitment that has been made, that is, meeting the specifications (Figure 5-4. See pg. 70). Doing it right the first time, every time, means meeting the same commitment for each request by the client. To do even better, one might set a realistic initial goal, capable of achievement. When that goal is achieved, another one can be set, with improved specifications. That is the "journey toward zero defects." It is this line of reasoning that prompted Crosby to say: "Zero defects is not a destination, it is a journey." Figure 7-1 illustrates the difference between "doing it right the first time" and the journey toward zero defects.

Why don't we strive for zero defects in our work?

The answer is because, in our work, errors are "budgeted," standardized (hence, the TQL defined in Chapter 3 is derived from a standard such as NF X 06-022), and therefore accepted. They are considered a misfortune that we must live with.

The illogic of this assumption is demonstrated in the following example. Some Japanese who had received an order for several thousand integrated circuits with the specification TQL = 1 percent, sent two packages – a large one and a small one. The small one contained the defects that had been ordered! Perhaps in our country we would have mixed the defective products in with the good ones: that is standardization! This may be another way of viewing things – or it may be a bad habit.

Until now, the work produced by a company was limited by this notion of an "acceptable" number of errors or defects. This thinking is laxness. Any error, any defect should be unacceptable.

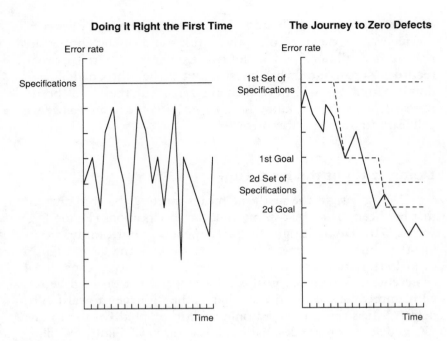

Figure 7-1.

Adherence to specifications, to requirements, and therefore to *commitments* entails allowing *no errors* with respect to the requirements that have been negotiated: that is *zero defects.* It is better to change the specifications than to permanently accept a 5 percent error rate because "it isn't serious." Managers should fight to end this bad habit, which has become deep-rooted in our companies.

Figure 7-2 shows that permanent actions taken with respect to the learning curve of a product make it possible to progress toward zero defects.

Parts per Million (PPM)

When embarking upon such a journey, one must recognize that the units of measure selected for use today must change in order to better evaluate improvement. Because 1 percent or 100 percent is used as a reference, percentage is often the unit of measure. However, the most advanced technologies quickly show that

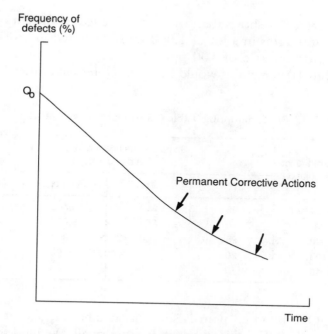

Figure 7-2. The Impact of Experience on Quality

this unit of measurement is in practice too large. In fact, when a subsystem is made up of hundreds and thousands of components, a 1 percent defect rate for each component precludes the creation of a properly functioning system. Furthermore, that fact would become evident only when the system is finished which not only would be too late, but would require that everything be redone in order to discover where the problem was. That would be appallingly expensive. And yet, 1 percent is "so little"!

Each product and each service require that tens, hundreds, and thousands of steps be performed during a process that includes detection of need, production, and use. If each operation is affected by a 1 percent error rate, no product will be satisfactory.

One unit of measurement that today makes it possible to perceive the goal to be attained is the *ppm* (parts per million): 100 percent represents 1 million of these units, which means that 1 percent is equal to 10 thousand ppm.

Table 7-1 shows that, with a confidence coefficient of 90 percent, 980 items in a lot of 1,000 must be tested in order to confirm a defect rate of 100 ppm. Given the level of uncertainty, which is 10 percent, it would be better to test all of them.

Table 7-1. PPM: Sampling Table (Confidence Level: 90%)

Size of the lot or population	Sample sizes needed to guarantee a defect rate of:			
	10%	1%	1,000 ppm	100 ppm
100,000 items	25	250	2,500	20,000
10,000	25	250	2,000	8,000
1,000	25	200	800	980
100	20	80	98	100
10	9	10	10	10

One hundred ppm is still a large amount, and yet it represents only 0.01 percent, which is quite small. We tend to consider any number less than 1 to be small and any number greater than 10 to be large. That is because we still count with fingers, even if only mentally. The advantage of the ppm unit of measurement is to transform the small numbers into large numbers: whereas the "small" numbers (0.01 percent) encourage passivity, the "large" numbers (100 ppm) create pressure for action.

It can be seen that, for example, with a 1 percent error rate for each step, only some 37 percent of the products are in conformance by the conclusion of one hundred steps. Nevertheless, for a simple but well-defined product, considering all that must be done between its design and its use – including development, procurements, manufacturing, and sales – one hundred steps are very few.

In this instance, one hundred steps lead to nonconformance in 63 percent of the products and goods. On the other hand, with a 0.1 percent error rate, only 10 percent of the goods are not in conformance. This analysis makes evident the importance of the number of errors.

In the design, production, and sale of complex items such as televisions or computers, the necessity of reducing the number of errors or defects in each step is immediately apparent. The more complex the product, the greater the number of steps to make it and the smaller the probability it will be in conformance. The only solution is to reduce the number of errors or defects, and to move toward zero. According to Figure 7-3, zero is not attained even with one hundred steps and an error rate of 0.01 percent, since one ppm = 0.0001 percent. But great progress has already been made if ppm is used as a unit of measure: nearly 99 percent of the goods (or products) would be in conformance for thousands of steps.

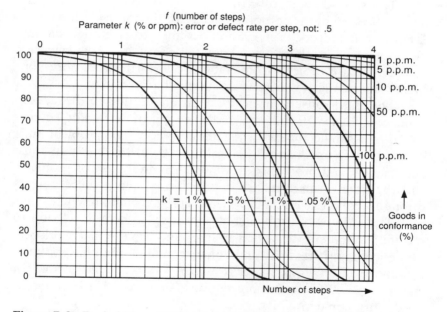

Figure 7-3. Probability of Obtaining Goods that Are in Conformance

Errors

The principal causes of errors fall within three categories:

• lack of knowledge

- a "know-it-all" attitude
- lack of attention

The first cause is the simplest to remedy, but there must first be awareness of this lack of knowledge. It is therefore essential to train those who need training, but with simplicity and humanity. This requires a deep sense of consideration and respect for the people to be trained, who are responsible adults and have their own particular experiences and abilities. If one single time they feel rebuked for not knowing something, they will never again ask for an explanation. There are few bad students, but there are many instructors who do not know how to deal with students. Teaching is a collective role that concerns us all.

The second cause of errors is more serious. Moreover, the higher the level in the corporate hierarchy, the more common it is. A know-it-all attitude is an evasion designed to save one's dignity: "I saw that once, therefore I know all about it." This evinces a mentality that is difficult to tolerate. It calls forth issues of responsibility and humility, which are discussed at a later point.

The third cause is more frequent and is due to distraction, confusion, lack of familiarity, and uncertainty. It cannot be corrected by a simple appeal for greater attention. The problem must be thoroughly understood. Critical points and trouble spots must be observed and procedures reviewed. An awareness of problems and their seriousness makes it possible to avoid these defects through a collective effort in which training is omnipresent.

The analysis of problems by subdividing them in relation to specific equipment, a particular step, and a particular work station encourages creativity and enhancement of the philosophy of prevention. Certainly, "to err is human," but it is *not* normal for errors to *recur*. The entire prevention system, as it has been developed, must come into play.

Excellence

The term *excellence* comes from the Latin *excellentia*, and *excellere*, which means "to be superior," "the finest."

Figure 7-4 summarizes what is meant by *excellence* in this discussion, and we are defining *zero defects* to mean "what we are completely capable of doing today."

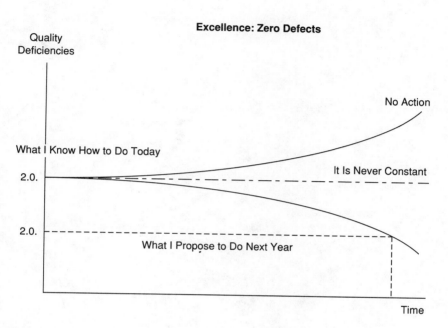

Excellence: Zero Defects

Quality
Deficiencies

No Action

What I Know How to Do Today

2.0.

It Is Never Constant

2.0.

What I Propose to Do Next Year

Time

Figure 7-4.

Excellence is an individual model that brings us toward a minimum of errors. It is also a collective model, in the sense that a group can research the error, identify its causes and correct it. Few of us wonder, when driving to work, why we don't hit a tree, a pedestrian, or another vehicle that day. Rather than being fatalistic about such errors, we do everything in our power to prevent them. We should do the same at work: let's not "budget" errors, create standards for them, or allow them at all.

Excellence is an attractive collective model that the entire company can follow, though patience is necessary. Behaviors and mentalities do not change with the wave of a wand, but that is no reason to delay action.

8
Measurement

If you wish to hit the center of the target,
you must aim a little above it;
all arrows are subject to the earth's gravity.

– H. Longfellow

The dictionary gives the following definition for *measurement*: the action of determining the value of certain magnitudes, using a fixed magnitude of the same nature as a reference term (and therefore, a unit). Notice the ambiguity of the terms: the *value* of *certain magnitudes . . .* with a *fixed magnitude of the same kind . . . reference (standard, unit)*. There is an immediate psychological short circuit, as shown in Figure 8-1.

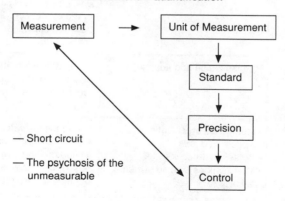

Figure 8-1. Measurement

115

If there is measurement, it is because there is a unit and therefore a standard. Hence comes the idea of precision, which leads to the notion of control. Suddenly, measurement = control is in everyone's mind. Now, if physical products can be effectively controlled, how, and by what right, could intellectual products be controlled? Table 8-1 gives several examples of the differences and similarities between administrative and production tasks.

Table 8-1. Similarities and Differences Between Administrative and Manufacturing Tasks

	Production	**Administrative**
Product	Tangible	Intangible
Quantification of time and charges	• Carefully measured and planned • Rejects, which are not readily accepted, are controlled	• Not well known • No work standards • Numerous special cases • Cyclical schedules • The smallest defect is considered an error by personnel
Superfluous tasks	Strictly controlled	Numerous survivals from the past foster a need to protect oneself with duplicate controls; or the lack of coordination between offices, drowned in a mass of procedures
Technology	Mechanization and automation	Computerization "in every direction" performed by technicians and limited to large-scale data processing
Operating procedures	• Methodical organization • Specialized jobs • Written instructions • Modifications studied systematically	Left to the discretion of operational managers, non-existent or limited methods, which are based on intuitive insights oriented toward routine

Among the dictionary definitions for the various terms of measurement – *value, magnitude, nature, reference, unit standard, and quality* – the most precise is for *standard*. *Quality*, for example, has numerous definitions. Nevertheless, even *standards* vary: for example, the definition for the *meter*, which used to represent one ten-millionth of a quarter of the earth's meridian, and whose standard is jealously guarded by the Pavillon de Breteuil in Sèvres, has been changed several times. Currently, it is the distance covered by light in a vacuum in 1/299,792,458 seconds. Isn't that simple?

This academic definition of standards has made such a deep impression on our attitudes that no one dares to measure anymore. Nevertheless, *there is no progress without measurement.*

Total quality is not an exact science, because we are continually in the process of discovering it; we should not be frightened of measurement. We should *count, compute, number, tally, enumerate, evaluate, and quantify*. In short, for purposes of total quality: *to measure* means *to quantify*.

To do so, we have *systems of notation* such as:

- Binary notation: yes or no, good or bad, accepted or rejected, and so on.
- Cardinal numbers: counting, numbering (1,2,3,4, etc.)

There are also reference tools such as:

- The nominal system: the use of numbers (codes) to designate objects
- The ordinal system: the arrangement of objects or events in a given order
- Intervals: the determination of distances (equal, logarithmic, etc.) along a scale (for example, a reference mark between 1 and 10)
- Ratios: the determination of relationships, expressed in the form of a fraction, between comparable values such as costs, time, units of measure, and dollars

Measurement requires a point of reference: the point where we are today. Imagine that I have decided to lose weight, beginning today. The first thing to do is to weigh myself. Do I need to know the exact weight? No, but I should always use the same scale. I could chose another method: placing a reference mark on my belt and seeing what progress is made in terms of that reference point.

What Should Be Measured?

Most often, those who measure are inspectors – police officers with their radar, government tax inspectors with their "surprise inspections." In French, the term inspector has a negative connotation that is undeserved.

If one goes beyond the academic definition that identifies measurement as a comparison with a reference, then everything is measurable. The analysis of human activities requires an attempt to evaluate; it is therefore essential to find the appropriate methods and units of measurement.

Collecting data and observations is like photographing the status of the problem. Will and imagination are the only components necessary for measurement. The crucial element is not precision, but the will to count. Progress, rather than control, is the goal, so many benchmarks, estimating factors, and indicators can be agreed upon to mark progress.

Measurement is usually concerned with conformance, but the principal concern here is *nonconformance*, that is, the failure to meet specifications or requirements. Everything is measurable, but only those terms that imply the "redoing" of something are relevant here:

- Rejects
- Returns
- Reimbursements
- Downgrading
- Errors
- Modifications
- Defects
- Corrective maintenance
- Unnecessary movements
- Overly long meetings
- The management of failures
- Delays in payment
- Inventory
- Stocks of semifinished products
- Failure to meet deadlines

- Poorly completed statements
- Poorly prepared invoices
- Incomplete purchase orders

Any and all of these can be measured and improved.

Some firms have even conducted brainstorming sessions in which they listed all undesirable items by division. These various items may, after they are given preliminary quantification, serve as reference points through the use of numbers or percentages. They may then be classified according to categories such as urgency, seriousness, and costs. It is even possible to combine the rankings.

Particularly in the case of administrative divisions, every activity should be shown to provide at least one product for which there is a quantitative evaluation (there is further discussion of this in chapter 12). Any event has a frequency of occurrence. If the phenomenon is variable, not only its central tendency but also its distribution can always be estimated. If it is a random phenomenon, it can be assigned a probability.

For example, absences (for illness or family reasons) or so-called unforeseen external commitments, could be "foreseen" if relatively large numbers are used as a basis for prediction and a certain level of errors is allowed. Therefore, a person's number of sick days is dependent on contingencies, but predicting the rate of absenteeism for 10 people to within about 10 percent is relatively easy.

The problem considered in this study is *quality* (error rate, number of claims, etc.), but it is also possible to document

- Quantities (volume, number, amount)
- Time (length of time between input and output, request and response)
- Costs (which often are the result of other factors, and may or may not include indirect costs)

It is a fact, especially since the creation of quality control circles, that *the simple act of measuring errors or defects has the immediate effect of reducing them.*

Measurement should stimulate action toward the goal of eliminating nonconformance.

The Purpose of Measurement

The purpose of measurement is to find evidence of any variation from the negotiated specifications. The role of measurement is to identify possible improvements and to indicate where to initiate action on failures. Above all, measurement should be a potent vehicle of success.

Indicators

Figure 8-2 shows four types of indicators. The first, at the top left, shows the trend in *quality deficiencies* as defined earlier. The goal is toward the bottom of the graph. It is represented as being nearly zero, but it is important to bear in mind the notion of ppm. The second, at the top right, is a *performance indicator* in the standard meaning of the term. The goal is to the top. Note that as the goal is neared, the difference between that maximum value, which is difficult to achieve, and the curve increasingly diminishes. It is a *management indicator* of undeniable usefulness.

As Figure 8-3 indicates, improving quality means reducing the items in the "low point of distribution" that exceed allowable values. To manage quality means to move the peak value. If the curves are often normal, it is because they are the result of many factors and operations.

Performance indicators are therefore management tools that indicate a trend.

Quality-deficiency indicators pertain to quality improvement. They play a role in the improvement of performance indicators even though the reverse is not necessarily true.

Management indicators show the results of collective action and indicate the tendency of the peak of a normal curve. Quality-deficiency indicators may be representative of individual actions and move in the direction of zero defects or 100 percent appropriate products.

It should be remembered that the quality indicator for 100 ppm is 99.99 percent. It is never appropriate to say "enough," because success requires inspiring the will to win by showing visible progress.

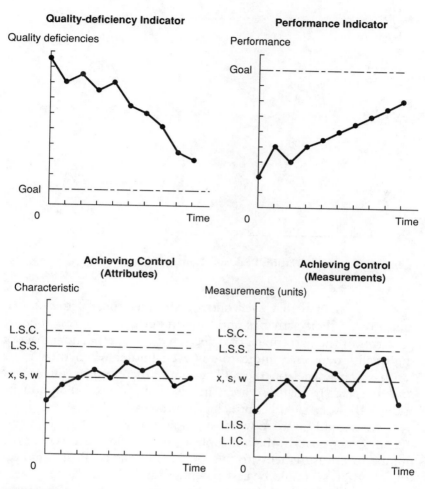

Figure 8-2.

The quality-deficiency indicators have the advantage of being adaptable to every type of management responsibility and therefore are also applicable to the technical, economic, and social fields. They are simple, trustworthy, and fair. Their preciseness is of no importance. They have a short response time: improvements are readily evident.

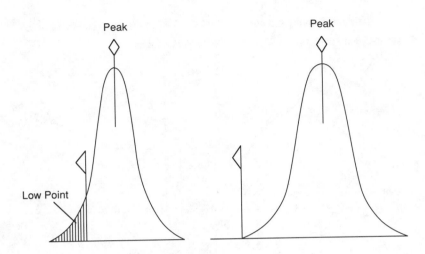

Figure 8-3. Distribution Peak and Low Point

It is essential that everyone see the relevance of the chosen indicator to their activities and determine their progress thereby (in terms of the percentage of defects, for example). The impact of the quality-deficiency indicators is even higher when their users can have an impact on them. They must therefore be *understood and accepted* by all those areas involved: Each person should be asking, "How can I affect principal indicators?"

We should improve what we know how to do before pursuing any other goal. In the initial phase, we should learn to limit the number of measurements to two or three per actor. Posted indicators of progress should be easy to understand with a glance.

You have no doubt noticed that analog watches (with hands) have reconquered the market, to the detriment of digital watches. Try the following experiment: if someone discreetly looks at his watch (during a meeting, for example), ask him the time, and you will see that he looks at his watch a second time before answering. During the first glance, he got an idea of the time from the angle of the two hands, but he did not note the exact time.

It is the same with posted indicators. Be aware of the *angle* or the general direction of change, because all day that is what workers will see. The specific scales will not be read. This important observation is even more valid when two indicators that originate from different places are viewed. For example, a data processing division that rarely monitors its quality improvement runs the risk, particularly at the beginning, of having an indicator with a steep upward slope, of which it would be justifiably proud. In contrast, any production division engaged in an attempt to improve quality will have a low upward slope. Comparing the two is unfair. With agreement by all parties, change the scales so that everyone sees their own progress and no one is frustrated by less tangible results.

The two other indicators at the bottom of Figure 8-2 are the *test charts for attributes* (qualitative characteristics) and *measurements* (measurable characteristics). The central line is the average, the range, or the standard deviation; the limits are for monitoring (which involves backup testing) or for a test that entails suspension of operation. The test charts for attributes have only upper limits. The test charts for measurements have both upper and lower limits.

Establishing test charts assumes that the measurement process is functioning correctly. It is active prevention, since anomalies become evident in the shape of the curve and trigger action before the implementation of corrective procedures.

Preparation of the charts is described elsewhere. The charts' purpose is to direct the process being tested toward stability by eliminating erratic causes of problems, to find abnormal causes, and to indicate actions to be taken in order to improve or optimize the process (change the average, narrow the limits, check the results a posteriori). In fact, a process cannot be improved if it is not "under control" since erratic variations mask the underlying abnormal problems and interfere with evaluation of the results of the changes made. In 99.8 percent of cases if a value is beyond the test limits, it is not due to chance.

It should be remembered that:

- The sample size is:
  - attributes: $n \sim 10/-p$ ($-p$ average proportion of defects)
  - measurements: $4 \leq n \leq 8$ (usually 5)
- The testing limits are calculated on the basis of background data from 15 to 25 samples
- If a testing periodicity of T is desired, the sampling periodicity shall be $T/4$

- If cyclical phenomena are suspected, the sampling period should be less than or equal to that of the cycle
- If the quantities produced during the sampling period are not sufficient to comply with the $n/-p$ rule, the quantities produced between the detection of two defects should be researched by using the "low proportion of defects" method

Some of the indicators are:

- The number of quality control circles in operation
- The number of presentations to the company's management
- The number of work groups assigned to quality (quality improvement groups in operation)
- The number of presentations approved by management
- Internal surveys regarding personnel satisfaction and their knowledge about total quality in the company
- External surveys of client satisfaction

Surveys and polls make it possible to discover the general situation, the internal and external images of the brand name, and also instances of nonconformance. The number of groups and circles at work reveals more about the perception of quality than about its staffing.

9

Responsibility

The current definition of *responsibility* is an obligation or a moral and intellectual need to correct a fault, to fulfill a duty, to meet a commitment. It implies that we accept and suffer the consequences of our actions according to particular moral and social criteria. In a company, employees are all responsible in relation to their subordinates (whose actions they vouch for), superiors (who vouch for their actions), colleagues, clients, and suppliers, but also with respect to third parties.

To be responsible is first of all to comply with the requirements of quality discerned in the previous four chapters: conformance, prevention, excellence, and measurement. Responsibility may be either individual or collective. A work group, for instance, must vouch for its own decisions.

About Management

Management, a magical and, since the late 1960s, somewhat tarnished term, means "ordering and arranging with care and skill." It includes all of a company's organizational and business techniques. It applies to all areas of the company as viewed from the broadest perspective. *Strategy* is the cornerstone upon which management conduct is based. Strategy, which is the aggregate of all choices, priorities, and commitments, includes:

- The creative effort that is responsible for the organization's existence and development
- The "direction of growth," which indicates how the company will continue to develop
- The company's financial, technical, and personal goals

- The synergies, or complementary relationships between functions and operations that the company will attempt to identify
- The different professional abilities upon which the company will focus its efforts

Any organization must define what it does, why and how it does it, and what it shall focus its efforts on. It should then set goals for itself in terms of market share, profitability, and social contribution. To attain these goals under the best of circumstances, it should direct its effort toward what it knows how to do well.

It is clear that the implementation of a strategy requires the use of a range of methods for transforming the organization's resources – personnel, equipment, financial assets, and products.

It is a reciprocal process: if strategy has a decisive influence on the type of management, then management also tends to affect the formulation of strategy.

The organization is no doubt the most visible part of management. Figure 9-1 shows the organization as the fruit of a dynamic process that is periodically called into question. As a reaction to the bureaucratic crisis, personnel will be more involved in decision making within the framework of interdisciplinary groups, which are supported by their own divisions within the organization and are linked together by streamlined formal procedures. Companies that today are progressing toward Total Quality Management are at this stage.

Both Crosby and Juran have said that management is responsible for 80 percent of all errors and defects. Figure 9-2 demonstrates the impact of an error by one operator on the quality of one product. The need for detecting the error as early as possible in the process has already been underscored.

Figure 9-3 demonstrates that a supervisory error broadens the impact of the error on the product. It has a magnifying effect.

What is true for operational matters is also true for administration (Figure 9-4). For example, in the instance of an area supervisor, an error by a production area may result in a significant product error. Moreover, an error in development, earlier in the process (Figure 9-5), may lead to complete loss of the product. What, therefore, could be said about an error in marketing?

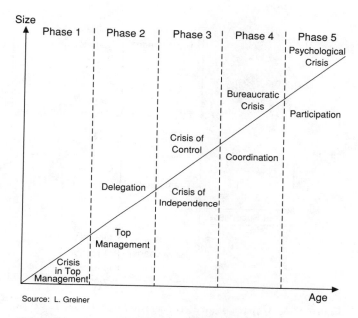

Source: L. Greiner

Figure 9-1. The Evolution of an Organization

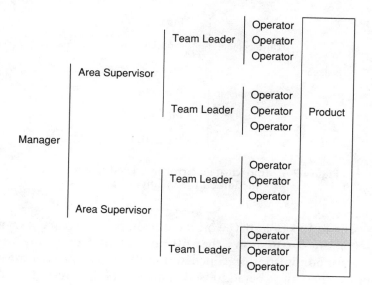

Figure 9-2. Impact of an Error by one Operator on the Quality of one Product

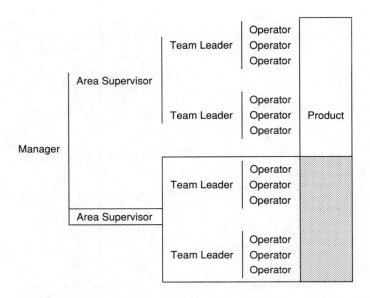

Figure 9-3. Impact of an Error at the Supervisory Level on the Quality of one Product

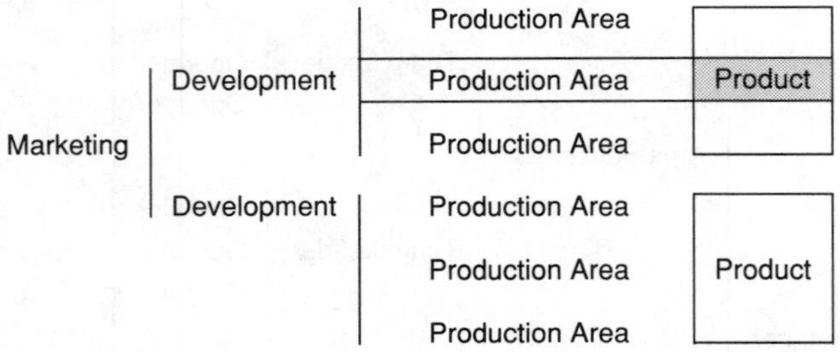

Figure 9-4. Impact of an Error in a Production Function on the Quality of a Product

The results of a survey on the distribution of errors in companies (Figure 9-6), shows that 50 percent of a company's total errors are administrative. Since administrative errors constitute a majority, they must be addressed. This will be discussed further at a later point.

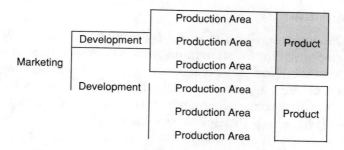

Figure 9-5. Impact of a Development Error on the Quality of a Product

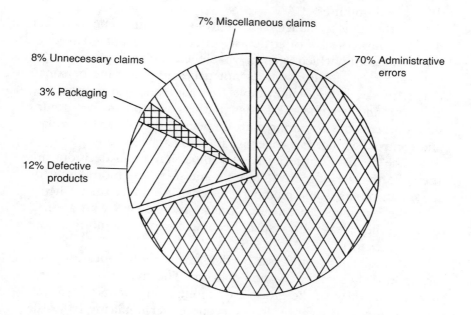

Figure 9-6. Delivery of Products — Distribution of Errors and Defects

AFCERQ claims that quality control circles only resolve 15 percent of the problems of private firms. But each day the circles show that they are capable of doing more. It is the company's duty to train circle members in prevention.

About Authority

The words *author* and *authority* connote initiative, will, creation, responsibility for something new. *Author* has been progressively reserved for the creators of a work while *authority* is currently used exclusively for social relationships. It refers to influence appropriate to participation in a structured organization.

Society, which in itself is not arbitrary or repressive, is a complex system of roles that has been endowed with certain regulatory and control mechanisms. Prescribed roles and functions are occasioned by the mere existence of an organization. Behavior in a given role cannot be contingent upon individual desires and impulses.

Authority is a characteristic of group structure. The mere fact that a group consists of structure, organization, and goals gives rise to authority, which is an inevitable and normal feature of the structure itself. Authority does not necessarily become personal; that is to say, it is not inevitable that someone will monopolize authority and become the leader. Rather, as soon as the spontaneous process of structuring a group begins, the power to regulate and control conduct as a collective function appears.

The birth of authority has an initial impact: if decisions are the collective act of a group (with some members more "influential" than others, some members "listened to" more than others), then the members cease being "private individuals" who are free to act as they please and instead become disciplined, and therefore obedient, actors.

Cohesiveness, universal participation, communication, and group goals become everyone's concern. The creation of such values and the birth of the group are simultaneous events. These values become an obligation for everyone either implicitly or in the form of rules or contracts. They imply the existence of a *leadership* that, since it is vested with authority, legitimize the "commandments" that govern the group.

How can *authority* be reconciled with *power* and *coercion?* Authority in an organized and structured group is accompanied by power because the group has the capability of ensuring compliance with the rules that have been agreed upon.

It is possible to imagine power held without consensus and therefore without authority. It may even be exercised by use of force. In that case, it is *unjust and pure coercion.* Power that tramples upon rights establishes a relationship based on force, not agreement.

There is a great intrinsic difference between authority and coercion, since authority refers to a value and coercion to force. There is, on the one hand, power without authority (intimidation), and on the other hand, authority without power (authority based on ability). Authority is limited by group boundaries, by group goals, by the powers assigned to it, and by any possible changes in the consensus.

Acceptance and agreement are at the heart of consensus authority relationships. Such relationships are based on *trust.* Without trust, power is nothing but coercion.

Within an organization, the problems of authority are of a different nature than in a society. Authority may be institutionally external to the group on which it is exercised; authority is indispensable when the agreement is contractual (as is the case with business organizations). There are also instances in which the purpose of the collective group is disputed even though affiliation is accepted for other reasons; instances in which there is no immediate or evident relationship between the purpose of the group and the orders of the leader; and instances in which there is a conflict between short-term and long-term goals.

Another type of authority is *statutory authority.* In principle, it is granted not to a person but to a social position. Power that is guaranteed and backed by higher-level positions emanates from the particular social position. This arrangement influences the rules of the organization, giving superiors the option to reward or punish depending on whether or not the role behavior of subordinates conforms to organization rules. Moreover, statutory authority controls the information and resources of the group. Because it possesses a power to punish and risks being used as an alibi for personal ambition, such authority is always suspect. Statutory authority is therefore in opposition to personal authority, gained through consensus and trust. It is impersonal and, like all other organizational roles, leads to technocratic behavior with obligations, constraints, limitations on free will, and spatial, temporal, and legal limits.

Moreover, statutory authority pertains to a position, which is established *before* the selection of its occupant. When that person arrives, he or she is accorded responsibilities that automatically determine the conduct of subordinates.

The Adaptation of Individuals to a Company

Building on the ideas of Hertzberg and McGregor, Chris Argyris (1970) argued that the organization should be adapted to the higher-level needs of the individual, which are those contained in Maslow's last category (Figure 9-7), and not vice versa.

The need for self-esteem, competence, and a psychological sense of success, is frustrated in the lower echelons of the traditional hierarchical organization. A new organizational structure should enable individuals to find more fulfillment in their work. The traditional organization frustrates psychological needs because:

- It does not offer persons in lower-level positions sufficient opportunity for internal promotion
- It rarely offers jobs that make full use of individual aptitudes and responsibilities
- It imposes relationships with superiors that are dependent in nature

This type of organization creates a vicious cycle: with no possibilities for self-actualization, personnel abandon their aspirations and needs for achievement, since such attitudes are incompatible with the organization's requirements (dependence, submissiveness, commitment, work, order, and conformity). The pressure of suppressed needs causes people to feel distant and withdrawn.

By contrast, if workers' psychological needs are fulfilled, progress toward synergy can occur. For this to happen, new structures must be established that challenge workers by testing their skills and ability to assume responsibility. The number of persons assigned to the same task should therefore be reduced so that each

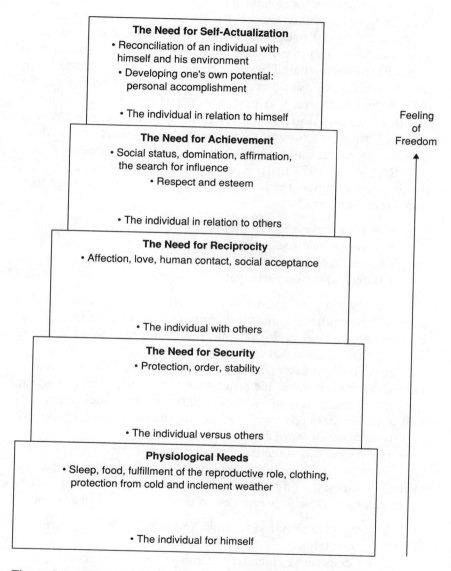

Figure 9-7. The Five Human Motivations (Maslow's Theory of the Hierarchy of Needs)

may have more responsibility. Participation in decisions, supervision, and responsibility should be instigated at every level. This requires changing procedures for supervision, compensation, incentives, evaluation, and recruiting. It also requires a structure in which functions are based on *participation*, interchange, and trust, rather than on imposed hierarchy. Companies need to change the old pyramidal structure so that power is shared by all, in such a way that each individual is able to influence the nature of essential activities. In such a system, there may be a consensus for the delegation of power and responsibility to one or several persons.

R. Likert (1974), developing this line of thought with a pseudo-experimental method, identified four types of organizational management:

- Authoritative and exploitative
- Authoritative and paternalistic
- Consultative
- Based on group participation

He argued that most effective structure uses coordinated groups. The entire organization should be composed of multiple overlapping groups, and each one should be capable of applying decision-making methods as a group.

According to Likert, an organization cannot exist without the individuals it comprises. He notes that companies often attempt to increase financial resources by discharging personnel, a practice that impoverishes collective intelligence, the value of which is difficult to calculate in immediate terms.

His system has three basic components: a participatory structure, a cooperative working method and a procedure for organizational analysis. The last component consists of seven measurements, which are reduced to five in the summary below.

1. Organizational structure and methods for exercising authority:
   - Cooperative/hierarchical and pyramidal structure
   - Autocratic/consultative authority
   - Cooperative/institutional authority
   - Group/bureaucratic control

- Hierarchical decision-making/consultative process
- Types of incentives used
- Nature of contacts between superiors/subordinates (trust/mistrust)
- Concept of the individual (Taylor/participationist)
- Accessibility or inaccessibility of information regarding the organization

2. The behavior of top managers:
   - Degree to which they exercise influence
   - Trust/mistrust vis-a-vis subordinates
   - Contacts with them easy/difficult
   - Interest or lack of interest in their subordinates' problems
   - Cooperative attitude (10-point scale)

3. Communication process:
   - Nature and quality of professional communication
   - Nature and quality of interpersonal communication
   - Direction in which information circulates
   - Nature, quantity, and quality of lateral communication
   - Dissemination of information
   - Interest in communication, information
   - Mutual ability of the parties to communicate

4. System of influence (and authority)
   - Importance of the nature of the interaction
   - Importance of working in a group
   - Influence of subordinates on their department's goals, methods, and activities (and subsequently on the organization as a whole)
   - Actual influence of superiors on goals (direct or indirect influence)
   - Existence of an effective structure for enabling one part of the organization to influence other parts

5. Status of the internal system:
   - Existence of a formal organization favorable to organizational goals
   - Integration of individual members
   - Acceptance of individuals and goals

- Interpersonal attitudes
- Personal attitudes toward data that is useful to the organization
- Degree of satisfaction enjoyed by its members
- Sense of responsibility among members
- Existence of conflicting motivations
- Underlying motivations for the work

Mistrust

Mistrust is the visceral, primal fear of being "owned." At the core of this mistrust is childhood experience, supported by the living tradition in the working world that believes one is always deceived by the person "higher up." Mistrust is expressed as prejudice. Our values and our hierarchy define stereotypes which condition our actions. Our mental perspective is strongly influenced by family, school, social background, friends, profession, beliefs, and prominent events in our lives.

Diversity of experience leads to diversity in modes of thought. For example, there is a great difference between those who entered the work force early and those who continued to pursue their studies. For the first group, concrete facts are what count: facts of lifestyle, action, and work. Those with less academic training will react negatively to abstraction, pure speculation, and distancing from reality. By contrast, those who spent more time in school are more Cartesian in orientation, more analytical and deductive in thinking, and less intuitive. For them, *truth* results from *logical* exposition rather than facts.

Figure 9-8, divides the hierarchical pyramid into a broken line (symbolizing the impreciseness of the boundary) in order to illustrate a typical phenomenon in business organizations. Above the line are the employees who use words, speech, and language. They wield abstractions, and their lengthy academic training has taught them to reason, that is, to use the "logic" of their school to express ideas, to give explanations. Managers often fall into this rational category.

Below the broken line are the employees who touch, who see, who observe what they are doing: the concrete. They are

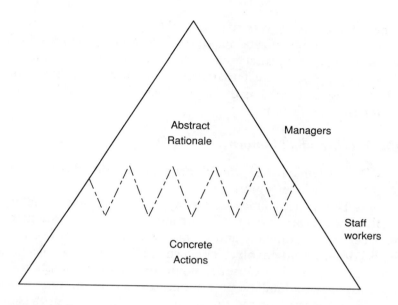

Figure 9-8. Mistrust

endowed with "intuition," that form of immediate knowledge that has no recourse to reason. Actions and not words impel them to act or to react. Workers and staff tend to action more than abstraction.

The difference in thought modes between workers and management fuels mistrust. Conquering workers' mistrust will occur only through the sincerity demonstrated by managers' actions, not their words, sustained over a long period of time.

Organization Structure and Management Styles

An organization is a human community, and the need for collective action arises as soon as a goal cannot be attained by a single individual. The act of joining together in a common cause appears to be fundamental to human beings. Within an interdependent community there is always an *organization*, that is, a distribution of tasks, powers, and roles. The awareness of goals and the will to attain them, and therefore an image of the action to be taken and to be achieved, is an important factor in the social organization of the group. The organization appears to be a *condition for effectiveness* and an antidote to anarchy; wastefulness of energy, time, and resources; internal and external discontent; fatigue; and stagnation. Effectiveness is defined as the achievement of goals and maintaining internal satisfaction.

The Qualities of a Manager

D. Chalvin (1985), in *Self-diagnosis of Management Styles*, identified a manager's most crucial qualities: *commitment* and *cooperation*. The same qualities are essential for any person in the organization. By *commitment* Chalvin means the commitment of a manager to his company and to his own professional objectives. Such commitment involves concern for individual projects, an interest in technical matters, a desire to be a good administrator, an intent to secure a fulfilling professional career, the ambition to succeed, and concern for the quality of work. In short, professional commitment involves everything that affects the management and success of both the company and one's own profession. (Table 9-1)

For the committed manager, cooperation means the creation of a community made up of committed individuals. Cooperation is concern for the commitment of others, the sacrifice of personal enthusiasm for the benefit of a collective organization. Making individuals cooperate even though their points of view and objectives are incompatible is not effective management. The basic function of cooperation is in fact to *make the various objectives of different employees compatible* (Table 9-2).

In the same book, Chalvin made the following points:

- There is no one management style. No style should be rejected since all of them may be valid depending on circumstances and particular instances. Managers should therefore be themselves and strive toward perfection within their own style.
- Beware of all management styles since all of them have a dangerous, ineffective, and unrewarding side to them. Nothing is achieved a priori, by simply adopting a certain management style.

Table 9-1. The Criteria for Commitment and Their Applications

Typical Criteria for Commitment	Effective Commitment	Ineffective Commitment
Interest in changing and improving the company	Sufficient freedom for effective criticism • Sufficient tension to improve individual goals and company objectives	• Excessive freedom • Incessant search for agreement • Severing of the relationship and departure
Identification with the company	• Interest in making the business progress • Fortunate connection between individual goals and company objectives	Coercion that encourages "objective" identification • Sole interest is preserving his or her own position
Motivation for work	• Enjoyment of responsibility and achieving results • Financial and career advantages are considered to be an overall incentive • Company spirit	• Priority is financial advantages and advancement • Search for stimulation outside of work
Contribution to the success of the company	• Achieving concrete results • Defining essential goals • Acquiring a team	• Careerism and personal gamesmanship • Utopianism and disinterested idealism

- The ideological war regarding management styles, with people reproaching colleagues for being mindless followers of "American" models, and others finding themselves accused of being traditional and reactionary, should be ended.
- A common ethic should be adopted: effectiveness. Anyone who attains the professional goals he or she is responsible for achieving, and does so in a spirit of realism and tolerance, should be considered effective, regardless of his or her personal mindset.

The following two examples illustrate Chalvin's point. The first shows innovations as a function of technical contributions and length of service in the position (Figure 9-9).

Table 9-2. The Criteria for Cooperation and Their Applications

Typical Criteria for Cooperation	Effective Cooperation	Ineffective Cooperation
Trust	• Sensible trust based on sound experience with human beings	Naive trust, trust only in persons with whom there are ties (seniority, education, family), or trust given only in order to better manipulate
Human Relationships	Based on • independence • freedom • flexibility • negotiation focusing on professional goals	Based on • strong dependence • excessive loyalty • inflexible stability • passive docility and principal focus on good human relationships
Working in a Group	• Making the group a way of life • Social proximity • Excellent technology • Work is process-oriented and allows for more applications and stimulating innovation	• Strong coercion • Identification with the leader • Conformity • Concern with the latest trends/fads
Communication within the Company	Awareness of the difficulty of communicating • Motivation to struggle to achieve communication • Precise structures and methods	• Snobbishness • Pseudo-communication • Illusion of ease in communication

There are three phases: familiarization, influence, and stabilization, which involve, respectively, a low, growing, and then strong level of technical contribution. These phases also correspond to the building of the position and its status, consolidation of the position, and, finally, maintenance of its status.

This diagram is theoretically interesting, but it only relates to a certain type of activity. It is certainly true for certain positions, perhaps the majority, but is it always valid?

The second example (Figure 9-10) divides management styles into four categories distinguished by whether a superior dic-

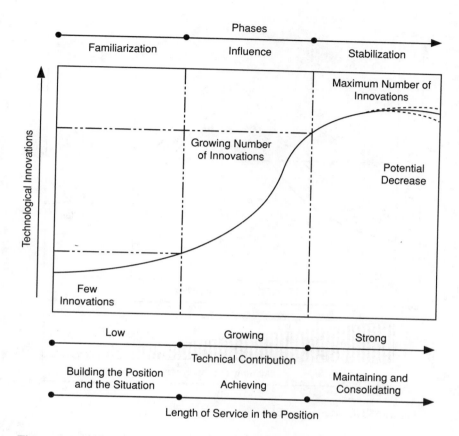

Figure 9-9. Innovations Related to Technical Contributions and Length of Service in the Position

tates, sells, participates, or delegates. All such actions have an impact on personnel interactions, which are at a maximum level when the superior sells or participates and at a minimum when he or she delegates, which can happen only if employees are quite mature. How is this determined? Aside from the fact that there is little supervision of activities, even with mature employees, what guides or motives them? This author believes that *to manage is, first of all, to motivate.*

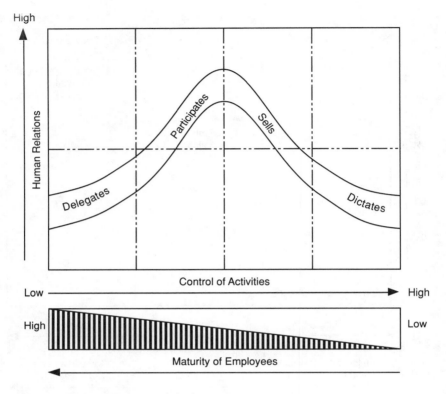

Figure 9-10. Management Styles

A Policy of Trust toward Employees

The theory of the "self-fulfilling prophecy" could be expressed as "You get what you ask for." If you wish employees to behave as adults, treat them like adults, but if you prefer them to be children, treat them like children. It can also be said that if you ask for accelerated output, or improvement in productivity, you will not necessarily obtain improvement in quality. Instead, the cost of returned goods will increase and often defective products will not be taken into account; they may perhaps even be concealed.

Companies must treat employees as associates, with dignity and respect. They must consider employees, not financial investments, as the fundamental sources of their profits. *Personnel are the company's most important asset;* their intelligence should be mobilized. *Respect for the individual* is more than a belief, it is a universal truth. As stated earlier, making this trust a reality requires not words, but *actions* in the form of structural mechanisms, systems, and values that are mutually reinforcing.

The quality approach is not a matter of paternalism, but involves an abiding respect for the individual. Thus one wishes to train employees, set clear and reasonable goals for them, and allow them the option of advancing and contributing directly to their own work.

The managers of high-performing companies are sincerely concerned with their personnel. Their enthusiasm is communicated. This attitude does not interfere with, but rather encourages strict standards, which are the result of mutual expectations and comparisons among peers. The feeling of being useful, needed, and held to high standards is a magic formula for doing well. Employees love to compete among each other, but they also want to measure themselves against requirements that are considered all the more reasonable because they have participated in establishing them.

One disaster is the mindless embrace of faddish solutions: the latest program for participatory management by objectives, quality control circles, and other independent groups for work enrichment. A system that is initiated without genuine and consistently deep interest on the part of management is bound to fail. To succeed, there must be perseverance, but above all there must be unconditional and ongoing support of the entire management team. The risk in taking on any technique is that if it fails, it will be difficult to revive it: there is increased mistrust. If it succeeds and is to endure, additional training refinements, and new programs must be injected into the system.

The emotional part of human nature must be accorded its proper place. It must be given the chance to be at its best, and thus an environment favorable to the quest for quality must be created. *Support, appreciate, reduce to a human scale, honor, reward, recognize, respect:* these are the strong verbs involved in the will to win.

Participatory Management

Figure 9-11, which is very familiar, shows how responsibility and influence is exercised with respect to employees.

There is no demagoguery in this. As previously explained, any organization needs a structure to combat anarchy and wastefulness. The hierarchy is not being called into question. It is simply being pressed to reap the fruits of the company's intelligence. Greater awareness can be achieved by teaching the corporate hierarchy to work as a group, which entails observing the five major principles set forth in Table 9-3. This involves harvesting new ideas, and also becoming more creative.

To collaborate, it is necessary to ask for help, contribute, challenge without bitterness, get involved, and share. None of these terms is in opposition to the term *management*. On the other hand, *management* is usually associated with orders, demands, laws, rules, authority, power, and management staff, and therefore it carries some rather heavy and negative connotations. Such connotations must be changed.

Earlier in this chapter I indicated our responsibility as professionals for the impact of our errors. We should therefore remind ourselves that when we point a finger, three fingers are turned toward us. Are we not ourselves responsible?

Participatory management is not laxness; it does not erase the need for formal meetings to disseminate information from the top of the organization, and it does not exclude the role of the hierarchy. It requires that authority based on ability not be limited to the technical area (technology, science, banking, administration, etc.), and it entails the need to motivate and train others, and form relationships with colleagues, subordinates, and superiors. We should nevertheless remain realistic and remember that, whereas in physics it is often possible to imagine 100 percent success, it is not a serious possibility in human relations. There, to attain even 70 percent success would be excellent.

A Policy of Information and Communication

Just as a company needs to make known to the outside what it produces and where the client can find its products – in other

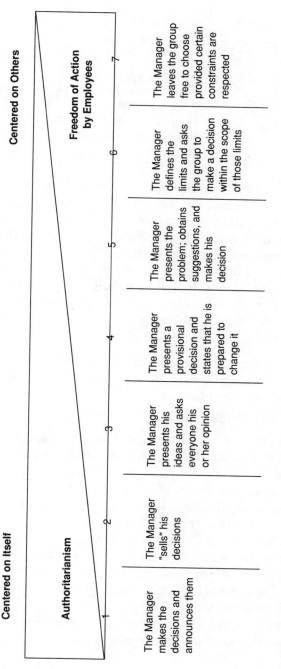

Figure 9-11. The Impact of Responsibility

Table 9.3. Working in a Group

Requires
- Knowing how to motivate
- Using a method and management tools
- Conducting effective meetings
- Training oneself in teaching methods
- Making listening a way of life

words, do external marketing – so must it disseminate to its employees, and receive from them, all pertinent information: that is, internal marketing. Internal communication requires the same high degree of openness, truthfulness, and credibility that is appropriate for messages sent outside the company. All media are useful and each part of the company should be able to not only communicate what it is doing, but also communicate with other parts of the company. Company newspapers, divisional bulletins, video and telephone information, and suggestions are some of the information media useful in

- Increasing the involvement of personnel in their work, that is, encouraging each person to make a stronger personal investment in his work
- Enhancing employees' sense of solidarity with the company

In the area of information, it is better to speak first than to have to issue a denial. Information should be meted out in doses and contain less bad news (25 percent) than good news (75 percent). It should give names of those who have outstanding accomplishments, those who have succeeded, those who are going away for training (and the training course should be specified), and those who are moving (whatever their rank in the organization). It should recognize the participation of employees in local activities, and should also inform families about events and activities in the company through normal local media. It is also useful to prepare press summaries dealing with economics, quality, and business; information from the left-wing press for those who do not read it, and likewise for other points of view. Written information must be published not only quarterly and monthly, but also in special "flash" bulletins.

Suggestions submitted should not only receive mention; they may also be a serious indicator of the climate within the company.

Figure 9-12 shows the languages used within a company. It is essential to speak the languages of not only a top manager but also a machine operator. If this elementary principle is not observed, information from below or above does not get through and mistrust increases.

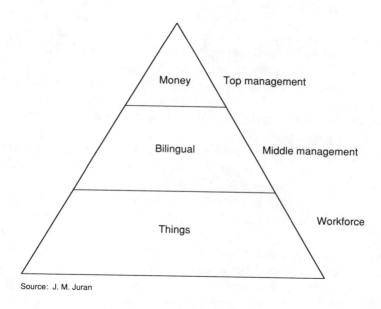

Source: J. M. Juran

Figure 9-12. Languages in a Company

Communication, that is, the sharing of information, is based on a simple truth: *there is no communication without interchange.*

In short, it is not enough to appoint a director of communication and information. All those who are willing to communicate and to communicate well should be encouraged to do so.

Spoken information is the domain of the hierarchy and originates from top management speaking to managers. Spoken information may be accompanied by one or two supporting documents that enhance its credibility. If the information is dense, the number of supporting media should of course be increased, but such situations should be the exception. Finally, the information should be organized on the basis of an internal marketing study of employee expectations.

A Policy of Training and Human Development

From this point forward, training needs will increase along with the growing complexity of the technological, economic, and social environment. Some companies have recognized this fact and have made a considerable investment not only in quality training, but also in professional training: the two are inseparable. Training in methods for resolving problems, in management tools, and in elementary statistics is accomplished through group motivation and pedagogy. Also emphasized are knowing how to express oneself, assert oneself, train the memory, and use every faculty of the mind. Organizations are confronted, sometimes in an acute manner, by problems of job restructuring and recycling, problems that require advance planning if the organization's survival and development is to be ensured.

Every organization must retain increasingly competent employees. Individuals who strive to become better informed evince a clearer desire to match their performance with their aspirations within the organization, or, if need be, on the outside. The optimal use of human resources is everyone's business. Individuals manage their own careers as a function of the organization's expectations while attempting to maximize their own advantages. Training takes them through the following logical sequence (a concept whose author is unknown):

1. Unaware of one's own incompetence
2. Aware of one's own incompetence
3. Aware of one's own competence
4. Unaware of one's own competence

Between phases 1 and 2 the person becomes sensitive to the function of training; it is impossible to know that learning is necessary unless a person takes stock of what is lacking.

Between phases 2 and 3, training itself occurs.

Between phases 3 and 4, practical implementation of what was learned takes place.

During phase 4, a person no longer knows what he knows, he simply does it.

Company employees use instinct and reason to assess the limitations of their surroundings and to optimize their personal strategies: What are their hopes for gain? What are their risks? Motivations? Aspirations? What are their chances of internal promotion or of making their services more valuable externally?

With the strength of their self-knowledge, they seek to negotiate in order to reduce the uncertainty of the future and secure assurances that the organization will take into account their personal and professional development. Secretly, they hope to be compensated with another job, the recognition of another qualification. Success depends on their objectivity toward others' perception of them and also on the subjective appeal the company has for them.

The organization's interest is in detecting the potential capabilities that are indispensable for its survival and development, a process integral to its strategy. Career management is part of organization management. In fact, an organization must have sufficient quantities of qualified personnel at the desired time, ensure a proper match between employees and work assignments, and maintain and, above all, increase motivation of personnel. Most companies are now attentive to the individual characteristics of the professionals who are recruited or promoted, to their capacity to deal with uncertainty, to adapt quickly, to innovate, to make decisions, and to acquire the entrepreneurial spirit.

The phenomenon is more complex for nonprofessionals. They do not always know how to express their desires because they are unaware of them, and they endure fast-paced technological changes without always understanding them.

Personal development requires self-awareness and self-improvement. The discovery of self is made in concert with others, and through others. Quality control circles and quality improvement groups become powerful tools for detecting needs and potential capabilities.

Decision and Consent

To Decide is to Choose the Action to Be Taken

"To choose" assumes that there are several options under consideration. The choice consists of selecting one option from among several. However, to choose one option is also to reject the others. Psychologically, it is more difficult to reject than to choose, but reticence about rejecting options may lead to indecision and therefore to no choice at all.

"The action to be taken": at the moment the decision is made, the action chosen has not yet begun. It will be performed at some point in the future, implying an inability to judge the decision's appropriateness until after its implementation. When the decision is made, therefore, information on the anticipated results is never complete. *To decide is therefore to make a choice in the context of incomplete information.*

The Decision-making Process

Making a decision consists of classifying the solutions according to the consequences of each option. The solution becomes self-evident: this can be termed a *pseudo-decision*. Unfortunately, nature is not always predictable, and unforeseen circumstances can easily undo this or that solution.

Most often, the future presents multiple facets and it is impossible to assign probabilities to the results of any solution. The difficulty increases when, in fact, there is no probability data for future results. One can only imagine the additional difficulty of numerous uncertain results, or even a situation in which results are hostile – but that does indeed happen.

In the face of such uncertainty, humanity has come up with many ways to make decisions. Some of the more sophisticated methods rely on mathematical criteria and bear the names of their illustrious inventors: Laplace, Hurwitz, Bernouilli, Savage, and Bayes, among others. A mountain of more-or-less serious books have wrestled with the problem of decision making, to little avail. All these methods are part of a pseudo-science that is termed *rational decision making.*

Rational methods notwithstanding, the future remains unpredictable. In the event that difficulties recur, a different decision must be made. Even if calculations provide some element of security, no individual will assign the same value, in the same situation, to the risks of winning and the risks of losing.

The *psychology of preferences* also enters into the process. On the one hand, there is the *fear of risk* brought on by choices between possible gains; on the other hand, there is *enjoyment of risk*. The higher the stakes, the more fear of risk prevails over enjoyment. Nevertheless, the results of the calculations are the same.

It can be said in summary that there is no simple, rational, and surefire method for decision making. Any decision is ultimately subjective, and therefore risky.

The Quality of the Decision

The future is always uncertain. By contrast, the past is documented, analyzed, and evaluated in terms of its consequences. As shown in Figure 9-13, the present tends to move toward the past (level 1). We wish to make a decision to achieve level 2 with a certain set of anticipated results. The decision is to be made at time t_0. Since it is impossible to foresee everything, despite experience and professional ability, we rarely attain level 2 precisely. Instead, we reach level A or level B, obtaining results that are different from those anticipated for level 2.

There is therefore a discrepancy of $\underline{d}_1$ or $\underline{d}_2$. The quality of the decision is inversely proportional to the discrepancy between the results achieved and the results anticipated.

$$Q_1 = 1/\underline{d}_1 \quad Q_2 = 1/\underline{d}_2$$

Here the quality of Q_1 is less than the quality of Q_2 for the same decision, with the same initial level, and with the same calculations for anticipated results.

This analysis is obviously simplified. The time required to move from level 1 to level A (or to level B) is never zero. This summary approach is sufficient at this point. It should be remembered, however, that "someone" made the decision to go from level 1 to level 2.

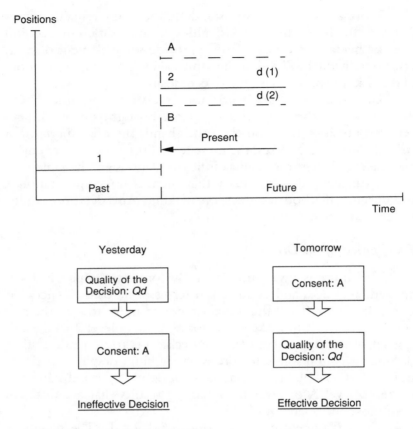

Figure 9-13. Decisions and Consent

Consent

A decision always involves human beings: those who make it, those who implement it, and those who are affected by the consequences. Each person responds to the decision differently. Those differences are exacerbated if people have not participated in the decision-making process. If there is a marked discrepancy between expectations and actual results, people affected by the decision may even become hostile, because they were not involved in a process whose results run counter to their goals. Thus, the results hoped for by the decision makers will be very different from the actual results. The quality of the decision will diminish. But what if we were to proceed differently? What if we tried to make our decision more *effective?*

N. R. F. Maier suggested a famous equation:

$$(\text{Effectiveness of the Decision}) = (\text{Quality of the Decision}) \times (\text{Consent})$$

The term *quality* implies the notion of *objectivity*: it only apparently depends on impersonal, objective data based on the facts of the situation (it has been "checked" for quality).

Whether those who must implement the decision agree with it depends on data that is necessarily subjective, affective, human: *consent.*

This terminology avoids adjectives such as *good* and *correct.* The adjective *good* may describe either quality, consent, or effectiveness, but it has no meaning for the decision as a whole. Similarly, the adjective *correct* should be avoided because it leaves room for the assumption that moderately effective decisions, decisions of average quality, or decisions that lead to only partial consent do not exist, which is untrue.

Each decision involving human beings is carried out by consent, which is a necessary prerequisite for quality (Figure 9-13).

Consent and quality are therefore two distinct goals of a decision. To aim for both goals *at the same time* is to achieve neither.

Aiming for quality first is the customary approach. However, to consider consent as only a secondary objective is to neglect it.

In contrast, choosing *consent as the first goal* does not mean sacrificing quality, because those who are involved may participate very effectively in defining quality, and thereby increase it. Working in groups is above all a *tool for consent* that has, among other objectives, the goal of working on quality.

Summary

Total quality results from using methods of implementation that are clearly defined and understood by everyone. It requires active participation by everyone in the prevention of errors and defects, whether administrative or technical. It implies awareness by everyone of his role in the application of any such method and of his participation in actions for improvement. It will fail if it is considered to be an activity connected with production or that pertains only to products. Making assumptions that "we've been providing quality for 20 years," or that "anyone knows what quality is, it's obvious, buddy" are destructive in the short term.

Efforts toward total quality will fail if they are concerned only with "problems of quality"; if directives are unclear or even nonexistent; if individuals do not understand their own responsibility to strive for quality; if there are different interpretations within the company for the same word; if indicators are not understood; if managers do not understand or do not wish to believe that they are themselves the sources of 80 percent of all errors or defects.

Total quality is the *willingness* and *ability* that emerges when a company instills *a sense of responsibility* in all the actors and secures their *consent*, especially, as we shall see, at the highest levels.

Figures 9-14 and 9-15, which come from "MIP and JOB" (management, innovation, productivity, and work) theory, show, by borrowing from Maslow, what quality control circles and quality improvement groups can contribute in terms of the employees' sense of power over and freedom in their environment, depending on the extent to which their needs are met.

The word *quality* is a mobilizing force par excellence because it channels energies and orients everyone's actions.

Total quality develops group projects, facilitates participatory management, and therefore improves human relationships. It creates dramatic change through the client-supplier relationship both inside and outside the company. It is applied collectively through new work methods and specially adapted tools, and it promotes the development of individual and collective training, and even self-training. It is a response to individual and collective needs (Table 9-4).

Everyone in the company strives for *excellence* by understanding and adopting this new quality strategy not only for their own tasks, but also for those they may act on or improve in concert with others (Table 9-5).

The development of new reflexes and individual involvement through responsibility, the development of management,

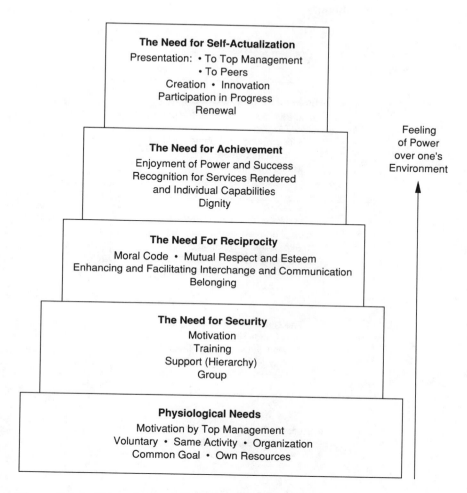

Figure 9-14. "MIP and JOB" Theory — The Motivations of Quality
Control Circles and Quality Improvement Groups

understanding of authority, and the matching of individual and
collective needs, produces new company responses to individual
needs. These are summarized in Table 9-6.

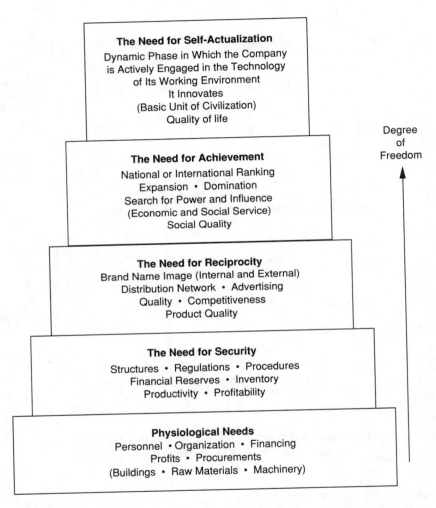

The Need for Self-Actualization
Dynamic Phase in Which the Company
is Actively Engaged in the Technology
of Its Working Environment
It Innovates
(Basic Unit of Civilization)
Quality of life

The Need for Achievement
National or International Ranking
Expansion • Domination
Search for Power and Influence
(Economic and Social Service)
Social Quality

The Need for Reciprocity
Brand Name Image (Internal and External)
Distribution Network • Advertising
Quality • Competitiveness
Product Quality

The Need for Security
Structures • Regulations • Procedures
Financial Reserves • Inventory
Productivity • Profitability

Physiological Needs
Personnel • Organization • Financing
Profits • Procurements
(Buildings • Raw Materials • Machinery)

Degree
of
Freedom

Figure 9-15. "MIP and JOB" Theory — The Motivations of the Company

Table 9-4. Individual and Collective Needs

Needs	Mutual Relationships For the Collective Organization	Expectations (Giving/Receiving) For the Individual
Physiological	• Flexible hours • Good working conditions	• Working late when necessary • Dealing with • stress • time pressures • rivalry of peers
Security	• Job security • Salaries and social advantages • Feedback/evaluation	• Learning the requirements of the position • Feedback/evaluation
Belonging (Reciprocity)	• Participation in decision making • Member of a team of winners • Cooperative colleagues	• Ability to work in a group • Dealing with the company's rules • Maintaining the internal and external images of the company
Rewards (Achievement)	• Opportunities for advancement • Recognition of merit • Power and responsibility • Stature and prestige • Representing the company with clients	• Being flexible • Assuming influence • Representing the company • Fighting for the interests and the goals of the company
Personal Development	• Opportunities for: • on-the-job training • education • Opportunities for • creativity • promotion • Freedom for personal development	• Ability to: • discover new methods of work • make decisions • suggest solutions • foresee problems, etc.

Table 9-5. The Requirements of Individuals, of Tasks, of the Group

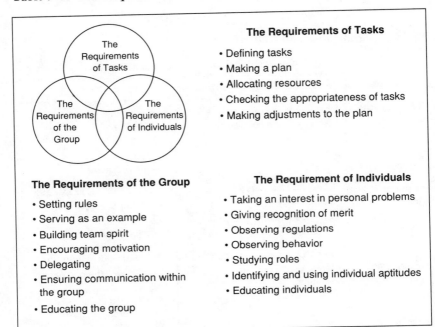

The Requirements of Tasks

- Defining tasks
- Making a plan
- Allocating resources
- Checking the appropriateness of tasks
- Making adjustments to the plan

The Requirements of the Group

- Setting rules
- Serving as an example
- Building team spirit
- Encouraging motivation
- Delegating
- Ensuring communication within the group
- Educating the group

The Requirement of Individuals

- Taking an interest in personal problems
- Giving recognition of merit
- Observing regulations
- Observing behavior
- Studying roles
- Identifying and using individual aptitudes
- Educating individuals

Table 9-6. The Principal Response of the Company to Individual Needs

Individual Needs	Principal Response of the Company	Procedures
Physiological	• Health and vitality	←
Security	• Full employment	• Opinion surveys
Belonging	• Participation by employees • Commitment by managers	• Open doors • Public speaking (presentations)
Recognition/ Achievement	• Stringent recruiting • Internal promotion	• Interviews with managers
Personal Development	• Continuing education • Building of qualifications	• Equal opportunity ←

Part 3

The Method and the Tools

*Society is like a ship – everyone should
join in steering the rudder.*

– H. Ibsen
An Enemy of the People

10
The Method

To succeed is not enough – one must do so
in the proper manner.

– J. Morley

All the Japanese who explained to me what is meant by Total Quality Management (TQM) gestured with their hands to imitate a mill wheel. For them, TQM is the wheel invented by Deming, their prophet and national hero.

The Japanese term *kanri* is translated as management and is concerned with maintaining the quality attained. The expression *hinshitsu kanri*, when used by K. Ishikawa, means not only maintaining the quality attained but also improving it.

The implication is that improvements come first. The stability of improvements is then ensured, which means maintaining what has been accomplished (management). Then, the process begins again with further improvements, and so forth.

The following statement has frequently been heard: "Let us begin by improving what we already know how to do, but not well enough, and then innovate, but not the reverse."

A first cycle for this process can be represented schematically by a gear with the following teeth:

- Finding the problems
- Defining an objective
- Planning
- Studying the problems
- Finding solutions
- Improving cooperation with everyone
- Checking the results
- Beginning the process again

A second cycle, and a second gear, would have the following components:

- Understanding what quality is
- Designing methods of implementation
- Learning operating methods
- Implementation
- Checking the steps performed
- Taking corrective actions
- Checking measurements
- Beginning the process again.

These two gears each turn in a unique direction. Between the two is a motor, which is shown schematically by a third gear that represents the quality control circles and other quality improvement groups in which the corporate hierarchy participates.

The first cycle is *improvement*, the second, *maintaining what has been attained*, and the third, the *motor*. This motor should operate continuously for all the company's actions, without starts and stops or switches into reverse.

These have been the teachings of Dr. Deming since the beginning of the 1950s: the PDCA wheel. Figure 10-1 shows that it is divided into four sections: plan, do, check, action.

This wheel, which can be used for all the company's activities, possesses greater complexity than is immediately apparent because there is a PDCA wheel in each of the four basic activities. In each section of these four wheels there is yet another PDCA wheel, and so on. It is therefore possible to plan the planning for the planning (Figure 10-2).

The wheel inexorably mounts the rising slope of successive improvements in every area of the company. Everyone strives diligently to make it turn in only one direction. On the symbolic level, this graphic representation derives its power from the perfection suggested by the circle, which implies constant flux, evolution, and unceasing improvement. The circle represents cycles, renewed beginnings, and re-creation.

Describing its use throughout the entire company would call for an exposition that would be too lengthy to provide here. The Deming wheel, with its perpetual ascent, provides a process for

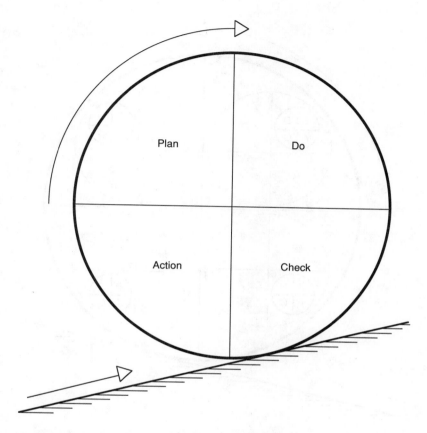

Figure 10-1. The Deming Wheel (PDCA)

permanent improvement as well as consolidation of achievements and motivation for all the actors in a company.

Defects: Accidental and Chronic

Figure 10-3 shows fluctuations in quality as a function of time. It is a random phenomenon with an initial average level that varies between two limits: intuitive upper limit of control (IULC) and intuitive lower limit of control (ILLC).

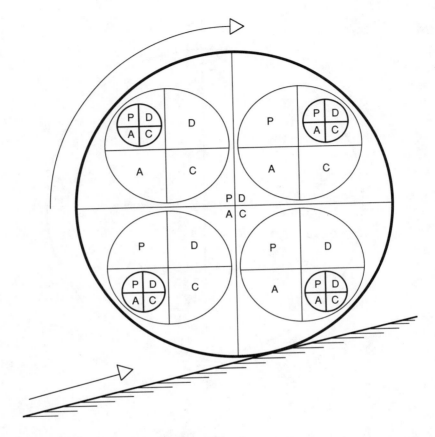

Figure 10-2. Use of the Deming Wheel

In other words, as long as quality deficiencies remain at an acceptable level, awareness that "something is wrong" is not possible. There is no action: "We live with it." One day, an anomaly suddenly occurs, which is point A at the left. Suddenly and clearly quality deficiencies become unacceptable. Rapid intervention is required in order to eliminate this intolerable increase. This is accomplished by a team of "firefighters," a special work group that must eliminate the accidental defect as quickly as possible so that the entire system can return to the "norm." The latter is located between the upper and lower limits of control, but it is not known

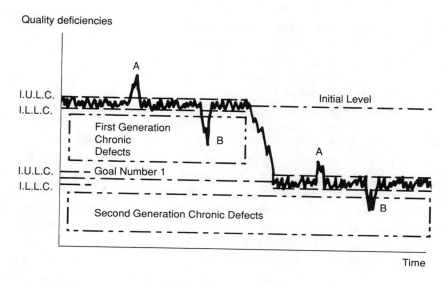

Quality deficiencies

I.U.L.C.
I.L.L.C.   Initial Level

First Generation
Chronic
Defects   B

I.U.L.C. — Goal Number 1
I.L.L.C.   A

Second Generation Chronic Defects   B

Time

A

Type A: things that suddenly degenerate
Type B: things that are suddenly improved

Figure 10-3. Accidental and Chronic Defects

precisely where. No matter: speed is of the essence, and the situation is serious. At another time, for unknown reasons, the process and the product are suddenly improved without anyone really knowing why: that is point B. No one worries about this, because things are "improved." Nevertheless, point B represents a much more revealing accident, suggesting that the process and the product could be permanently improved. It is symptomatic of another category of defects: the company's *chronic defects.* Here they are termed "first generation" in order to show what is happening in a firm that has not yet initiated a total quality program.

Maintaining the level of quality between upper and lower limits of control is commonly termed *quality assurance.*

Beyond the initial level, the level indicated by goal number 1 is termed *quality improvement.*

To maintain the level set by goal number 1, which does not prevent accidental defects such as A or B, is to maintain the improvements achieved in accordance with the Deming wheel theory. But B now reveals new chronic defects, which are termed here "second generation" defects. There is no reason not to set a second goal and therefore to continue making improvements: that is the *zero-defect* philosophy.

It should be noted that, while eliminating type A accidents is indispensable and urgent, such defects are superficial rather than chronic. The situation is urgent and speed is essential; "the fire must be put out." In contrast, type B accidents reveal an enormous hidden substratum of quality defects and are concrete manifestations of "improved" processes and products. Why not work on this phenomenon? There is all the time in the world to analyze, scrutinize, and understand these sudden improvements, and the outcome would be rich in results. Therefore, pay special attention to something that suddenly improves.

The Curative Approach

There are two ways to approach problems. One begins with symptoms and results in a remedy, the curative process, and one begins with a remedy and produces a means of prevention, the preventive process. Both of them demand consideration of all available factors:

- Environment
- Symptoms
- The problem
- Diagnosis
- Analysis
- Causes (which conceal other effects: microbes, viruses)
- Remedies (which do not take everything into consideration)
- Vaccination

which combine to form two processes.

The curative process, which precedes the preventive, consists of nine phases.

1. Gather all the symptoms connected with an *effect*: observe. The *effect* is *nonconformance*.

2. Describe the effect: *define* it.
3. *Analyze* the effect.
4. Search for *all possible causes.*
5. *Confirm* the probable causes. If the confirmation is negative, the process must be reinitiated at the analysis phase.
6. Propose a solution.
7. *Check the chosen solution.*
8. Implement the solution.
9. *Monitor conformance* of results with the anticipated goals.

All errors, all human or equipment failures must be listed and only one should be chosen, so that the efforts made will not be dispersed. This choice is possible through the use of Pareto analysis.

Figure 10-4 summarizes the methodology for the curative path and alludes to the preventive process.

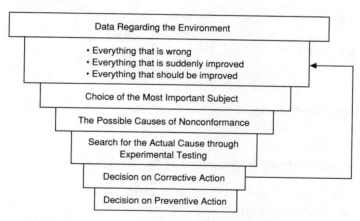

Figure 10-4. Standard Sequence for Handling Defects

Figure 10-5 gives the frequency of use for the tools. Table 10-1 summarizes the principal phases of the curative path and the tools involved. Table 10-2 lists the step-by-step procedure for accidental defects that require speedy action: "firefighting teams."

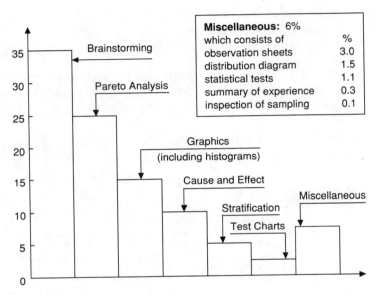

Figure 10-5. Frequency of Use for Tools

An Example of Implementation of the Methodology

Figures 10-6 and 10-7 make it easier to appreciate the difference between the curative and the preventive processes. A detailed analysis of nonconformance was made in a particular division of a company. After Pareto analysis and weighting according to costs, a Pareto graph (which is not to be confused with the analysis of which it is the result) was made of the division's nonconformance (Figure 10-6). On the same occasion, a pareto graph for conformance was also prepared (Figure 10-7). One group then set to work on the type A failures and completed the nine phases previously described. Since the B, C, D, and E types of failures were

Table 10-1. The Stages in the Resolution of a Problem and the Tools Used

Identification of the Problems	Brainstorming Individual report
Selection of the Problem	Majority vote Weighted vote Consensus Observation sheets Pareto analysis
Analysis of the Problem	Cause/effect diagram Brainstorming Individual report Pareto analysis Observation sheets Histograms, correlation diagrams "Multi-vari" charts Stratification Experimentation Sampling
Confirmation of the Solution	Pareto analysis Observation sheets Data collection Sampling
Presentation to Top Management	Histograms Cause/effect diagrams Correlation diagrams Graphs and charts "Multi-vari" charts Pictograms Test charts Pareto analysis

independent of type *A*, only the column for type *A* defects was reduced, up to the broken line. This reduction is the total savings, which includes the final savings plus the amount appropriated for investment in prevention. Such independence is a hypothesis whose validity was assumed for purposes of simplification; in practice, it is far from being proven. In reality, there would have been

Table 10-2. Step-by-Step Procedure for Accidental Defects

Step	Mental or Methodological Resources
Choose a single problem	• Selection of one of the phenomena • Pareto
Define the usual standard (considered to be appropriate)	• Observation, systematic tests
Describe the defect	• Scientific research: collection of accurate and precise data
Compare the defect with contrasting phenomena	• Distinguish
Deduce the special circumstances or characteristics	• Compare
Research the change	• Thoughtful consideration
Formulate a hypothesis regarding the possible causes	• Cause-and-effect method
Confirm	• Experimentation

another Pareto graph in most cases, if only because measurement was performed, as explained in Chapter 8.

It is then voluntarily decided that a fraction of the total savings obtained will be invested in prevention. The question that arises is, where?

Pareto analyses of costs, such as those encountered in Chapter 6, show that, for conformance, the largest expenditures for evaluation (which are for testing and inspection) are located to the left, while the expenditures for prevention are located to the right. Therefore, the investment will be made in prevention in the columns on the right of the Pareto graph for conformance, as shown in Figure 10-7. If costs had not been involved, the reasoning would have been the same: save on failures, invest in prevention.

This obligatory investment in prevention after elimination of nonconformance may be termed *vaccination*. Reference can also

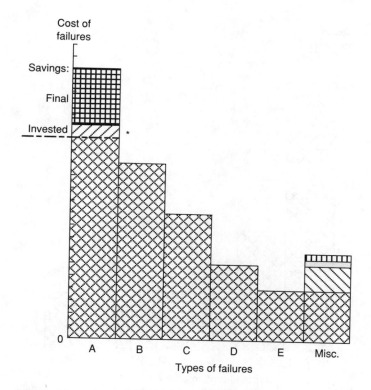

Figure 10-6. Nonconformance Pareto: Corrective Action Taken on Failures

be made to *therapeutic serum*, by analogy with the antibodies obtained from an immunized (or convalescent) animal and used either as a cure (final) or for prevention (active and ongoing).

Goals

Human nature is such that individuals who set objectives generally set the bar of the hurdle too high. They want to go directly from situation *A* to situation *B* (Figure 10-8).

A goal is a measurable result within a given period of time. It consists of two quantities: a number and a period of time. This pair is inseparable. Remember that the goal is determined before

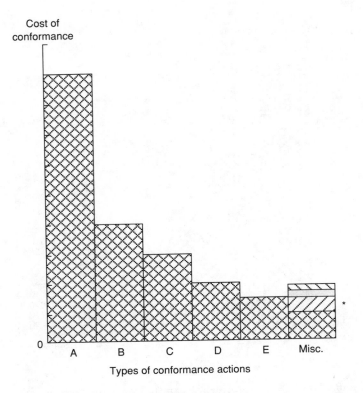

Figure 10-7. Nonconformance Pareto: Investment in Prevention

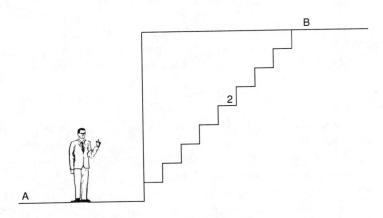

Figure 10-8. The Individual vis-a-vis His Objectives

deciding on the means. The latter is only a consequence of the goal. Furthermore, to create and maintain the attitude of a winner, the goals set must be easy to attain. It is better to set a goal of 12 percent and achieve 15 percent than to plan on 20 percent and fall short. According to the methodology for the curative process, goals for resolution of the problem are set after the second phase. A second goal is set after the fifth phase: confirmation of the causes. A third goal is set after the seventh: checking the solution chosen. A fourth is set after the eighth phase, which is implementation, and a fifth for monitoring. The first of all these goals in fact concerns what one wishes to achieve, and during what period of time, in order to reach the seventh point.

To summarize: in order to be achievable, a goal must be:

- Precise
- Measurable
- Realistic
- Attainable within a definite time frame

Active Prevention

Active prevention results from improvements: after achieving savings through a reduction in failures, what can be done so that this failure never again occurs?

Regardless of the actor involved or the point at which the failure was detected, there are products entering and exiting that point that can be measured. Within the actor's unit, as defined in Chapter 5, the measures taken may also involve that person's mission, activities, and tasks. These terms will be explained more precisely later.

In summary, the curative process consists of detection, definition and description, analysis, search for causes, corrective action, solution, and checking. Active prevention appears in the center of this curative loop (Figure 10-9).

Active prevention involves committing to memory all the measures originated by the unit and its environment, the characteristics of the defect, the causes, and the solution(s). This method is all the more effective because of the availability of microcomputers,

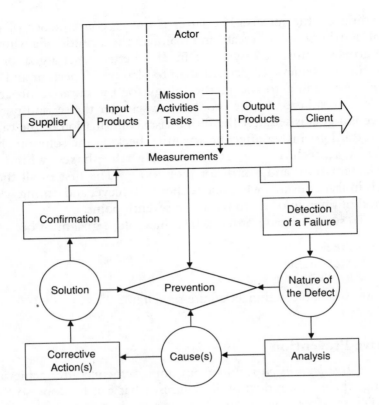

Figure 10-9. Process and Prevention

which constitute an artificial substitute for, and an extension of, our memory. Once a failure has been eliminated with a particular solution, the group may challenge its creativity by immediately dealing with methods of prevention. The solution becomes, in effect, part of the daily routine. When the solution goes well, no further thought is given to the issue.

There are two methods of prevention. The first is to immediately process all the data to be put into memory, even if it appears to be useless subsequent to prevention, because it may later serve "the historian" (see the following section). The second method consists of using the systems described in Chapter 6: mistake-proofing and fool-proofing.

An example of poka-yoke, or mistake-proofing, is a system that triggers an alarm or shuts off a machine in the event of an accidental defect. Shutdown of the machine should occur if the consequences would quickly lead to ongoing defective production. Another example can be seen in the following situation. Two parts are identical, one of which is to be mounted to the right and the other to the left. The only difference between them is the position of an opening. Since errors in folding are common, a press is fitted with a micro-breaker placed in the area of the opening, which shuts off electrical power in the event of improper positioning. The number of movements performed if certain phases of production have been properly performed could also be checked.

In any case, the approved system is made available to the operator. The purpose is to prevent him from forgetting, or to alert him that he has forgotten. His sense of responsibility, his honesty, and his ability are not being questioned: he is simply being given a useful aid.

The "Historian"

Particularly today, private firms have need of an "historian" who maintains a record of everything that is produced over a period of, for example, five years. He may make use of artificial memory and therefore, when a problem occurs, may recapitulate the points illustrated by Figure 10-9 with respect to similar problems in the past. His usefulness comes fully into play when he makes it possible to build a bridge between active and anticipatory prevention. In fact, managers waste an incredible amount of time in tackling problems without devoting the amount of time necessary to resolve them. Furthermore, the memories of managers do not have the reliability of modern computers and, with both confusion and conviction, they fail to distinguish between cause and effect, between definition of the problem and solutions. The presence of a historian is particularly justified in the case of products that are new or have only been produced in small quantities. He could supply data on what had already been produced in this or that other instance, and on whether such products were related to the company's products. His role could extend from knowledge of specifications up through implementation of production, with authority that had formerly been entrusted only to experts. The historian's usefulness would be indisputable not only in resolving the difficulties encountered, but also in identifying additional causes. His assistance would be valuable in modeling and simulation, in which it would be possible to include restrictions and parameters not thought of by harried managers. He could be a wise and stabilizing influence who would enhance and maintain the aggregate knowledge of the company.

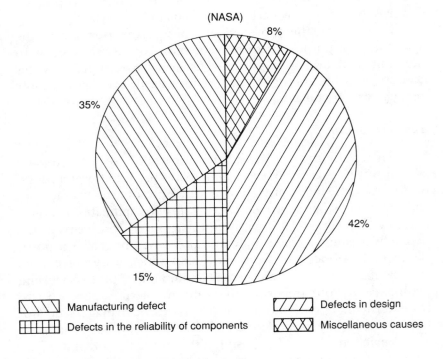

Figure 10-10. Causes of Failures

Anticipatory Prevention

Anticipatory prevention involves everything that is done before producing a product or implementing a procedure or process.

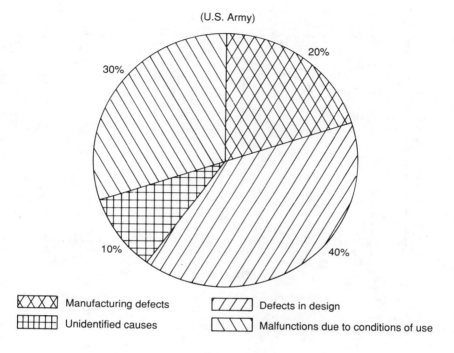

Figure 10-11. Causes of Malfunctions

Objective Life Cycle Cost

Figures 10-10 and 10-11, which cover causes of failures found by NASA and causes of malfunctions (which are tantamount to the same thing) provided by the United States Army, reveal that the principal causes arise from *defects in design.*

This finding contains a fundamental problem that requires special attention. Leaving these professional fields to one side, discussion is facilitated by focusing on ordinary products. Figure 10-12 shows what is called the "objective life cycle cost curve."

More simply stated, it is assumed that there will be five phases in the sequential progress of a product from its design through its use. These are (1) specifications, (2) research, (3) development, (4) manufacturing (or production) and (5) utilization (therefore, after-sales service). At 100 percent of the total time, all products

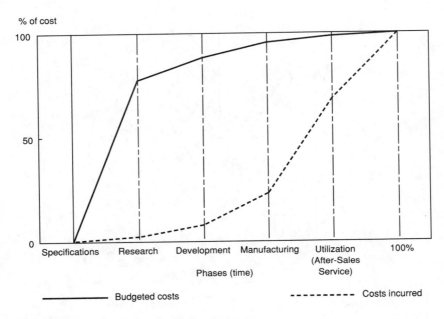

% of cost

Figure 10-12. Objective Life Cycle Cost Curve

are unusable. The lower curve shows the percentage represented by costs incurred. It can be noted that specifications, research and development are relatively less expensive, amounting to 10 or 15 percent of the total cost expressed on the vertical axis. Certainly production entails costs, but during the subsequent utilization phase, it is the user who incurs expenses in order to operate the product and to provide for its maintenance. It is specifically noted that technical considerations are not relevant. The analysis is the same for the launching of any new product: in leisure, banking, insurance, and so on. The upper curve illustrates budgetary commitments, that is, the amounts to be invested when the decision is made for each phase. It is immediately apparent that, whether the specifications are good or bad, the budgeted costs amount to 70 percent, if the decision to continue is made. In general, budgeted costs are high at the beginning of the cycle. The budgeted cost is low for the client, since he or she fortunately is not the only one to buy the product. This situation creates the imperative need for active prevention to be undertaken at the earliest possible point in the life cycle of the product. Figure 10-13, which is based on this factual premise, shows the relative distribution of responsibility for generating quality achievement costs among the divisions that conduct the operations of the organization. A scale is intentionally withheld for the vertical axis, because it is an approximation that essentially depends upon the type of organization. For this reason it can be seen that, for NASA, manufacturing defects are in last position, and, for the U.S. Army, they are in the penultimate position.

It is therefore imperative to completely eliminate likely causes after the specification, research, and development phases, and at the installation stage.

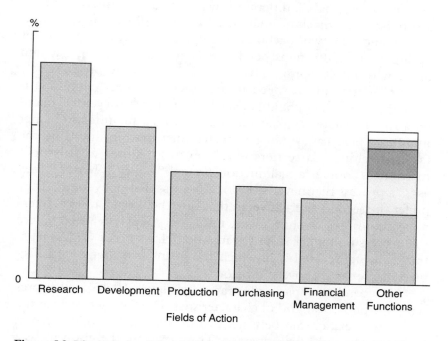

Figure 10-13. Relative Distribution of Responsibility For Generating Costs

Two Examples of Anticipatory Prevention

The first example of anticipatory prevention involves the design for a high-speed production machine. Its production is defined by the quotient: number of items/period of time. We Westerners have become accustomed to building or purchasing machines bearing quotients with a large numerator and a small denominator. For example, we prefer a machine that operates at a speed of 60 items per minute (or 3,600 per hour), rather than 50 per minute (3,000 per hour). In other words, we demand a great deal from equipment, techniques, and technology. However, what counts is not the speed of the machine, but the length of time during which the machine operates without needing adjustment or troubleshooting.

Easterners have a different way of thinking. Rather than have a sophisticated machine that operates at 2,800 items per hour, they would take two machines that operate at a slower pace – for example, at 1,500 items per hour – but keep working day and night without stopping. That would not exclude progressively increasing the rate of speed in a prudent manner. While one is operating, the other could be checked and given preventive maintenance. In that way, the number of items manufactured per month or per year would be greater than that produced by the faster machine. Easterners would even go so far as to stop a machine as soon as a malfunction occurs! "Which is better," they ask, "a process that never stops or a process that does stop?" They prefer the second alternative; in that case they could at least determine the causes of shutdowns, until the point is reached where the process no longer stops because no defects occur. This is illustrated in Figure 10-14, in which the quantity of items manufactured is the same above and below.

A second example is illustrated by Figure 10-15, which presents a hypothetical grid of characteristics. One characteristic in the grid is the relationship between two magnitudes: in this instance, V for voltage and I for amperage. The curves for the grid vary as a function of a parameter. This example is valid in electrical engineering, electronics, industrial physics, and many other fields. Technicians learned in school that in such a grid there is a "power

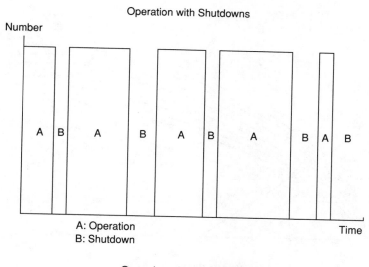

Operation with Shutdowns

A: Operation
B: Shutdown

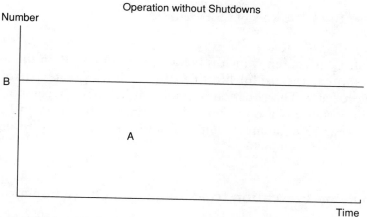

Operation without Shutdowns

Figure 10-14. Operating Time for a Process

hyperbola" and that the "load line," which passes through P, must be a tangent of that hyperbola.

To best use the efficiency of this motor, component, or whatever (it is not important which), point P must be chosen as the "working point." In the East, another line is drawn that is, above all, not tangent to the "power hyperbola." In addition, another

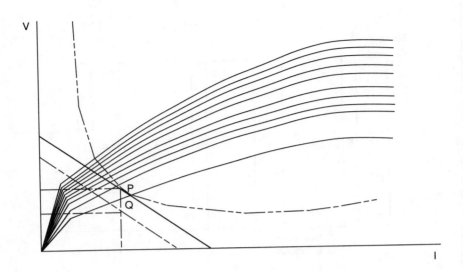

Figure 10-15. Network of Characteristics

point, Q, is chosen, which is below the maximum P. In the example shown, the useful life of Q is 10 times greater than that achieved at P. This situation is significant for strategic components. Its importance is also recognized with respect to professional high-performance equipment, but not always in the case of everyday products or machines.

Applying Prevention to a Company's Other Functions

The following is only a quick sketch of methods that all go in the same direction: the "zero-defect philosophy" for the prevention of defects or errors.

Zero Inventory

In traditional Western approaches to quality, there is in the course of any process a whole succession of steps between the initial point and the end of its sequence. This means that there are work-in-process (WIP) inventories between two consecutive work stations, partially for purposes of inspection, and partially to "regulate" production time and supplies of semifinished goods.

This operating method entails handling, and therefore the risk of deterioration; it also increases production time, delays, and cost prices.

During a trip to the United States, Taiichi Ohno, one of Toyota's top managers, observed in a supermarket that the customers themselves took the products they desired from the shelves. The customers then transported the products to the cash register, which reduced the labor for handling even more. He also noted that the shelves were restocked only to the extent that products were removed by customers, which avoided the buildup of unneeded inventory. He then had the idea of adapting this procedure to automobile production – the basic principle was the elimination of inventory. With the Western method, production management still often considers inventory a necessary evil that constitutes the only solution for fluctuations in demand.

If the point of departure is that only *transformation operations* impart added value to the finished product, inventory represents a loss that is in the same category as scraps of raw materials or production rejects. Moreover, such inventory entails not only the handling of large quantities, but also the risk of deterioration as a result of phenomena such as oxidation, for example. Inventory must be limited to an absolute minimum, which is to say a level approaching zero.

This goal is perfectly realistic provided (1) demand does not fluctuate excessively, (2) all phases in the production of each product are linked together in a tight and unbroken sequence, and (3) the process is sufficiently flexible to adapt itself immediately to changes in production.

In our Western system, functions are located and grouped according to very specific tasks (with mechanical processes: stamping, machining, milling, lathe work, etc.) so that the largest possible series can be worked on. Work is therefore done on series or lots.

In the Eastern system, the specific pieces of equipment for each function, and therefore for each step to be performed on the same product, are lined up one after the other. The product then undergoes the entire production process without interruption.

Kanban

In Japanese, *kanban* means "label" or "sign," but the term has been applied to a specific method.

In the Western system, everything is planned in advance, including inventories and so-called margins of safety, which are designed to anticipate accidents in each phase of production. Kanban is one of the most rudimentary procedures for implementing a production process. Its characteristics are the following:

- *Time frame*: each actor must produce and deliver at the appropriate time (just-in-time).
- *Quality*: any defective product must be eliminated immediately.
- *Reliability*: no machinery breakdowns should occur.
- *Versatility*: machinery and personnel must be adapted to various tasks in order to eliminate "downtime."
- *Balancing of production*: duplication of equipment must sometimes be permitted in order to synchronize different steps in production.
- *Engineering*: automation should extend to every possible part of the process.

All these conditions are strictly required; if any single condition is not met, production must be stopped.

Easy-to-read cards (labels) are posted and accompany the products throughout the production process. Each actor is considered the client of the actor immediately preceding him or her in the production sequence. The cards transmit the orders of one actor to the next.

These cards are of two types: the supply kanban (SK); and the production kanban (PK). When operators complete their procedures on a product, they remove the SKs attached to the product and post them on a board, for example. At regular intervals, other operators remove the SKs and find the corresponding products at the work stations upstream. They remove the PKs from the products they find there and replace them with the SKs destined for the work stations downstream. The PKs are placed on the production board and are returned to the upstream work stations as production orders.

This explanation has been somewhat oversimplified, but it is the principle involved that counts. Through kanban, work is initiated at any given moment only on the products necessary for immediate utilization. *Downstream always controls upstream.*

The downstream part of the process, which is based on demand for finished products, thus succeeds in adjusting production to the orders actually placed. There is therefore no unsold inventory and the number of semifinished goods is kept to a minimum.

It should be pointed out that it is the actor-producer who controls and possibly eliminates excess inventory. External suppliers, who are responsible for supplying the upstream part of the production process, must obviously follow this system. The SKs that they receive specify the quantities to be supplied, the date, and even the time. This raises the notion of partnership, in which clients, subcontractors, and suppliers are integrated into the production process.

Just-In-Time

Kanban is a philosophy that puts the client in control and requires that production be based on that reality. Production and delivery must occur at the appropriate time: *just-in-time.* Orders must be firm and final, and inventories must be nonexistent. Time frames become the fundamental basis for regulating production. Kanban depends on an appropriate match between delivery time frames and production time frames. It is particularly important to shorten the production cycle which reduces the time required for delivery, thereby luring new clients. To accomplish this, any equipment changes must be greatly expedited; otherwise, they will become problematic for the production of small series. Moreover, the reduction of waiting time between steps is particularly advantageous: production of small lots (while maintaining a continuous production flow) becomes possible, thereby reducing the number of semifinished products. If a lot of 1,000 products is produced by each of the actors in the process, it follows that, while the first is being produced, 999 others are waiting. Most often, it is the storage time for semifinished goods between steps that absorbs more of the total time frame for production than the actual time required for manufacturing. Machines that are too rapid cannot be made to pause in order to "align" themselves with slower equipment. It would be better to select less modern equipment or accept duplication of slow machines.

There is a wide gap between the several hours in France and the eight minutes at Toyota that are required to change the die in a stamping press for automobile roofs! Changing equipment requires both:

- Internal steps, which require that the machine be shut off
- External steps, which can be performed in advance

If internal steps are converted into external steps to the maximum extent possible, which may be done "off the clock," a machine would only be shut down for the period of time strictly necessary for removing one piece of equipment and replacing it with another. The operator, who is normally alone in front of the machine, could be assisted by another operator, whom he or she would in turn assist.

Adjustments made after installation of a new piece of equipment may take 50 to 60 percent of the time necessary for a standard operation of this type. Reducing this time requires that a maximum of adjustment be accomplished in advance. For example, clamping mechanisms using levers could replace screws. Of course, automation should be as extensive as possible.

How can the fixed nature of production capacities be reconciled with fluctuations in orders? It has been explained that the Western tendency has been to increase the number to time ratio and to run machines at maximum speed in order to produce in a minimum of time. This point of view necessarily entails the buildup of inventory. Action must be taken, not on the operating time for production systems, but rather on downtime. It is therefore unwise to establish a level of production that is consistently at maximum capacity, using high-output machines; the higher their performance, the more often they would be inactive. It would also be absurd to base production on minimum capacity, because orders could not be filled.

The solution consists of adapting production resources to a planned average volume, with the freedom to rely upon duplication of equipment. To set machine capacity at an even level is not enough. The work load must also have been evenly proportioned, and the best distribution over time must be found for the different types of production that have been ordered.

The client cannot absorb his entire order in one day. By agreement with the client, production should be drawn out in small lots over a longer period of time. It is therefore useful to divide up production in smaller lots and to complete it jointly with other types of production, which have also been divided up. In this fashion, an average permissible value for each piece of production equipment can be arrived at.

Comments

The principal ideas from these methods – which could be improved, computerized, and applied to companies in France – are:

- Budget base zero (BBZ), which shall not be described, but that expresses the same idea: *meeting the commitments undertaken*
- The client order
- Quality, reliability, time frames
- Downstream directs the upstream; *production is pulled*
- Consistent and regular production
- Deduction of inventory of semifinished products (handling, errors, accidents, incidents, intermediary inspections, costs, deterioration of products due to the environment, stacking, and other conditions)
- Rapid changing of equipment
- Reduction in inventories of finished products (costs, obsolescence, etc.)
- Added value comes from transformation, not from handling
- Versatility by the actors
- Self-disciplined group work

It is important to accept these ideas and to adapt them to Western attitudes and computer capabilities. To do so will require self-examination, an enormous training effort, and particular improvement in systems of communication and the promotion of decompartmentalization in organizations. Total quality can assist in this effort.

MRP

Created in the United States, MRP (material requirement planning) and its complement, DMRP (distribution material requirement planning), constitute a system that is practically the opposite of the kanban philosophy. They may be translated as: *management of production resources* and *management of production and distribution resources.*

This system has met with great success in Europe and is found there in various forms, although the overall principle is the same. It is a method for planning production (and distribution, if need be) that is based on technical data that is as reliable as production nomenclature and documentation. Planning, which is determined by computer as a function of production cycles, requires a lengthy period of time: from several months to one year. The production load is balanced as a function of the maximum capacity of each machine. The purpose is to achieve the maximum output of every piece of equipment. Once the production plan is established, the production and procurements necessary for each phase are planned down to the tiniest detail, and production orders are issued on that basis.

This is a system that pushes production. To ensure that the hypothetical plan withstands any chance events (breakdowns, delays by a supplier, etc.), reserve stock and a margin of safety between each step are mandated. Such provisions lengthen the production cycle, and therefore place a burden on fixed costs.

This method makes it difficult to respond to fluctuations in the market, particularly short-term variations. Instances in which a factory is overproducing one product and failing to meet delivery dates on another are not unusual, since the two products are produced on the same production line.

MRP is *a system for planning*, whereas kanban is *a system for prevention.*

Prevention as Venture Capital

Just as improvement in quality can be translated into palpable and quantifiable facts that are expressed as gains, prevention – and especially anticipatory prevention – is difficult to perceive *a priori*.

To purchase an extinguisher for one's car or apartment is an act of anticipatory prevention. It does not mean that some day there will be a fire, and even if there is a fire, it does not mean that the extinguisher will be able to put it out. Using different terminology, how can the profitability of the investment be justified? Of course, true prevention would be to avoid creating conditions that could cause a fire in the car or apartment. At this stage, one difference is already apparent: in one's home, vigilance and foresight may be enough to prevent a fire, because one has nearly absolute control. In a car, however, the situation depends not only on the driver but on other drivers, who cannot be controlled. In the event of a fire in another vehicle, the extinguisher may be used to put it out. If several drivers carry an extinguisher in their cars, the combined forces would increase the chances of extinguishing any fire at the outset – thus, it becomes a civic duty. Of course, there is always the risk that the assets committed to the process will not be used. Should the situation therefore be neglected? Foresight should be accompanied by prevention. One should always consider the "what ifs" and "unforeseeable circumstances." Moreover, prevention is an ongoing process. One must not only have the extinguisher but must remember to change it before its expiration date. In short, one never knows until after use whether or not assets should have been committed.

Pyralene is a contrasting example from current events. It is a trade name filed by the Prodelec Company, which produces chemicals for use in transformers and condensers. The development of these products was strongly pushed by Electricité de France for several purposes, including the replacement of dielectric mineral oils that are designed for use in electrical transformers. This was *active prevention*. In fact, the mineral oils had a "flash point" – a temperature (around 150° C) at which their vapors ignited in the presence of, for example, a spark. At such a high temperature, mineral oil can quickly burst into flame (think about deep fat fryers). Thunderstorms and short circuits frequently touched off fires in the transformers that distributed electrical power to an entire district. To avoid such hemorrhaging of the system, Electricité de France ordered only pyralene transformers, which had the advantage of being "nonflammable." This was true in practice for temperatures below 250° C. The engineering costs for installation of large power transformers in districts or in large buildings was considerably reduced, as was the cost of insurance premiums. From that point forward, pyralene became the universally accepted dielectric liquid, not only for transformers, but also for condensers (both large and small). The purpose of the latter is to improve the power factor in motors used, for example, in fluorescent systems. The considerable quantity of this product today, both in France and abroad (under other brand names), can therefore easily be imagined. It is estimated that there are nearly 150,000 power transformers and more than 100 million condensers currently in service in France, which would require more than 200,000 tons of pyralene.

The first alarms regarding pyralene were sounded in 1975, when Sweden used its derivatives in the conservation of plums and as plasticizers for paint. The use of these products in such applications was prohibited both in France and abroad during the 1980s.

The incident in Seveso (Italy), and the subsequent disaster in Bhopal (India) with dioxin, occasioned a huge debate, but it was still not known whether pyralene could produce such toxic substances. A fire in a transformer in Rheims settled the question. Due to pyrolysis, which is chemical decomposition from the effects of heat, pyralene gave off traces of dioxin. Extremely high temperatures were necessary for this to occur, but the fact remained. A double danger therefore existed as the result of active prevention: certain molecules of pyralene in the ecological chain became lodged in the livers of animals (and therefore those of humans) and, furthermore, after decomposition at very high temperatures, traces of terribly dangerous products appeared.

This example illustrates how prevention was neglected in three ways. First, prevention is a "capital risk" that may be initially beneficial but subsequently catastrophic. This is a contradictory effect similar to those occurring in the economic sphere: unforeseen uses of a product that in the long term may produce the opposite of what was anticipated. Second, the choice of pyralene for fire prevention was not subjected to an exhaustive analysis of the type described in Chapter 6. Left unanswered was the third question: "What could happen to make my client dissatisfied?" In this case, it would have been appropriate to imagine what could happen with a new product that was nonflammable but decomposable through pyrolysis. Third, no one thought about the destruction of the components in which this product was used, even though such destruction is a frequent occurrence. Prevention requires imagining not only long-term destruction, but also the consequences of such destruction.

Failure Mode and Critical Effect Analysis

The importance of anticipatory prevention has been discussed in the preceding paragraphs and in Chapter 6. One method of working in a group consists of analyzing failure modes in an exhaustive manner, component by component and subsystem by subsystem, during the specification, research, development, and prototype phases. Such research may be based on several different criteria, for example: mechanical (reliability, feasibility of production, process) or electric (reliability, feasibility of production, process). For each failure mode, the group would give the causes (falling, assembly, crushing, flame, smoke, water, etc.), then describe the effects on use (Table 10-3).

For standard and commonplace goods, the group would use a subjective scale of probability P and assign a grade of from 0 to 10 to each failure mode that involves, for example, one component of the product. Subsequently, the multi-disciplinary team of specialists would determine a grade (also subjective), which describes the seriousness S of the defect, taking into account the function of the particular component (mechanical, electrical, etc.) in the final product's application.

The sum of the two grades, $X = P \times S$, describes the *risk factor*, which is the significance attributed to the seriousness of the

Table 10-3. Failure Mode and Critical Effect Analysis

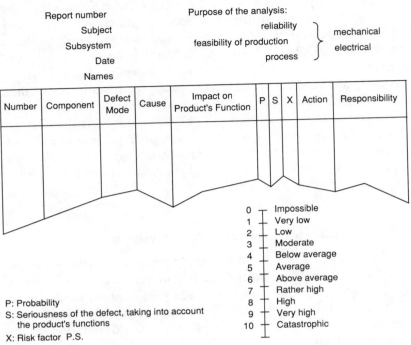

Number	Component	Defect Mode	Cause	Impact on Product's Function	P	S	X	Action	Responsibility

0	Impossible
1	Very low
2	Low
3	Moderate
4	Below average
5	Average
6	Above average
7	Rather high
8	High
9	Very high
10	Catastrophic

P: Probability
S: Seriousness of the defect, taking into account
   the product's functions
X: Risk factor P.S.

failure mode during production, during the process, or during use. The X values for each failure mode would be different. The highest values should then be eliminated by designating managers who would be responsible for eradicating or attenuating them.

This is quite clearly a systematic method that can be applied to the various phases before production is initiated. It may involve not only the product itself, but the process or the means of production. Precise figures may often be available. For example, in aviation, it is considered that an event with a probability of:

- 10^{-3} occurs from time to time in the service life of each aircraft – it is probable
- 10^{-5} does not occur in every aircraft, but may occur several times in the life of a fleet – it is rare

- 10^{-7} does not generally occur in the life of a fleet, but is considered possible – it is extremely rare
- 10^{-9} will not happen – it is extremely improbable.

At the same time, the seriousness of the consequences may be:

- *Minor*: slight degradation in characteristics or slight increase in the work load of the crew
- *Major*: significant degradation in the margin of safety, noticeable increase in the work load of the crew
- *Critical*: dangerous degradation in safety margins; dangerous increase in the work load of the crew; marginal conditions for the occupants
- *Catastrophic*: loss of the aircraft and/or deadly accident

Predictions are therefore possible when the appropriate figures are available. However, the most desirable thing in this particular situation is *prevention*, in other words, finding the critical points in a component that has several failure modes, thus creating a problem in the entire product or system. Next, every effort should be made to improve the results by eliminating the critical points and (for example) choosing other components.

Modeling and Simulation

A *model* is that which serves or should serve as an object to be imitated in order to reproduce something. In this sense, it is a *sample*, a model in the sense of a sewing or dressmaking pattern. A plan, a rule, a formula, a template, and a mold are therefore all models.

The same term has another definition: a person, event, or object possessing certain qualities or characteristics to such an extreme degree that they become representative of those qualities. This is the meaning of *type, specimen, example*, and *master*, in the sense of a leader, captain, or chief.

A *scale model* is an object that reproduces another object in a smaller size; in this sense, the model and the object are homothetic.

Finally, a model may be a *simplified representation* of a process or a system. This is the case with economic forecasting models, for example.

It can be said in summary that a model is an example to be followed, an ideal to be attained. The term *ideal* implies perfection, or abstraction, which explains why intangible models (such as those used in mathematics or forecasting) can only be imitated or copied. For such models, the neologism *simulation* is used to mean matching the appearance in the absence of an actual likeness.

On the human level, dealing with problems is more subjective than objective (hence the value of working in a group in order to both consider results and challenge the imagination). It is an intuitive process that, if overly personal, may lead to maladjustment or contradictory behavior. It is difficult to find models.

In the technical area, modeling makes it possible to study and optimize complex procedures for both products and methods, processes and systems.

The challenge of industrial expansion is part of the economic context and requires not only *modeling* but *simulation*. Great economists have taught us what contradictory effects and unforeseeable circumstances lurk behind all forecasts. It is only possible to work by an iterative manner on the basis of gross trends. This is the case with a relative upsurge in sales prices in connection with a policy of lowering of the sales price in relative terms. Increasing costs for investments in technology and new facilities also belongs in this context. Likewise, the pressure of international competition upon profit margins, the need to preserve employment, competitiveness, and the expansion of markets are all compelling phenomena whose influence needs to be conceptualized, and all the more rapidly if their momentum is decreasing.

If a model is defined for business purposes as a simplified representation of the structures and events of a complex reality, it is possible to:

- Better understand and discriminate between fundamental characteristics and influential parameters
- Better attain the goals set by two types of analysis – comparative analysis that compares hypotheses and solutions; and iterative analysis, that permanently transforms policies into strategies, while proceeding in a prudent manner.

Simulation becomes an aid to decision making but does not replace it. It is that much more effective when it yields rapid results that are immediately confirmed and that serve to improve the effectiveness of the decision.

Various types of models aid anticipatory prevention, strategic thinking, and decision making. *Scale models and prototypes* are appropriate for describing tangible products. *Samples and plans* are preliminary generalizations. *Intuition*, preferably collective, and guesswork are utilized for subsequent adjustments, and are approached in phases. They can only be used, in the instance of excessively high costs, for a gross overall approach, to detect the weak points to be eliminated, clarify anticipated performance, and describe technical and time requirements. They are used because a prototype would be too costly, and imagination and creativity is desired in the initial stages.

- *Forecasting and decision making models* have the essential purpose of refining and improving the preceding approach, which provided a general orientation. The desired results may be the forecasting of the company's needs and activities, improvement of a management system, or evaluation of profits and losses for different sets of figures. Difficulties may arise if growth phases are not linear, there is a change in the social context, or the implications are financial in nature. It is therefore wise to refer to the past and use imagination in incorporating both random events and unchanging situations. This approach aspires to be more rational. Forecasting is restricted to the short term (with slight extrapolations), but is extended in space. These models should include external constraints, the degree to which variables are connected, and any conceivable changes such as in the overall objectives, for example. The company is often considered a system in this instance, and an effort is made to display its structures and functions, flow patterns, regulation process, control system, and hierarchical structure. The decision making aid consists of an image of the actual phenomenon. It is an observation made concrete by measurements – it is a frame of reference. The actual system to be visualized poses a problem and requires analysis, or even theoretical explanations, from which a conceptual model can be derived. The latter is a logical and mathematical representation of the assumed behavior of the actual system. This representation has the advantage of indicating two processes: one that results in a solution, and another that leads to simulation and therefore programming (by means of a computer, for example, or with a set of scenarios). These two processes yield results that can then be compared with the measures developed by the preliminary review. The conceptual part of this model may be qualitative and therefore may involve predictions based on certain aspects of actual phenomena (the theory of catastrophes). When possible, *predictions* are to be made with the quantitative variables of the actual phenomenon, perhaps even with precision.

- *Descriptive models* are concrete and closely connected with observable facts. They enable one to better perceive reality through observation and communication. In addition, useful variables, relationships, and results for tangible items can be detected. Econometrics, statistics, and data analysis are a few examples of the descriptive model.

- *Abstract models* are based on general principles, on laws that, if they are not made into paradigms, provide opportunities for analysis and manipulation. Such models make it possible to optimize the object of study through the discovery of the most effective actions as a function of various criteria. They may be analytical, symbolic, mathematical, and heuristic models, with single or multiple criteria. When used for simulation, they enable one to use iterative methods, which clarify the consequences of an action.

The initial phase consists of presentation of the *problem*, which should include external factors, disturbances, events, and constraints. Next to be considered are current and anticipated situations and their characteristics, along with production doctrines, policies, and strategies. The purpose is to complete a dynamic behavioral study of the system in order to make a decision and derive the pertinent strategies. In this instance, the model is solely a schematic representation to spur analysis, understanding, and description. The behavioral study is amplified with a study of risks, which provides a basis for deciding which risks should or should not be incurred.

There are two categories of abstract models: those that are analytical and those that are concerned solely with simulation. The principle used by the first category is the solving of equations. The exact results show the optimum level. Its advantage is speed, and its restrictions are the low points of the distribution curve (Chapter 8). The second category provides a more precise representation, yields more complete data, requires an iterative approach, and accommodates a high degree of complexity, but with the limitation of being more time-consuming and more expensive.

Given the enormous advances in data processing, the usefulness of abstract models increases every day, provided their flexibility can be maintained. It should be stated once more that they are *decision making aids*, but do not in themselves constitute decision making. As explained earlier (Chapter 8), decision making first requires *consent*.

The fields of economics, sociology, psychology, and organizational studies may use such simulations if

- The objectives are extremely well-defined
- The data is grouped by the most homogenous populations
- The institutions are disciplined and enduring
- The behaviors are regular and stable

The decision itself will always be in the domain of intuition, experience, insight, and consent. The validity of simulations is based on prior observations that rely on measurements of actual phenomena, within the scope of variations following well-defined parameters. Bear in mind that, while in physics precision may reach or exceed 10-6, in social technology and the social sciences, 10 percent is rarely achieved, despite the rigor of the preceding conditions.

Summary

The scale model and the test or final prototype are particularly relevant to anticipatory prevention, and make it possible to perform failure mode and critical effect analysis, for example. Forecasting begins at the transition point between the concrete and the abstract. It is in itself indispensable, but answers only question number one of the prevention strategy: "What does my client need from me?" Simulation makes it possible to refine forecasting and to better define expectation. For purposes of prevention, simulation today answers only part of question number three: "What could happen to make my client dissatisfied?" Only creativity, working in groups, and the synergy of ideas permit at every stage the use of imagination to "foresee the unforeseeable." Perhaps one day it will be possible to simulate the unforeseeable, which occurs in a random fashion, but it is doubtful that such an analysis could be exhaustive – the number of criteria and constraints would tend toward the infinite. It is more reasonable to anticipate that simulation in the future will at least allow us to work on events that could occur in an erratic manner, and to take into account unplanned, and therefore unforeseeable factors.

11
Determining the Cost of Quality

With time and patience, the mulberry leaf becomes silk.

– Chinese proverb

The cost of quality (Chapter 6) can be divided into two costs: tangible and intangible.

Each of them has a cost of conformance (evaluation + prevention) and a cost of nonconformance (internal failures + external failures).

Tangible COQ is defined here as the COQ pertaining to anything concrete, palpable, and physical – objects that have precise specifications.

Intangible COQ concerns everything that is not concrete, palpable, and physical. It essentially takes into account functions, intellectual work, administrative work, and the like. It is more difficult to discern. On the other hand, as Figure 9-6 (see pg. 129) shows, it is far from being negligible and represents 50 to 60 percent of total COQ.

To determine the first category of COQ, use of an AFCIQ grid or its equivalent is sufficient in most cases, as will be demonstrated later. Determining the second category of COQ requires dealing with a more complex phenomenon, as indicated in Chapter 8.

The Administrative Environment

The effectiveness of administrative work, which is essentially a process of supplying data to others as a product, is not enhanced in direct proportion to an increase in staffing, as might be imagined in production. For purposes of discussion, it is assumed that an administrative unit has 10 employees. One-third of their time is dedicated to exchange of information. If the unit hires an 11th employee who is as competent as her colleagues, she will also need to reserve a third of her time for giving and receiving information. However, she will consequently immobilize her colleagues for a third of the others' work time.

The calculation is as follows:

The initial productive time was $^{(10 \times 2)}/_3$ of the day, per working employee, per day. Like the others, the new employee dedicates one-third of her time to information and coordination activities, and, by virtue of that fact, takes up at least one-third of the time of at least one other person in the unit. The effect of her arrival on production would therefore be $(^{20}/_3 - ^1/_3) + ^2/_3 = ^{21}/_3$ of the day, per working employee, per day, for this new team. This translates into $^1/_{20}$ additional production, for an increase of $^1/_{10}$ in staffing and therefore in fringe benefit costs.

In other words, an increase of 10 percent in this team's staffing leads to an increase of 5 percent in the personnel's work capacity. The result of this is that work increases as a function of the time available for its completion, and that, as a consequence, increases in expenditures have the mathematical tendency to overtake increases in revenue.

Although this is true for small staffs, one must also consider what C. H. Parkinson (1979) coined the *law of thousands*:

> Any organization, whether in government, business, or higher education, whose administrative staff reaches or exceeds one thousand persons, has no need to undertake any other activity or to employ any other category of personnel in order to perpetuate itself. Administration is self-supporting. It can sustain itself by its own work: administration for the sake of administration. This is a general law, a law of nature, just like the law of gravity. It is easy to prove the validity of this law since there is an abundance of examples.

Parkinson does not mean that administrative work is lacking in usefulness but rather that it too often serves only the administrators.

The thoughts of Parkinson have had only a limited practical impact, for several reasons:

- The 1960s and 1970s were decades of expansion. That growth was the result of a disorderly forward impetus and proliferation.
- The tendency toward centralized control was reinforced by the traditional attitudes of top management, who wished to maintain direct supervision of management by employing different administrative procedures.
- Technological limitations imposed by large-scale computers made it necessary to focus first on the development of management tools. Recent innovations such as microcomputers and office automation created the option of affordably priced components that could be placed in decentralized locations within the organization.
- In the context of economic development, the effect of excessive costs was blurred by constant growth in demand. The issue of profitability and productivity was relatively secondary.

Today personnel have increased requirements: working conditions, participation, consultation, and so on. Also, even if a person does not always manifest his aspirations because of a difficult job market, and even if he is alienated from his work, conditions such as stable employment, equality, upgrading of job classifications, excellent fringe benefits, convenient working hours, and freedom from rules and regulations are trends that are already a reality for administrative personnel. They add to the increased cost of fringe benefits.

The essential requirement desired by administrators is that the company survive, thereby preserving their seniority and job security. Hence, they strive for adaptability to change. This commitment to change will without doubt be the critical factor for companies in the future.

External Factors For Change In the Administrative Environment

- An increase in the diversity and variability of problems posed by the operating environment

- Uncertainty, which creates the need to process more data, and therefore more administrative work
- The problems of internationalization, and therefore export and foreign standards
- Variations in currency exchange rates, which require processing financial, commercial, economical, and even political data
- The multitude of documents demanded by government authorities
- Regulations, prohibitions, jurisprudence, and so on.

Internal Factors For Change In the Administrative Environment

1. Taylorian and bureaucratic criteria, whose characteristics are:
   - The separation of the *assignment, supervision, and execution of work* into distinct functions, and hence a significant vertical information flow
   - The dividing up and proportioning of tasks at the implementation level, which gives rise to a second, horizontal information flow
   - Development of the two flows through the give and take and *feedback necessary* for managers
   - A proliferation of written procedures (in addition to the flows previously described)
   - The centralization of decision making, which means that any instances not contemplated by procedures must be referred high up in the organizational pyramid, which prolongs the time necessary for a response
   - The inflation of paperwork

2. The closing in of the administrative environment on itself:
   - Those in company A do not feel that they are in competition with those in company B, and yet they are;
   - There is a distance from the actual market, often tied to an absence of economic incentive;
   - Competition, by forcing companies to design higher performing products, to manufacture them better, and sell

them faster, has protected administrative activities, because company management did not have the time to give them any attention;

- Top management, preoccupied with products, has not been able to concern itself with the competition or the pressure on administrative divisions because it did not have the data or figures.

The following is a list of these administrative behaviors resulting from growth, borrowed from J. Roy:

- The search for increased power and prestige (personnel and functions) through increasing staff, and the impact on resources.
- Hoarding of information (including information that is extraneous to the function) because:
  - Information equals power;
  - People fear having to say "I don't know."
- Excessive perfectionism.
- Manipulation of information by withholding it in an abusive manner under the pretext of "confidentiality"), by leaking it (often for personal ambition), and by distorting it.
- The desire to make the work more complex in order to:
  - Enhance the importance of individuals;
  - Create greater security for individuals.
- A growing trend toward conflict (between individuals, between functions).
- "Defensiveness" toward new organizations, which discourages innovation (and is tied to a feeling of insecurity about any change).
- Conspicuous indifference toward administrative expenditures, of which there is generally little or no awareness.
- Blind belief that the size of the company guarantees performance (through economies of scale). In fact, in administrative matters there are "diseconomies" of scale.

The danger is that these behaviors will increase by reinforcing each other. Thus, the prestige of a function (particularly for its manager) is often measured by the size of the staff it has; the search for complexity creates inflation in tasks and staffing.

What Corrective Action Should Be Taken?

Companies may take corrective action through:

- Technical means, without falling into the error that M. Crozier denounced as follows: "After the problem with 'meetingitis,' the danger of the 'computeritis' is at hand and quite serious. In other words, use figures and statistics, of course, but do not omit their subjective aspect";
- Structural changes, decentralizing functions, and transfer of staff with decision-making power to the various operational units (the creation of versatile teams);
- Methodological innovations, including those with participatory aspects (methods and tools);
- Use of the behavioral sciences, including their use in creating acute awareness of competitive pressure, particularly external competition.

The Processes

A process is a series of tasks performed with the assistance of resources such as personnel, facilities, equipment, information, and procedures. The anticipated final result is a product. It assumes:

- Measurable inputs
- An added value
- Measurable outputs
- The option of being repeated

There is no product without a process nor a process without a product.

Functional and Interfunctional Processes

Two major types of processes in an organization can be identified as follows:

- The functional process, which is a complete set of tasks for a single function. It is generally vertical in nature (Figure 11-1).
- The interfunctional process, which involves a combination of tasks pertaining to various functions. It is generally horizontal in nature (Figure 11-1 and 11-2).

The following are examples of functional processes: accounting, data processing, personnel, maintenance, advertising, development, production, inventory management, marketing, and training.

Examples of interfunctional processes are: product quality, committees, processing orders, forecasting demand, plans for investment, product changes, payment, replacement parts, contracts, invoicing, litigation, safety, prevention, taking inventory, and materials management.

Process Categories

Category 1 is termed *one-dimensional.* In other words, for each input there is one and only one output. This is the case for

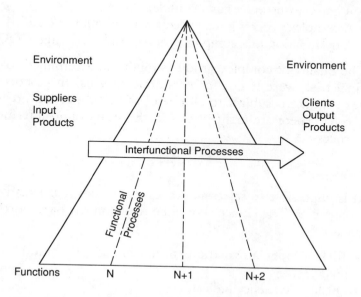

Figure 11-1. Functional and Interfunctional Processes

"technological" types of production such as metallurgy, semiconductor production, and machining parts. (Figure 11-2).

Category 2 is termed *multidimensional* because, for each output, there are several inputs, which in turn come from either one-dimensional processes or complex processes. This type of process is termed "assembly" and pertains to mechanical, electrical, and electronic parts.

Category 3 is termed *complex* because it may have any number of inputs and outputs. It is characteristic of administrative work such as orders, invoices, planning, and management of personnel, clients, and equipment.

Category 4 is termed *artistic*. It is difficult to represent in a simple fashion because it engenders a product that is usually unique and does not conform to any formal methodology. It is the process used by inventors, painters, composers, and other creative individuals.

For purposes of their analysis, processes 1, 2, and 3 may see some of their privileged paths lead to an elementary process of the one-dimensional type. In general:

- A complex product has a complex process
- A complex process has a process with a high value added
- A dysfunction in a complex process results in a high COQ

The quality of complex products might be determined solely by a final trial, were it not for economic reasons. In practice, a complex product is subject to all phases of the inspection process (Table 6-3). There are eight phases in the study of an interfunctional process:

Selection

It is impossible to select all processes to study, particularly in large companies. The choice should be made on the basis of criteria such as

- Risks (financial, to the external or internal brand name image, etc.)
- Quality-deficiency indicators

One-dimensional: I = 1, O =1

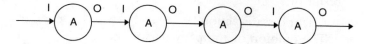

Technological Type of Production
Semiconductors, Machining of Parts, etc.

Multi-dimensional: I = n, O = 1

Assembly Type of Production
Mechanical, Electromechanical, Electronic, etc.

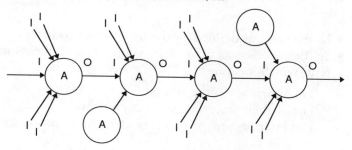

Complex: I = n, O = p

Administrative Type of Work
Orders, Planning, Invoicing, etc.

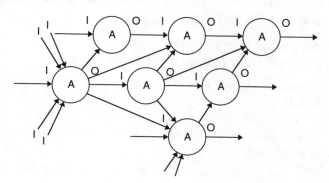

Figure 11-2. Elementary Processes

- COQ
- Negative data from surveys or opinion polls that are the result of
  - Client dissatisfaction
  - The opinion of company personnel
  - The number and significance of corrective actions from audits
  - The strategic goals of the company

Setting the specifications for the process chosen

Once the process has been chosen, specifications should be established for

- Its purpose, as defined by the product it produces
- Its boundaries, as defined by suppliers and clients its content, which includes
  - The functions of the actors
  - The elementary processes it comprises
  - The intermediate products of elementary processes

Responsibility

In the case of a functional process, the manager of the function with which it is concerned is by definition responsible. For an interfunctional process, a manager of one of the key functions involved would be in charge. This manager

- Is designated by top management
- Is responsible for management of the process
  - Through direct operational control within his own function
  - By performing his function in collaboration with the other functions with the support of the management committee
- Seeks arbitration of any disputes that may arise through the higher echelons of the company structure
- May not delegate

The managing committee

The managing committee consists of

- The manager of the process, who is chairman of the committee
- A representative of each function involved, who is an authorized representative of the manager if the latter chooses to send a deputy
- Experts in finances, accounting, management, quality methods and procedures

This committee is responsible for improving the quality of the processes and its mission shall be to determine

- Goals
- The functional processes and their managers
- The principal details and methods for measurement
- Priorities for the actions to be taken
- Key indicators for the process
- The process itself (soliciting assistance regarding methods and management from the units involved, the manager of the process, and several work groups if necessary)

Segmentation

Segmentation entails

- Identifying not only suppliers but also *all* clients
- Identifying the products
- Identifying the details of measurement (method, instrument, person responsible)
- Documentation

It mandates

- Purity, which is attained when each elementary process has the characteristics of a complex process
- Respect for the specific nature of the products produced by the process under study

- The definable elementary products that make up the final product (so as not to make a division by function when doing so is unnecessary)
- Details of measurement that have already been established or are easy to define
- Classification by product rather than by function

Measurements

- Measurements that are peculiar to the process must be made upon entry into and exit from it.
- On every possible occasion measurement will be subject to statistical testing.
- Both the capabilities of the process and the frequency of measurement must be determined.

Management of the process

During design, management means doing things well, designing an error-free process, and commiting oneself to satisfaction of the client. In other words, things are done well by proceeding in the proper manner. Improvement of the process must be permanent and ongoing.

Improvement of the quality of the process

Companies can improve the quality of the process by measuring both the quality of the product and the satisfaction of those who receive it. Frequency of measurement is a direct function of the degree of control desired.

The Purposes of Studying Processes

This type of study, which follows the Merese method, may be performed by using ideas from *A Systems Approach To Organizations*. It demonstrates that some complex processes generate dysfunctions. It also proposes an effective system of decompartmentalization designed to detect, improve, and control the interfunctional processes that are the most difficult to analyze, since everyone "guards his sacred site" like a Knight Templar. It is also possible to perform an analysis with another tool, the GRAFCET which, as complete as the description may be, makes it possible to establish indicators in practically every area of the company, even the tertiary sector. The important thing is to determine several indicators (3 to 5) that have significance with respect to improvements that could be made. The goal here is improvement in quality rather than in COQ.

COQ Analysis in an Elementary Process

A functional division within an organization can serve as an example for purposes of discussion. First of all, it has a *mission*, an assigned duty for which it is responsible, which is its *function*. Its manager is assigned this function and needs employees in order to accomplish it. Each person in this division will be responsible for *activities*. An activity is a precise action that contributes to the creation of a product (service, document, advice, and so on).

For each activity, there is one input product and one output product. *If an activity has no output product, it is useless.* The mission is, in fact, the coordination of the activities of the division in order to add value to the input products, which then become output products. The transformation performed between input and output is the value-added for the activity. The total value-added, which is the mission of the division, is the sum of all the value-added in each activity related to the mission.

The transformation of an input product into an output product (the activity) is itself the result of a *process*. The phases of this process are *tasks*. There are five types of tasks:

- Prevention (P)
- Evaluation (E)
- Internal failure (Fi)
- External failure (Fe)
- Useful value-added (UVA)

The total costs connected with these tasks is the value-added for the process, and therefore for the activity.

Take the example of a secretary's office: there is a function, and therefore a mission.

The principal activities of a secretary can be broken down as follows. Each activity transforms an input product into an output product.

- Answering the telephone (input product: the call; output products: the greeting, information, screening, routing, connecting the call)
- Arranging a meeting (input product: a request; output products: communicating and confirming the time and place, recording this data)
- Filing (input products: documents, notes, reports; output products: reference system and filing locations)
- Typing a letter (input product: the original issued by the manager for the function; output product: letter on company letterhead, etc.)

The activity of typing can be analyzed in terms of the five tasks.

- Reading the manuscript (to understand, proof, paginate, correct errors, check paragraph order, and consider the page format) is a *prevention* task.
- Typing the letter (finding a sheet of paper, placing it in the machine, typing or entering the text) involves *useful value-added.*
- Rereading the letter is inspection and therefore *evaluation.*
- Correcting typing errors involves *internal failures.*
- Submitting it for a signature involves an *external failure* (if the author discovers an error that the secretary did not catch; in this instance, he or she is the secretary's client) or an *internal failure* (if the author corrects his or her own text).

Working as a Group

To accomplish its mission, and therefore its function, a department or division must carry out several activities, each consisting of several tasks.

A document may be prepared for the group, listing:

- Principal activities: what the division does.
- Finished products: what the division supplies to its clients.
- Tasks: what each person does.
- Suppliers: what the division needs for its activities, and therefore for its tasks.
- Clients: those to whom the division supplies products, which are the results of its activities.
- Frequency and quantities (estimates).
- The time necessary for each task, as an annual percentage (estimate).
- The time necessary for each activity, as an annual percentage (estimate).
- The cost of each task, obtained by multiplying the percentage of time spent annually by the cost of the personnel involved (salaries, fringe benefits, other costs). Expenditures that do not vary by activity, such as investments and work areas are not at issue here.
- The costs for each activity.
- All other costs, not including personnel costs, which directly relate to the activities of the division (subcontracting, market studies, printing, data processing, photocopying, travel, mail, telex). In the case of machines, the annual costs for equipment (depreciation, maintenance, preventive maintenance) and its use (fluids, raw materials, corrective maintenance) must be tallied. Costs that vary as a function of activities – such as investments and work areas – are relevant here, and should be combined with those for activities, with an accuracy of +20 percent.
- The classification of each task, according to whether it adds value to the product (UVA) or adds costs to the product. Included in the latter are:
  - P: Prevention
  - E: Evaluation: anything that is inspected, monitored, or otherwise evaluated within the division
  - Fi: Failures that are internal to the division (anything that is redone, corrected, or modified *before* going to the client)

- Fe: Failures that are external to the division (anything that is redone, corrected, or modified *after* going to the client)

COQ = Prevention + Measurement + Management of Failures

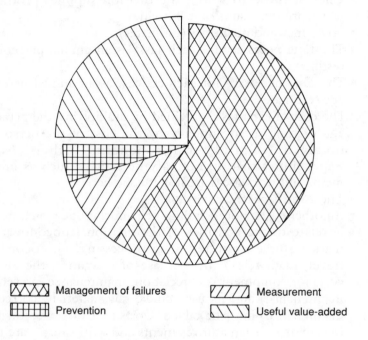

Management of failures   Measurement
Prevention   Useful value-added

Figure 11-3. Our Daily Work

Figure 11-3 demonstrates how the total value-added for an administrative function should be subdivided, according to specialists in time management. For purposes of managing dysfunctions, there are two types: those due to the employees performing the function and those due to others. Employees spend approximately 25 percent of their time committing errors and about 25 percent correcting them. In this instance, the term *measurement* concerns evaluation of one's own work.

Prevention includes documentation, for example.

Figure 11-4 shows the leveraged effect of prevention, which has the same effect on individual work as on collective efforts.

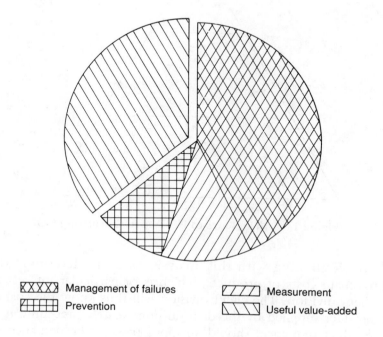

| XXXX Management of failures | ///// Measurement |
| ⊞ Prevention | \\\\\ Useful value-added |

Figure 11-4. Our Daily Work: "Leveraged Effect" of Prevention

Personnel costs may be *normative*; that is, they may have related categories, each of which may be assigned an average value. This procedure produces three or four normative costs per function, or even a single cost for a division: the rates for a section, for example (Figure 11-5).

The sequential order should be noted: *mission, activities, tasks.* An analogous sequence would be *policy, strategy, tactics.*

For each activity, separate totals can be derived for UVA, P, E, Fi, and Fe.

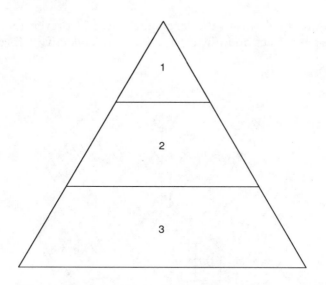

Figure 11-5. The Rates to Be Used in Calculating COQ

By continuing with this analysis, one can determine the approximate costs of products, which is of particular interest to the client division. The client division will thus know the cost of the product supplied by the division immediately preceding it in the product sequence, should an input product be damaged or spoiled by the client division itself.

Tasks that absorb more than 10 percent of total time annually are termed *principal tasks*. Tasks requiring less than 10 percent of annual time are not taken into account.

Presenting all of the above costs in the form of matrixes enables the group to arrive at cumulative totals for conformance (evaluation and prevention), and nonconformance (internal and external failures). This cost breakdown makes it possible to determine what actions should be taken with respect to prevention, once the most important problems have been resolved.

This analysis may initially be performed in a rough and approximate manner. The principal requirement is that it remain the same throughout the entire improvement process. While this method is well known to many in the field, it is generally not used with respect to the cost of quality. Rather, it is all too often applied only by "commandos" or ad hoc teams. That type of application has given it a bad reputation.

I suggest that the situation be turned around. Everyone should be familiar with and use COQ analysis. It does not require monitoring or any means of pressure, but rather is a *system* that extends prevention to all levels of the company. It is the voluntary act of a group that is committed to participation and success through quality improvement.

Tracking the group's own progress

To document its own progress, the group should:

- Prepare an exhaustive list of clients
- Prepare a list of output products
- Prepare a list of input products
- Prepare a list of tasks by activity
- Classify the tasks as P, E, Fi, Fe, and UVA
- Tally the number of each and the time spent on each
- Disregard tasks that absorb less than 10 percent of time on an annual basis

Estimating

It may be very useful to evaluate tasks directly before resorting to more sophisticated techniques. It is enough that the definitions of tasks be approved by everyone and that accuracy be nearly + 10 percent, which is adequate if the activities, the five types of tasks, the clients, and the output products are known. Sometimes, extrapolating on the basis of data from the past leads to estimates with an accuracy of ± 15 percent, in which case the question arises as to whether it is useful to devote additional time to a more accurate estimate.

It is important not to draw conclusions regarding the individual output of employees – that is not the desired purpose.

For example, the focus should be on a problem rather than a particular activity. In any case, do not attempt to achieve total accuracy – that is perfectionism and a waste of time. In fact, it is a delusion to think one can estimate with an accuracy greater than 5 percent. What counts is awareness of prevention. Figures are less

convincing than actions. On the other hand, giving encouragement and informing others that progress has been made creates a
great sense of satisfaction.

Estimating is a simple and practical way of quantifying.
Everyone should participate in it and, for the initial analysis, can
provide correct information on volume, time frames, quantities,
delays, error rates, and costs.

Penduluming is a valuable method for correcting the skewing
of data (distortions caused by systems): it yields excellent results
when used by individuals who are thoroughly familiar with the
work or field under study, even if they do not have quantitative
notions about the issue. This is all the more true if they themselves
normally perform the work under consideration.

This method consists of making a series of three approximate
estimates: a minimum m, a maximum M, and the most probable x.
These are based respectively on an optimistic perspective, a pes-
simistic perspective, and normal conditions. The corrected average
(the closest to what would occur if the operation were performed
a large number of times) is obtained by the following formula:

$$x = \frac{m + 4x + M}{6}$$

This formula comes from what is termed a normal distribution and is most often found to be appropriate. Weighting can be
used, if need be, when the observers do not work in a random
fashion. Note that the greater the distance is between m and M
(minimum and Maximum), the more uncertain the estimates are.
If an assessment of the degree of uncertainty u of the corrected
average obtained is desired, the following formula may be used:

$$i = \frac{M - m}{6}$$

The following example is an evaluation of the average number of telephone calls received per day by one person. If the evaluation results in the following figures: minimum = 6, maximum =
20, and probable = 12, the average number would be:

$$\frac{6 + (12 \times 4) + 20}{6} = 12.33,$$

or approximately 12.

The degree of uncertainty would be:

$$\frac{20 - 6}{6} = 2.3, \text{ or approximately 2.}$$

Therefore, the average number of calls per day would be 12 ± 2.

There are 95 chances in 100 that the person would receive between 10 and 14 telephone calls. This is not very far from 12, but to have the best chance for accuracy, 14 is used. The amount of time spent on the telephone can be determined in the same manner. If the evaluation gives the following time indications: minimum = 3, maximum = 15, and probable = 5, the same type of calculation would result in an average of 6 minutes, with an uncertainty factor of 2 minutes. It can therefore be concluded, with a confidence level of 95 percent, that the person spent approximately 72 minutes on the telephone during the day.

Quality Improvement Projects

Even with administrative divisions, for which advance analysis is rough and approximate, it is possible to ask certain questions regarding each activity:

- Is there a specification or requirement by our client?
- What is it?
- Is the product in conformance?
- What is our client's opinion of its conformance?
- Is the product truly necessary?
- What is our client's opinion about the need for the product?

The answers to these questions require a dialogue with clients and a joint setting of priorities:

- Have we determined what we need from the supplier?
- Is there a specification or a requirement?

- What is it?
- Is the product in conformance?
- Is it actually used?
- Is it used correctly?
- What is our client's opinion on this subject?

The answers to these questions require a dialogue with suppliers. The client-supplier relationship has systemic virtues. If it is not based on conformance and specifications, then it is a relationship between a person and a document. Thus, it is purely bureaucratic, which is necessary but not sufficient because, no matter who we are, we have little or no influence on a piece of paper. If, in contrast, conformance arises from an actual need that is expressed by a genuine client-supplier relationship, there is *communication*, therefore feedback, and therefore a system, which is human, necessary, and adequate. Feedback makes joint progress possible. That is the virtue of a negotiated specification, which, within a company, is termed a *requirement*.

The parties should arrive at a commitment to comply with the specifications or requirements that have been jointly established. Such an arrangement does not exclude the responsibility of divisions with respect to their own jurisdictions. Recourse to an arbitrator is always possible. If there is a subsequent problem, it is settled not through waiving of principle, but through the setting of a new specification, or even through the cancellation of a recognized but less reliable product.

The client-supplier consensus makes it possible to establish representative and useful indicators of quality, while creating the means for measuring quality. These indicators are designated only with the client's agreement.

- Is the activity measured?
- Can it be measured?
- If not, does the activity actually have any usefulness?

Next is the improvement phase, to be followed by prevention.

- What would have to happen in the division to make the client dissatisfied?
- What must be done to prevent that from happening?

- What do we not want to receive from our supplier?
- What is the supplier's opinion?
- What do we not want the client to receive?
- What is the client's opinion?
- Where does our action begin (one action at a time)?
- What is the time frame for the action taken?
- How strongly do we want to succeed?

Each project would have a duration of between 60 and 120 days. It is important to have a fixed time limit with a precise and quantifiable goal to be achieved.

Any positive results should be publicized so that everyone can appreciate them. Each person will tend to continue his efforts if his participation is recognized and appreciated by all.

"Guide Charts" for Calculating COQ

Any attempt to impose on a company or companies a set of standard charts for use in calculating COQ could not be taken seriously. Guide charts are meant to serve as examples only, as rough cuts that can then be tailored to individual functions.

Nonconformance affects a company's revenues in two ways:

- Directly, through the losses it entails and through the costs budgeted for achieving quality in the company's activities;
- Indirectly, through lost profit opportunities that are the result of the difference between actual sales volume and what could have been achieved without nonconformance. Lost profit opportunities might include a diminished internal and external brand name image, lowered sales price, delay in launching products, loss of potential clientele, and reduction in market share.

The costs of nonconformance must therefore be measurable for each function, which may be either generated or experienced by a function (for example, costs from errors arising further upstream in the production process). It should be recalled that conformance consists of prevention and evaluation, whereas nonconformance consists of internal and external failures.

Lost profit opportunities are difficult to measure in the short term. Though it is possible to take into account foreseeable factors such as seasons, shows, and fashion, it would be difficult to measure the difference between sales forecasts and reality. Moreover, numerous subjective factors would have to be included that could not be accounted for in a formal manner and for which it would not be possible to set limits.

How in fact could the following reactions be estimated?

- Reduced confidence by regular clients as a result of excessive rigidity or flexibility in (technical or commercial) negotiations
- Reduction in the number of clients as a result of missed deadlines
- Reduction in the number of clients as a result of press or information campaigns that were too easy on the competition
- Reduction in the number of regular clients as a result of advertising that they considered unwarranted or frivolous
- Inadequacy or lack of dynamism on the part of distributors or sales personnel
- Loss of prestige, and therefore of external brand name image, as a result of another of the company's activities
- The company's absence from certain shows

Market share lost as a result of industrial espionage, pirating, or theft cannot be reduced to accounting entries except those for costs generated by lawsuits or by internal investigations or countermeasures. Therefore, only measurable costs due to direct losses shall be considered.

The following functions will be covered:

- Product (upstream marketing)
- Research and development
- Materials
- Production
- Marketing (downstream marketing)
- Quality
- Personnel

- Administration
- Information systems
- Accounting

The 10 charts provided at the end of this chapter are intended to serve as a source of inspiration only, not to be applied in their present form. The major headings for the charts and the sequence in which they are listed must be approved by the parties involved. They are no more than a basis for reflection, in which items listed under the four major COQ headings are not listed in order of importance.

Once these charts have been agreed upon by the personnel involved, the group can make a final, definitive version of a grid such as the one presented in Table 6-2, which was prepared by the AFCIQ. The company's grid should have its own codes and become one of the standards for calculating COQs. Each year, it should be revised as necessary to avoid compromising the validity of the calculations as a whole.

The Limitations of COQ

COQ and its importance obviously prompts attention from higher level professional employees. COQ makes possible the determination of quantifiable indicators for improvement in quality. It would appear to direct corrective actions in more profitable directions, and could also be useful providing a basis for setting priorities.

Today, experience shows that it does not have all these virtues, for reasons inherent in its calculation and the accuracy with which it has been determined.

It should be so simple to determine the COQs for large functions and then add them up. In reality, things are more complicated. Even though each function can identify prevention, evaluation, and internal failures, it is not always easy, because of the existence of interfunctional processes, to identify external failures. They are found downstream in the process, often within several other functions (Figure 11-6). This leads to an important conclusion: *COQs by function cannot be added together.*

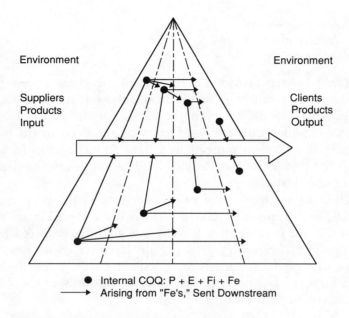

● Internal COQ: P + E + Fi + Fe
→ Arising from "Fe's," Sent Downstream

Figure 11-6. COQ Totals by Department

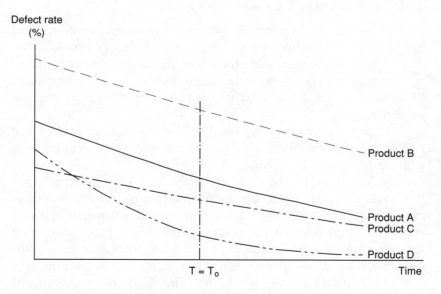

Figure 11-7. COQ Totals by Products

Now, as has been previously noted, products have a learning curve, and permanent active prevention measures should be taken with respect to these curves (defect rates as a function of time) after the failures have been dealt with. Furthermore, in any company that is not a single-product business, some products die and others are created, usually in short order. Hence, the reference to time $(T = T0)$ in the calculation is no longer comparable with the COQ obtained for another period, and the figures obtained are no longer a frame of reference. This leads to another important conclusion: *COQs by products cannot be added together.*

COQ nevertheless has a contradictory effect, which occurs within a function. During the process of improving quality, everyone is dedicated to reducing the COQ caused by internal failures. Because of habit, the tendency is to initially increase evaluation, whereupon "hidden" internal failures increase. This is the contradictory effect of COQ illustrated in Figure 11-8.

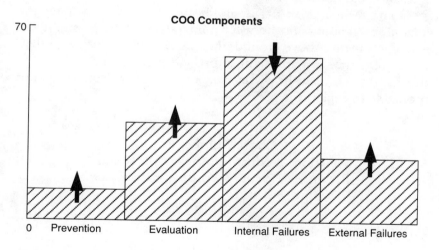

Figure 11-8. The Contradictory Effect of COQ

What Should Be Done?

Rather than attempt a minutely detailed analysis that will never be completely accurate, it is better to use a long- term cycle that progresses toward greater accuracy. Year after year, each division, each function, each department, and each unit determines the scale of accuracy for the COQ. As a metaphorical example, consider the sequence of tools used in an excavation job:

- The first year, a truck
- The second year, a shovel and wheelbarrow
- The third year, a soup ladle and soup pot
- The fourth year, a soup spoon and soup bowl
- The fifth year, a teaspoon and cup
- The ninth year, a dropper and glass

These may be termed the successive *substrata* of quality deficiency, which should be conquered year by year by setting goals.

Nothing should obstruct the quest to permanently improve COQs by working on failures and constantly increasing prevention. This approach requires drawing the two Pareto graphs: conformance and nonconformance.

The term *substratum* is significant: it clearly illustrates the analogous relationship between minerals and the feasibility of extracting them. Above ground, they are easy to remove. At a shallow depth, they require slight effort and investments. At average depths, they demand heavy investments. At great depths, it is not profitable to exploit them.

Chart Number 1
Function: Product (Upstream Marketing)
Research • Product Marketing • Promotion

A. Prevention

- Review of the draft plan
- Studies of the client's needs in terms of the product's quality
- Description of tasks
- Studies of the range of options with respect to aesthetic design
- Description of methods
- Participation in the creation of internal quality standards

- Participation in reviews of the design
- Value analysis during the design stage
- Participation in the creation of the testing plan for the products
- Participation in COQ summaries
- Development of the upstream marketing structure for quality
- Preparation of any possible internal audits

B. Evaluation

- Cost of initiating quality evaluations of competing products
- Inspection costs for the product
- Studies and surveys regarding the quality of the design (the product/need match)
- Verification of the use of supplies
- Participation in the evaluation of new technologies
- Participation in the validation of research methods for the production function
- Monitoring of the implementation of field marketing studies

C. Internal Failures (Measured by Function)

- Cost of redoing marketing studies on account of unfeasibility of the product or the system selected
- Modification of the design
- Cost of redoing market studies because constraints were overlooked in design or production or because new constraints emerged
- Changes in purchase orders necessitated by modifications in product function

D. External Failures (Measured by Function)

- Cost of repeating studies upstream because product was repositioned as a result of problems connected with:

- product policy (performance specifications, warranties, etc.)
- distribution policy (channels, networks, direct sales, etc.)
- communication policy (advertising, promotion, etc.)
- pricing policy (price level, price lists, discounts, etc.)
- failure to meet sales goals

Chart Number 2
Function: Research and Development
Technology • *Advanced Methods* • *Studies* • *Prototypes*

A. Prevention

- Participation in the creation of internal quality standards
- Client relations
- Participation in the preparation of inspection plans and procurement specifications
- Participation in packaging design
- Participation in reviews of the design (preparation of specific documents)
- Preventive maintenance
- Participation in reviews of production and inspection documentation
- Determination of the capabilities and appropriateness of the process for production of the product
- Participation in quality studies (reliability, maintainability, safety, failure mode and critical effect analysis, quality metrology, etc.)
- Production of equipment for special tests
- Development of research and development structures that reflect and are conducive to quality
- Participation in summaries regarding COQ
- Monitoring of the preproduction process
- Preparation of annual quality improvement plans
- Planning of defect prevention
- Participation in any possible internal audits
- Approval of production specifications

B. Evaluation

- Review of forecasting
- Participation in trials for evaluation and validation of the design
- Examination of procedures
- Participation in the evaluation of new technologies
- Cost of modifications
- Checking of plans and drawings
- Acceptance trials for samples
- Formal inspection of research documentation
- Inspection of production standards
- Participation in the approval of various suppliers
- Tests of samples of semifinished products
- Cost of the calibration of measurement equipment in research laboratories
- Testing of the final product
- Laboratory tests and analysis
- Tests for errors in insertion
- Training for special tests
- Evaluation of personnel

C. Internal Failures (Measured by Function)

- Cost of redoing marketing studies as a result of design errors detected by tests and measurements performed on scale models or prototypes and during the start-up of production
- Warranty expenses incurred by modifications
- Cost of redoing studies because of new constraints (product constraints, production constraints, and internal standards)
- Analysis of products returned by clients
- Costs created by delays upstream (specifications, resources, administrative approvals, or other causes)
- Corrective actions
- Participation in repetitions of evaluation/validation tests pursuant to studies that were redone (see above)
- Reports on defects

- Cost of various unusable purchases and investments caused by
  - Changes in the specifications for products and systems (obsolescence, prototype)
  - Cancellation of the project

D. External Failures (Measured by Function)

- Repetitions of unscheduled studies for the product carried after the first delivery or deliveries
- Participation in studies with new evaluations and their validation pursuant to the above-indicated repetition of studies
- Lack of product reliability in relation to the study
- Participation in studies for the analysis and detection of the causes of failures occurring at the client's premises, and repairs, if necessary (time spent for technical support during after-sales service)

Chart Number 3
Function: Materials
Purchasing • Procurements • Preparation for Launching of Production • Warehousing of Materials • Acceptance Inspections

A. Prevention

- Setting of firm prices
- Preparation of inspection specifications for components, materials, and software purchased in accordance with the quality plan
- Forwarding of correct specifications to suppliers
- Periodic meetings with suppliers
- Preparation of a schedule for supplier audits
- Provisions for heavy or fragile materials
- Participation in reviews of design and manufacturing documentation

- Costs incurred by the existence of several sources
- Development of the structure for the function
- Participation in COQ summaries
- Preparation of annual quality improvement plans

B. Evaluation

- Examination of the suppliers' quality procedures
- Acceptance inspection, including those for materials consumed during testing
- Inspection at the suppliers' premises
- Participation in the evaluation of products purchased
- Inspection of inventory items, including reinspection of surplus from production
- Monitoring of compliance with deadline dates
- Calibration of measurement equipment
- Participation in audits of suppliers
- Inspection of orders (technical specifications, signatures, etc.)
- Monitoring of invoices and payments on account
- Monitoring of procurement sources (reliability/longevity, dual source)
- Destructive tests (loss of components)

C. Internal Failures (Measured by Function)

- Excessive inventory necessitated by lack of confidence in suppliers
- Reinspection of component lots
- Renegotiation of purchases pursuant to errors, oversights, and modifications in pertinent documentation
- Reissuing purchases on account of supplier inefficiency or errors
- Rejects: materials that are ordered by error, unusable, or out of date (obsolescent or unusable because of modifications in specifications, for example)
- Screening performed pursuant to errors in the setting of specifications, a lack of specifications, or an error by the supplier that was not billed

- New inspections necessitated by rejections and the waiving of requirements
- Extra transportation needed because of delays or errors
- Time spent in redoing work
- Reshipment and reprocessing of rejected lots or sub-assemblies
- Inventory losses (differences between actual and theoretical)
- Cost of excess inventory created because of lack of confidence in the supplier
- Supplementary time and tasks required for the data processing needed to manage these dysfunctions
- Cost of precautionary reordering done because of lack of confidence in the supplier

D. External Failures (Measured by Function)

- Changes in an order pursuant to errors
- Repetition of various procedures after transfer of ownership in the event of recall of the product
- Losses incurred by supplier errors
- Screening performed and returns handled by the materials warehouse because of a product recall
- Preparation of new versions of outgoing order forms
- Transportation costs for direct claims to the supplier
- Trips and visits to suppliers to resolve problems
- Rearrangement of deliveries by telephone

Chart Number 4
Function: Production
Methods • Manufacturing • Warehousing • Subsystems • Inspection

A. Prevention

- On-the-job training

- Preparation of plans and documentation for the inspection of products, subsystems, and the like, in accordance with the quality plan
- Study of critical points in manufacturing and inspection, establishment of standards for the various phases of the process, documentation of general procedures
- Identification of specifications, search for incorrect documentation
- Preparation of reviews of production documentation
- Zero defect program
- Training in general information regarding COQ
- Determination of goals
- Participation in design reviews
- Preparation of annual quality improvement plans
- Preparation of work orders
- Maintenance of the premises

B. Evaluation

- Inspection of documentation for procedures and equipment (including precautions for maintenance and storage)
- Monitoring of overtime
- Inspection of production, with specific tests subcontracted to laboratories
- Inspection of semifinished products, entry inspection at warehouses for surplus subsystems
- Certifications
- Participation in evaluations of product specifications and production
- Participation in product and production audits
- Evaluation of client data
- Calibration of devices and equipment used for measurement
- Modification of prototypes
- Checking the capabilities of machines, tools, and personnel regulating the machines (initial inspection and periodic inspections)
- Inventory audits

- Examination of the flexibility of equipment and machinery, especially for slower-paced phases of production

C. Internal Failures (Measured by Function)
- Expenses incurred by questionable absences
- Rejects from manufacturing and warehousing
- Repetitions and corrections performed by production in order to bring a product or subsystem into conformance
- Costs due to damaged equipment
- Searches for defects and implementation of corrective actions
- Costs for corrective maintenance and returned goods
- Reinspection of corrected products and subsystems
- Obsolete products
- Repetition of, or modifications to, the production process because of malfunctions or miscellaneous problems

D. External Failures (Measured by Function)
- Costs for repetitions, adjustments, or other procedures performed by production pursuant to, for example, a product recall
- Time lost because of lack of equipment reliability
- Time lost because of accidents
- Time spent solely on discipline

Chart Number 5
Function: Marketing (Downstream Marketing)
Sales promotion • Sales • Distribution
• After-Sales Service • Technical Support

A. Prevention
- Plan specifications

- Expenditures budgeted for study of the quality aspect of commercial proposals and for the preparation of quality plans or specific inspections
- Aesthetic design of forms
- Participation in review of the plan, detailed analysis of documentation
- Monitoring of exchange rates
- Expenditures for the dissemination of internal and external information on product quality (precautions for installation, placement in service, use, taking into account the critical points of products)
- Market forecasting
- Insurance premiums
- Client research (financial status, monitoring, and so on.)
- Conferences for promoting quality
- Monitoring of product reliability and legislation
- Investment expenditures for the establishment or operation of an office to administer client claims
- Data for calculations regarding market prices
- Expenditures for quality training of switchboard operators, sales personnel, installers and after-sales service personnel
- Preparation of possible audits
- Identification of market segments for the launching of new products
- Costs for participation in COQ review meetings
- Market studies by region
- Preparation of annual quality improvement plans

B. Evaluation

- Expenditures for corrections to evaluations of clientele performed before final marketing
- Promotional sales made at a loss
- Cost of the inspections performed by the marketing division to avoid the generation of errors
- Inspection of price lists and documentation
- Inspection of orders, payments on account, invoices, and shipments

- Inspections related to merchandising
- Inspection of inventories of finished products and replacement parts
- Expenditures designed to avoid assuming responsibility for unnecessary (warranty) work (for testing subsystems returned from clients, inspections, and installations)
- Expenditures for the licensing of installers and distributors
- Expenditures relating to monitoring the perception of quality; surveys, opinion polls, and reviews performed or initiated by marketing, especially for correlation with internal data
- Costs of the calibration of measurement devices for after-sales service and for technical support teams

C. Internal Failures (Measured by Function)

- Incorrect recording of orders
- Expenditures for repair and preparation of products before sale
- Repetition of administrative work
- Cost of the reprocessing of finished product inventory
- Production by units
- Rejections and losses of finished products
- Excessive costs due to special products
- Losses due to the downgrading or cancellation of finished products
- Reprinting of poorly prepared documentation
- Expenditures for reprocessing of orders (reissuances, etc.)
- Unforeseen expenses
- Expenditures budgeted to mitigate the consequences of production or supplier delays (negotiations, substitution of other products, special transportation)
- Financial charges for inventories of finished products
- Costs for reprocessing of erroneous orders, payments on account, and invoices
- Costs for the reprocessing of erroneous master plans
- Costs for reassembly of commercial documentation
- Expenditures budgeted for unprofitable or poorly defined commercial proposals

D. External Failures (Quality Deficiency as Perceived by the Client)

- Costs for replacements, repairs, and service calls, pursuant to warranties
- Costs due to delivery errors
- Measurable losses in market share
- Costs for losses due to errors in routing and shipping
- Nonbillable work
- Costs for product recalls
- Insurance premiums budgeted to cover civil liability for failures of products or systems
- Penalties for delays
- Expenses occasioned by partial or incorrect shipments, including costs for documentation
- Expenditures budgeted to cover delays
- Losses due to discount or price list errors
- Costs for repairs approved (by error) after the period of warranty
- Expenses for reprocessing of erroneous orders, invoices, and payments on account
- Expenses for the preparation and issuing of new documentation to replace erroneous documentation
- Losses due to legal disputes and expenses budgeted for collection

Chart Number 6
Function: Quality

A. Prevention

- Quality management (cost of operating the department)
- Preparation of the quality manual, internal standards, and miscellaneous rules
- Participation in the preparation of inspection plans
- Preparation of quality plans in accordance with the schedules for the company's various activities (medium-term plan and quality improvement plan)

- Organization of or participation in COQ review meetings
- Internal audits and recommendations (effectiveness of the quality system)
- Preparation of audits of suppliers and subcontractors
- Organization of reviews
- Quality studies (reliability, safety, maintainability, component analyses)
- Participation in the quality training of the company's organization
- Campaign to promote quality
- Preparation and establishment of quality control circles, self-inspection, and other systems
- Participation in annual quality improvement plans
- Preparation and implementation of new methodologies (FMCEA, reviews, value analysis)

B. Evaluation

- Total or partial evaluations of:
  - Products and systems in the design and production phases
  - Products and methods (design/production)
  - Technologies and software
- Audits of planning
- Assistance in inspection for the purpose of evaluation, or as an aid to decision making
- Monitoring of internal procedures
- Costs for inspections of processes and products (apart from production)
- Product audits
- Costs for statistical inspection
- Inspection of prototypes
- Costs for metrology and calibration of equipment for unit measurement (operation of the metrology division)
- Test for durability and reliability
- Audits of suppliers and subcontractors

C. Internal Failures (Measured by Function)

- Analysis of erroneous inspection plans
- Monitoring of items pertaining to nonconformance generated by the entire unit (coordination, inspection, interdepartmental consolidation), for example:
  - Monitoring of the processing of incident cards
  - Monitoring of actions taken pursuant to certain inspection reports
  - Monitoring of the quality improvement plan
  - Analysis of rejects
  - Quality measurement of the cost of the quality structure involved in the analysis of problems and their resolution, as well as the monitoring and validation of the final solutions
  - Analysis of waivers
  - Measurement of instances of nonconformance generated by the quality function, examples of which are:
    - Delays in technical trials or evaluation testing
    - Prohibitive approval trials
    - Excess quality mandated by an inspector
    - Certain quality requirements that are unclear
- Analysis of warranty costs

D. External Failures (Measured by Function)

- Same procedures as for internal nonconformance, except as perceived by clients of the function

Chart Number 7
Function: Personnel

A. Prevention

- Time spent listening to personnel firsthand
- Interviews and hiring techniques

- Promotion of action to combat accidents in the workplace
- Career management
- Development of a policy of participatory management (quality control circles, groups, etc.)
- Promotion of and participation in the implementation of a merit recognition system
- Training
- Participation in COQ review meetings
- Job and task descriptions
- Training the personnel department in quality
- Monitoring of labor and safety legislation
- Preparation of annual quality improvement plans

B. Evaluation

- Monitoring of attendance
- Examination of job, mission, and responsibility descriptions
- Personnel career audits
- Inquiries and surveys regarding personnel involvement, motivation, and opinions
- Tracking of accidents during work and travel
- Evaluation of the quality of relationships maintained within the corporate hierarchy
- Quality control of information on personnel benefits

C. Internal Failures (Measured by Function)

- Cost of the rotation rate for personnel
- Costs for additional staff generated by absenteeism
- Costs generated by the failure to listen to personnel
- Costs for strikes experienced by the company
- Inappropriate job appointments
- Costs for unnecessary or unused studies and analyses of personnel benefits
- Audits of personnel benefits
- Costs for redoing studies (failure to define policy, etc.)
- Training audits

- Excess salary costs generated by careless personnel management:
  - Discrepancies between the remuneration for a position and the person occupying the position
  - Functions with little effectiveness (no precise job or mission descriptions)
- Excess salary costs generated by discrepancies between the results of labor negotiations and the objectives of the plan or budget
- Costs generated by administrative or other delays in hiring (direct costs only: reissuing announcements, initiating new consultations)
- Expenditures generated by accidents on the job
- Cost of corrective actions implemented to reduce the above nonconformance

D. External Failures (As Perceived by Personnel)

- The use of outside consultants for serious situations
- The use of service companies to take over the personnel function
- The cost of accidents on the job (additional external insurance contributions)

Chart Number 8
Function: Administration
Management • Accounting • Finance
• Cash Management • Insurance Legal Affairs
• Organization • Security • General Services

A. Prevention

- Monitoring of information issued by government agencies (new products, patents, etc.)
- Establishment and implementation of quality indicators adapted to the particular function (document duplication

services, telephone, reception, and miscellaneous error rates)
- Critical review of administrative procedures and regulations in force
- Maintenance of the library
- Research into simplification of procedures
- Monitoring of advertising announcements
- Preparation of plans for preserving company assets
- Preventive maintenance plans for buildings and equipment
- Preparation of preventive maintenance plans for general services
- Inventory of depreciated equipment
- Expenditures for increasing awareness of problems of safeguarding (technical assets and achievements, resources, products, etc.)
- Monitoring of the frequency of preventive maintenance for equipment
- Reviews of insurance policies (duplication, unnecessary premiums, risks that are not covered)
- Expenditures for training personnel in quality
- Preparation of audits of the administrative function
- Participation in the formulation of COQ and in summary reviews
- Preparation of annual quality improvement plans

B. Evaluation

- Audits regarding accounting rules and regulations in force
- Audits of procedures (routing, signatures)
- Monitoring of compliance with written regulations concerning data issued or received (numbering, coding, classification, references)
- Confirmation that financial summaries are consistent with reality (fixed assets, operating value, third party accounts)
- Measurement of administrative volume and errors
- Checking of errors on working documents
- Evaluation of legal (fiscal) and operational risks (debts, inventory, etc.)

- Monitoring of contacts
- In general, any action designed to validate financial entries and to justify them

C. Internal Failures (Measured by Function)

- Faulty time allocations
- Financial charges resulting from errors in estimating (sales, inventory) or from poor planning of expenditures
- Delays in investments that result in losses on the basis of the planned cost price
- Delays caused by machines that are out of service for corrective maintenance
- Lack of cost-effective amortization (premature replacements, errors in estimating amortization periods)
- Deterioration of assets apart from normal wear and tear
- Implementation of warranties or guaranties
- Fines for failure to implement safety measures that pertain to the environment
- Downtime for machinery
- Operating losses in the event of an insufficiently insured or inappropriately appraised accident
- Additional insurance premiums or penalties as a result of inappropriate declarations of risk
- Equipment depreciation (obsolescence, overly sophisticated technology)
- Cost of retrieval of administrative documents as a result of poor filing or storage
- Cost of retrieval of supporting documentation required as a result of errors by the company
- Cost of reissuing statements on account of noncompliance with administrative standards
- Cost of any type of corrections to records

D. External Failures (Measured by Function)

- Administrative disputes (banking, administrative, property, third party, etc.)

- Penalties for delays
- Legal settlements (errors in payments or appropriations, VAT, etc.)
- Product recalls
- Losses due to administrative errors (orders, remittances, etc.)
- Loss of clientele due to faulty administrative behavior (inappropriate collection letters, lack of discipline and uniformity, etc.)
- Legal disputes caused by patent, copyright, or trademark infringements

Chart Number 9
Function: Information Systems
Data Processing and Office Automation
• Documents and Printed Matter • Documentation
• Internal Dissemination of Information • Archiving

A. Prevention

- Written description of tasks
- Establishment and implementation of quality indicators
- Reduced documentation and testing for transmission of information
- Establishment of written information regulations (type of originator, type of distribution, standardization of memoranda, reports, confidentiality)
- Contacts with schools and universities
- Conferences for promotion of quality in written information and creating awareness of external constraints (legal, governmental, accounting documents, etc.)
- Project risk analysis
- Conferences to increase awareness regarding information security and the implementation of data backup measures
- Screening of data intended for distribution
- Preparation of a:
  - Data processing system inspection plan
  - Data backup plan in the event of a momentary shutdown of the system

- Preventive maintenance
- Participation in the formulation of COQ
- Preparation of possible audits of the information function
- Implementation of indicators (preparation and display)
- Monitoring of local and national press
- Preparation of annual quality improvement plans

B. Evaluation

- Examination of data processing facilities (periodic inspection)
- Examination of information to be disseminated
- Entry (acceptance) inspection of data processing facilities
- Evaluation of office automation facilities
- Inspection of the transmission of interdisciplinary information

C. Internal Failures (Measured by Function)

- Repetition of data processing pursuant to errors (of any type) detected downstream
- Corrective maintenance
- Restoration of files on the basis of previous data as a result of data processing failures
- Development of criteria for rejects
- Cost of searching for listing errors
- Repetition of programming work
- Excessive consumption of books, subscriptions, and fees as a result of poor management of documentation, lack of coordination, and so on
- In general, expenditures generated by failures in data process and office automation equipment

D. External Failures

- Cost of reissuing statements, etc. (errors and format problems)
- Excess costs and losses caused by lack of information regarding outside parties

- Claims by personnel
- Costs of errors or penalties generated by faulty printed matter (orders, invoices, receipts)
- Consequences of loss or theft of information

Chart Number 10
Function: Accounting

A. Prevention

- Forecasting performance
- Planning of accounting software
- Designing and ensuring the reliability of accounting software
- Training and procedures
- Systems analyst's queries
- Monitoring of documentation, legislation
- Monitoring of the profit and loss ledger and the balance sheet
- Detection of the needs of internal clients
- Preparation of budgets
- Training of data entry operators
- Long-term planning
- Participation in annual quality improvement plans
- Description of tasks
- Participation in the formulation of COQ

B. Evaluation

- Monitoring of time frames
- Analysis of correlations
- Copying and checking of accounting software packages
- Monitoring of general expenditures
- Testing of software
- Verification of coding
- Monitoring of total expenditures and delegation of authority

- Depreciation of accounting software
- Verification of accounts
- Monitoring of data entry of orders
- Standards for product costs
- Cost reduction
- Cost of monitoring quality
- Report on data processing of, and follow-up on, the financial report
- Monitoring of ledgers
- Monitoring of billing

C. Internal Failures (Measured by Function)

- Monitoring of defects caused by accounting software
- Revaluation with clients
- Correction of accounting errors
- Accounts not inspected
- Incorrect account entries
- Bad debts/arrears

D. External Failures (Measured by Function)

- Requests for changes submitted by clients
- Changes in documentation, lists
- Errors in billing
- Incorrect payments to vendors
- Payroll errors

12
Other Methods and Tools

It is impossible to cover in a single volume all the methods and tools used for quality. Only the most important ones will be discussed. It is fundamentally important that everyone participate in this movement; thus particular priority should be given to working in groups. An overview of significant points regarding methods will be given. As for specific techniques, there is an extensive bibliography that enables everyone to find books at their own level and for their company's particular field of activity.

For a discussion of the simplest methods, the reader is referred to my book *Les outils des cercles et de l'amélioration de la qualité* (*The tools for quality control circles and for quality improvement*).

Ideas on Measurement: Standardization

Table 12-1 summarizes the advantages of *standardization*, which may be either internal or external, and hence national or international.

The AFNOR publications cover practically all areas of French industrial, governmental, and commercial endeavor. The contacts this major organization has through the International Standards Organization (ISO) enable it to publish international standards. In its monthly *Enjeux*, AFNOR publishes proposed standards and standards that have already been published or modified; it also reports which standards have been canceled. The standards have a reference number (NF-LETTER-XX-XXX) as well as an effective date.

249

Table 12-1. Standardization

All rules and techniques for the purpose of
• creating proper matching and uniformity among products (effectiveness)
• simplifying tasks (quality)
in all commercial and industrial activities

Enables Communication Without Ambiguity

Throughout France; between France and international clients
• Terminology, symbolization, etc.
• Coding = objectives: create a common language, facilitate operations through the use of data processing
• Qualities: accurate, concise, expandable, practical

Enables Product Compatibility and Interchangeability

• Success: phonograph records, audio cassettes, plugs for television peripherals, etc.
• Failures: power supply cards, automobile lights, etc.

Makes it Possible to Reduce the Range of Diversity in Materials, Products, Subsystems (Inventory, Purchasing)

Improves Safety, Health, Well-being

(Household electrical products: fire, noise, electrical shock, etc.)

Protects the Interests of Consumers

• Methods of measurement (facilitates choice)
• Suitability for use
• Voluntary or compulsory certification.

Standards are not discussed here as instruments of coercion, but rather as inexhaustible mines of information on:

- Metallurgy (A)
- Quarries, ceramics, heat-resistant glass, wood, cork (B)
- Electricity (including electronics, data processing, telecommunications) (C)
- Home economics, the hotel trade, furniture, interior decorating (D)
- Mechanics (E)
- Railroads (F)

- Textiles and leather (G)
- Physical distribution of merchandise (H)
- Aeronautics and space (L)
- Fuels, nuclear energy (M)
- Construction and civil engineering (P)
- Paper, cardboard, graphic arts (Q)
- Automobiles, motorcycles, bicycles (R)
- Miscellaneous industries (including medicine and surgery) (S)
- Chemical industries (including water testing) (T)
- Materials and items used in agriculture (U)
- Agricultural products, fishing, and food industries (V)
- Basic standards, general standards (X)
- Government, commerce, documentation, data processing (Z)

There are approximately 12,000 documents in all, ranging from the general to the particular, which have been prepared by commissions made up of the best French specialists in each field.

This documentation represents a national treasure. It is an extraordinary source of ideas, methods, and observation techniques ready to be put to use.

The principal standards pertaining to quality are the following:

NF X 50-109: Quality Management. Glossary.

NF X 50-110: Recommendations for a quality management system for use in private firms.

NF X 50-111: Guide for the selection of provisions for quality assurance in client-supplier relationships.

NF X 50-112: Quality audits within the framework of client-supplier relationships.

NF X 50-102: Suppliers-Users: questionnaire and survey to be used within a supplier's firm.

NF X 50-104: Suppliers-Users: advanced quality assurance program.

NF X 50-120: Quality. Glossary.

NF X 50-151: Guide for the preparation of an functional list of specifications (1984).

NF X 50-152: Value Analysis. Glossary (1985). RC Aéro 00018: Guide for the preparation of a quality manual (general recommendations).

NF E 10-020: Instruments for measurement and inspection. The metrological function of geometric and mechanical magnitudes.

NF E 10-021: Idem, part 2: basic principles.

NF X 06-001: Equivalent French and English terms.

NF X 06-002: Glossary for probability computations.

NF X 06-003: Statistics glossary.

NF X 06-006: Symbols for computations involving probability, statistics, quality and reliability inspections.

NF X 06-021: The use of statistics. Principles for statistical testing in lots.

NF X 06-022: The use of statistics. Selection of sampling plans for inspections which use tallies (proportion of individual items not in conformance and average number of nonconforming characteristics per unit) (1983).

NF X 06-023: Rules and sampling tables for inspection that measure the percentage of defective items.

NF X 06-024: Progressive sampling plans for inspections that use tallies (proportion of individual items not in conformance and average number of nonconforming characteristics per unit).

NF X 06-031: Inspection during production. Test charts.

NF X -6-501: Introduction to reliability.

NF X 06-502: Reliability and after-sales service.

With a minimum of motivation, it is possible to find in this national data bank an impressive amount of knowledge as well as techniques for every field. Moreover, a detailed examination of the standards reveals not only an enormous quantity of measurements of every type, but also the means with which to make the measurements. There are even standards for sensory analysis:

NF V 00-150: Glossary (experimental standards).

NF V 09-012: Testing by comparison in pairs (1983).

NF V 09-013: Triangular testing (1983).

NF V 09-014: Testing by recording observations of quality (experimental standards).

These are applicable to the testing of organoleptic properties (which involve organs to a lesser degree) and focus on the senses – sight, hearing, smell, taste, and touch – for the purposes of discerning differences and preferences.

Marketing

Marketing is not only a function or subject area, but a way of thinking. It is the awareness of a company that its survival depends on its relationship to the economic context as well as on the needs it serves. It must orient its actions solely toward conditions external to the company.

The distinction must therefore be made between marketing and *commercial distribution*, which is the process of moving products into commercial markets. The product is therefore a given.

Marketing Overview

The marketing overview is concerned with *need*; it is formulated by discovering the product, and subsequently the marketing program of action, through analysis of *the overall needs of users.*

The nature of the product is deduced from a list of specifications that is determined as a function of needs (a deep frozen cooked dish + "low-calorie" food + the name of a famous cook).

The product should appeal to every motivation (a line of equipment with a "professional" look for the general public). The product is based on a *formula* because it is the result of a compromise between contradictory factors such as: perfection, simplicity, strength, light weight, quality, and price. *Balance* should be a function of needs, even if the product must therefore include characteristics that are inconsistent with the technical tradition of the company that creates it.

Concepts

The market comes first

- The client is the *user*, not the wholesaler, sales representative, seller, retailer, or central purchasing office.
- The true sale occurs when the actual client (the one closest to the user) purchases the product.
- The market is specific to the company: it should be within the reach of its technical resources and its commercial capabilities.

The market must be researched

- Needs can be detected by listening to and observing users, not intermediaries. Surveys, opinion polls, and other tools establish contact with the user outside the sales network.
- Future needs remain to be discerned and are not revealed by the current market. This requires a search for "the invisible": *it is a dynamic process.*

The market must be conquered

- Sales are made directly to the principal user in accordance with the policy for the brand name. The tool used is *advertising*, which is a direct appeal to the public. Its purpose is to seduce but also to create an identity for the producer and to generate loyalty if the product marketed satisfies the user. It is also a means of exerting pressure on distributors.
- Sales are generated by joint action with the intermediaries of the final user. The most common form of such collaboration is point-of-sale advertising: contests, special offers, promotional material, etc.
- Middlemen are nothing but links in the chain. A product is sold only when it reaches and satisfies the user.

Objective research and measurement tools

Conquest of the market and detection of needs involve risks in researching data, decision-making, and testing decisions.

Marketing is a science engaged in by business professionals who need the greatest possible number of tools for analysis and measurement. The "data bank" is made up of permanent information:

- Regarding current products (source: after-sales)
- Regarding defects and, especially, warranty costs (source: after-sales)
- Regarding the quality of and defects in competing products (source: marketing)
- From surveys of actual clientele, preferably by neutral specialized organizations (source: marketing)
- Regarding reliability, maintainability, durability, availability, safety and suitability for use, respect for the environment, and cost of utilization (source: after-sales and marketing). The tools used are data analysis, modeling, regression, techniques for estimating reliability, techniques for estimating maintainability, and quality measurement techniques.

Profitability

This concept is indispensable because it:

- Places limits on requirements that tend to increase marketing costs through studies and promotion
- Serves as a counterweight to need and keeps it within reasonable proportions in relation to a given optimal level
- Is an instrument of measurement regarding the user, and consequently the client – subjects of vital concern to the company

Marketing Research

The marketing sequence:

1. Begins with users and clients, whose needs it measures and analyzes
2. Subsequently requires a decision by the company
3. Performs tests regarding products, pricing, and advertising, etc.
4. Finds a test market, if necessary

5. Launches the product
6. Returns to point 1 after having measured client and user satisfaction

In this circular sequence, each transition between stages is marked with a two-way arrow. There are numerous methods available for dealing with every step except the second.

The Method

The given factors are:

- The needs of the market
- The company, with its limitations and its commercial and technical capabilities

The goal is commercial. It requires a policy based on the four P's: product, placement (distribution), promotion (advertising), and price. The marketing sequence includes the given factors and the goals.

The needs of the market are discovered by comparing needs, which constitute demand (expressed or not), with the characteristics of all products presently available, which constitute supply.

The limitations of the company are imposed by the company's production equipment, technical experience, commercial position (both in the market and in the field of distribution), personnel, and financial status.

The company's goals within the market segment to be conquered are established by comparing and analyzing the above data. Each step in the process must be handled delicately: assessing unsatisfied needs in the markets requires the use of general psychology and social psychology.

Estimating volume and demand trends entails the use of econometric techniques.

The components of marketing policy are identified by comparing:

- Unsatisfied needs in the market segment selected with the technical limitations of the company in order to determine the product to be designed: feasibility, quality/price ratio, etc. (product policy)

- The needs of the market and product characteristics with the commercial limitations of the company and its distribution network (distribution policy)
- The needs of the market, product characteristics, type of distribution, and program for promotion (and advertising) with the company's cost and profitability limitations (pricing policy)

The last item, pricing policy, represents a synthesis of the entire marketing policy, which integrates contradictory factors: it sets the lowest possible sales price while allowing margins for the distributor, budgets for sales staff, and profits for the company.

Since a circular sequence is involved, determining a marketing policy implies decisions both upstream and downstream in the process. The term *basic constraints* is used to describe the past history of the company, its type of distribution, and other factors that can be changed only in a slow and gradual manner. A decision at a certain level depends on the reconciliation of needs with constraints, which may be either basic or upstream. *Upstream constraints* is the term for decisions that were made prior to, and are more important than, the current decision. They can be altered if there are compelling and significant reasons that relate to the current decision.

This sequence culminates in a "marketing mix," or marketing policy. It optimizes the various marketing steps to be taken while taking into account limits with respect to capabilities: the company's personnel, money, and time.

For example, in the case of women's clothing, the important factors are a collection that is fashionable and well-tailored, a good distribution network, and reasonable prices. Advertising plays only a small role because a brand name cannot make poorly tailored clothing sell. The reverse is true for detergent, for which the most important thing, other than distribution, is advertising.

Value Analysis

Value analysis came into being in 1947 at the General Electric Company, under the influence of H. D. Miles. A. F. Osborn published his book *Constructive Imagination* in 1953, and this magnificent tool assumed a position of importance, first in the United States between 1966 and 1968, and subsequently in France. The first value analysis congress took place in Japan. The movement is led in France by the AFAV (Association Française pour l'Analyse la Valeur), French Value Analysis Association.

Definitions

In citing only the major definitions available, I note that H. D. Miles of the United States and C. Joineau (1976) of France have each provided definitions, but I prefer the one proposed by the AFNOR (NF X 50-152, May 1985). "Value analysis, a method of achieving competitiveness, is designed to obtain the best match between the product and the user's need."

It has three major components: functional analysis, a method, and working in a group.

The definitions for product and value given in Chapter 3 will not be recapitulated here. It should only be noted that *value* is a quantity that increases when the fulfillment of the user's need increases or when the expense incurred by the product decreases.

Function is the effect of a product, or one of its components, expressed solely in terms of reliability.

For the producer, the basic functions are:

- *Principal functions* or service functions: those which meet the need without omitting the need for the proper image
- *Secondary functions*: a choice must be made as to which cannot be sacrificed
- *Functions related to constraints*: those which are mandated by regulations or the environment

Hence, there are two perspectives on value:

- That of the client: value = function/price
- That of the producer: value = function/cost

Value, Quality, and Costs

Figure 12-1 shows where value analysis is located in the trihedron of functions, quality, and costs. Value pertains to the plane for costs and functions. Conformance occupies the function and quality plane. Costs, and COQ in particular, are situated on the costs and quality plane. In his book *Production Management and the Kanban Method* (1983), Shingo insists on the fact that companies who base their management on the equation

$$\text{Cost} + \text{Profit} = \text{Sales Price}$$

rather than on the equation

$$\text{Sales Price} - \text{Costs} = \text{Profits}$$

are in error. In the first instance, if the product does not sell, it will be said that sales methods were bad or that the product was not a good one. Efforts to eliminate waste will be made without conviction because any increase in costs is seen as quickly recovered by the sales price; there is no attempt to see whether a reduction in other costs would permit a reduction in the sales price. In the second instance, the consumers' choice determines the sales price and cost reductions. Efforts are therefore made to improve quality. Even governments, who should take responsibility for financial issues, seem to give in to the ease with which government rates or fees can be increased instead of first reducing their expenditures.

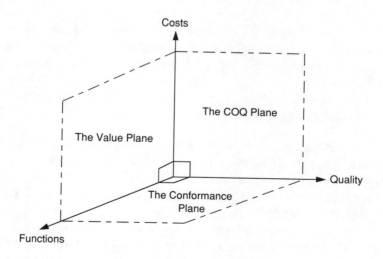

Figure 12-1. The Various Planes

The Method

The method is the result of the work of H. D. Miles and has the following seven phases:

1. Orientation: choice of a subject for study
2. Research: documentation; comparison between needs and limitations.
3. Analysis of functions and costs: functional analysis.
4. Search for ideas and solutions.
5. Study and evaluation of solutions.
6. Draft summary and proposal for the solution chosen.
7. Monitoring of implementation, summary.

The Actors

The *decision-maker* is the person for whom the group is working — he or she initiates the analysis and is the group's driving force.

The *facilitator*, who is specially trained, should ensure the objectivity of the results and maintain a logical approach during analysis of the subject.

The *members* bring to bear their technical abilities by using creative techniques, which requires cohesiveness, a spirit of openness, desire to communicate, and self-confidence. They are most often representatives of clients: after-sales service, quality, and marketing; who may be joined by purchasing, manufacturing, and research.

Functional Analysis

This is a basic concept that has its own tools and whose fundamental purpose is to identify the characteristic functions of the product. Functional analysis should make it possible to "break down" the product into its component parts in order to arrive at a common language within the group.

This phase is completed only when the product can be described through a listing of its functions. This process makes it possible to check conformance with the client's requirements.

A simple method for identifying the functions of a product is to consider its relationship to various factors in the external environment. It may be a physical phenomenon, a relationship with the user, a relationship to regulations, social customs, or company rules. At this stage, no solutions are entertained.

Assigning Values

A judgment as to the value to be assigned to the functions is made only after the functional analysis, on the basis of a subjective quality criterion that is derived by using two parameters.

The first concerns the functions' importance.

The second concerns the degree of satisfaction achieved by the functions as a result of the use of technical (or organizational) resources that are allocated to solve a problem.

The result is a grid for assigning values such as the one given in Table 12-2.

These grids can be extended to include the equation Value = Function/Cost. The results come from a preliminary calculation function by function as a percentage of the total or from a breakdown of costs obtained from functional analysis. The preparation of an evaluation table provides a summary (Table 12- 3).

If the value index is greater than one, the qualitative output is good, but if it is less than one, greater effort is necessary.

The Role of Value Analysis in a Company

Value analysis encompasses all of a company's functions, including administration, in the following descending order of importance: research, development, preparation for production, production, purchasing, and so on.

Related methods are:

- Design to cost: design for a cost objective.
- Design to life cycle cost: design for an overall cost.
- Budget base zero: BBZ
- Value analysis: registered trademark.

Value analysis has been put to use in the United States Department of Defense (DOD), Japan, the French aeronautical

Table 12-2. Grid for Assigning Values

A: Importance by Function

Function	F_1	F_2		F_i		F_n		F_p
No importance :0								
Average importance :1								
Great importance :2								
Indispensable :3								
Coefficient with respect to :2 principal functions	x	2		x		1		2
Importance rating	A_1	A_2		A_i		A_n		A_p

B: Degree of Satisfaction

Dissatisfied :0								
Moderately satisfied :1								
Quite satisfied :2								
Very satisfied :3								
Satisfaction rating	B_1	B_2		B_i		B_n		B_p

C: Quality of the Function

Quality	A_1B_1	A_2B_2		A_iB_i		A_nB_n		A_pB_p
Weighting $F_i = \dfrac{A_iB_i}{\Sigma\, A_iB_i}$	$F_1\%$	$F_2\%$		$F_i\%$		$F_n\%$		$F_p\%$

Table 12-3.

Functions	F_1	F_2	F_3	
Quality of the function	F_1 %	F_2 %	F_3 %	
Distribution of costs	C_1 %	C_2 %	C_3 %	
Value index	V_1 %	V_2 %	V_3 %	$V_i \% = \dfrac{(F_i \%)}{(C_i \%)}$

industry, electronics, industrial equipment, automobiles, domestic electrical appliances, and the tertiary sector, among other places.

Table 12-4 gives a comparison of the characteristics of value analysis in Japan, Europe, and the United States.

Functional List of Specifications

The expression of need is the first rational step in the design of a product, as previously defined in this book. The fundamental elements of a product's costs are implicit in the need expressed by the requesting party. Value analysis has shown in practice that *the functional expression* is a determining factor in competitiveness.

The functional list of specifications (standard NF-X-50-151, 1984), a rigorous methodological tool, allows detection and formulation of need. In the early stages, it can also justify the technical requirements contained in a sales contract for procurements, a research contract, or a request for proposals.

Functional in nature, it has flexible rules. The act of preparing it facilitates the search for an optimal technical and economic definition of the product. It promotes client-supplier dialogue, restores to each party its own responsibilities, and encourages innovation.

In the functional list of specifications the requesting party expresses its need (or the need it has the responsibility for conveying) in terms of functions, services, and constraints. Assessment criteria and levels are set forth for each of these. Flexibility is permitted with respect to each of these levels.

Table 12-4. Value Analysis in Japan, Europe, and the United States

Factor	Japan	Europe	United States
Introduction of VA	• Initiated by private, public, and large-scale industry; hence: • participation by everyone in VA activities	• Use of committees; hence: • VA activity handled by internal teams	• Initiated by government agencies such as DOD; hence: • VA practiced by outside or internal consultants
Implementation	• Promotional apparatus organized in detail • Ability to motivate • Coordination with quality control circles • Demonstration by citing successful cases (very little theory)	• Awareness of VA by the corporate hierarchy • Expansion subject to testing and prudent measures • Standardization (DIN, AFNOR, etc.) • Growth within multinationals • General application in companies on a partial basis	• Systems orientation of VA implementation through the use of manuals • Growth • Use of a group of specialists • Mutual interchange of information on VA
Focus of Interest	Moving gradually in a pragmatic manner from physical aspects to conceptual aspects	Combining the physical and conceptual aspects	The accent is placed on design and development phases
Future Trends	Concentrating on cost reduction; expressing needs better through the use of practical VA techniques	Extending the fields of application; adapting the methodology to each type of organization	Applying VA to saving energy, especially in construction; increasing value rather than reducing costs

Establishing this list of specifications presupposes the use of a survey that makes it possible to discern the needs of users with precision. Its purpose is to respond to the need by obtaining a proposal for the product most appropriate for the service desired, under the conditions provided for, and for the minimum price (or cost). To this end, the specifications express only requirements for results, but, in principle, no stipulations regarding the means employed. Each qualitative assessment criterion is accompanied by a scale that indicates its quantitative level.

The fundamental differences between a simple list of specifications and a functional list of specifications are cited in Table 12-5.

Table 12-5.

List of Specifications	Functional List of Specifications
• Description of needs • Description of solutions to be studied	• Description of actual needs • List of functions associated with these actual needs: - principal functions - secondary functions - functions related to constraints - functions related to image
• Description of requirements (anticipated solution, standardization)	• Expression of criteria for the functions - Quantification - Prioritization - Standardization - Conditions for acceptance - Limits - Flexibility
• Request for estimate (pricing)	• Cost objective

Profile Method

The profile method identifies the actions to be taken with respect to a product. Although there are no precise means of measurement, it is possible to draw comparisons, list the functions, and assign a rating to each function (after a survey, if necessary).

For this purpose, there is an evaluation table (Table 12-6) in which

- Column 1 lists the functions in descending order of importance

- Column 2 reports the ratings assigned by the client to each function – the expression of the need in the market
- Columns 3 and 4 report the ratings assigned by the client to our competitor
- Column 3-2 compares the ratings assigned to our product by the client with those assigned to each function of our product
- Column 4-2 compares the ratings assigned to the competing product with those assigned to each function of our product

The client may be represented by the quality, marketing, and after-sales service functions. The competing product can be considered to be the ideal product.

Table 12-6. Profile Method

	1	2	3	4	5	6	7					8
	F	Ratings			Signs		Product profile					
		M	OP	OC	3-2	4-2	0	1	2	3	4	
1	F1	4										
2	F2	4										
3		3										
4		2										
5		1										
6		1										

M: Market
OP: Our Product
OC: Our Competitor

The above profile is the result, if the signs for 3-2 and for 4-2 are:

−	−	:research and development
−	+	:advertising
+	+	:value analysis
+	−	:marketing

Audits

An audit is a methodical examination of the status of a product, process, or organization with respect to quality, which is performed in cooperation with the interested parties for the purpose of verifying the conformance of this status with preestablished provisions, and the appropriateness of the latter with respect to the objective that is to be achieved. (Standard NF-X-50-109, -112)

The "interested parties" are the persons who have direct responsibility for the situation being examined.

"Cooperation" is the act of participating in a common task – it is collaboration. The audit should have the approval, assistance, support, participation, and contribution of the manager of the situation being examined. The "status of the product" relates to three areas that are usually addressed separately. There are, therefore, three types of audit:

- *The product audit*: as noted previously, the term *product* is used in its broadest sense to mean a material, piece of equipment, or service – including those things necessary for its use, packaging, and maintenance. It should be noted that a product audit is not limited to conformance but is also concerned with the appropriateness of the product for the intended use.
- *The process audit*: the operational methods and sequences used to produce and inspect the product.
- *The organizational audit* or *systems audit*: a method concerned with the principles and regulations that govern the resources involved in the production and inspection of a product or service (for example, a particular process, procedure, or any other part of the quality assurance system of the supplier).

The "preestablished provisions" encompassed by the audit may pertain to:

- The definition or description of a product or service contained in its reference documents: regulations, standards, orders, specifications, lists of specifications, and other contractual documents

- Specific documents for processes and methods
- Internal written procedures or regulations for the organization that were set forth by the supplier and that determine the functions, responsibilities, and actions involved in achieving the desired result (for example: quality manual, quality plan)

These provisions constitute the frame of reference on which the audit should be based.

In organizing a quality audit, the emphasis should be placed not only on a comparison between actions actually performed and the preestablished provisions, but also on the appropriateness of these provisions for the intended purpose. The findings made by the audit should enable managers to undertake corrective or preventive action, if necessary. To determine or propose such actions is not part of the audit function. Use of the audit's conclusion for such purposes is the function of the interested parties' managers.

General Classification of Quality Audits

Since the situation under examination involves conformance and discrepancies with respect to the preestablished provisions, both should be brought to the attention of the manager of the situation. Such communications are considered *reports*, but never *tests* or *inspections*. There must be a climate of trust between the auditor and the persons or organization audited.

In an *internal audit*, the report is prepared by an internal organizational unit of the company that is functionally independent of the department or division concerned.

In an *external audit*, the report is prepared by an organization that is external to the company being audited.

Since any organization departs over time from preestablished provisions, the sole purpose of this methodical examination is *progress*, which is achieved by confirming what is correct and detecting discrepancies. The auditor is therefore a *third party*. Legally, an auditor is a person who is not and has not been a party to a contract or a judgment. A third party is *neutral*.

An internal audit enables the head of a company or the manager of the area concerned to check:

- The implementation of preestablished provisions
- Their appropriateness for the intended objective, in order to maintain or improve the quality assurance system

An external audit offers the client a basis for confidence in a supplier. There are three levels for external audits:

- *The evaluation audit*, whose purpose is to confirm for the client the ability of the supplier to produce the desired quality
- *The follow-up audit*, intended to confirm the implementation of the contractual provisions agreed to pursuant to the evaluation audit
- *The qualification* or *certification audit*, which recognizes a supplier's fitness to be included in a particular category that has been defined in advance

Table 12-7 summarizes the two phases of supplier quality assurance (SQA): the combination of the evaluation audit and the follow-up audit (measurement of performances) illustrates how the various components of external audits work in harmony and establish trust between supplier and client.

Responsibilities

In an internal audit, which is most often part of systematic monitoring of company activities:

- The audit is initiated by company management or the department or division concerned.
- A specialized division (or unit), persons external to the area concerned, and persons from outside the company are responsible for conducting the audit.
- The conclusions are submitted to the manager of the area audited, who determines appropriate action as necessary.
- The audit is used internally.

In an external audit, which involves evaluation, follow-up, or certification:

- The audit is initiated by the client with the agreement of the supplier, or by the supplier if there is a request for certification.

Table 12-7. Supplier Quality Assurance

SUPPLIER QUALITY ASSURANCE (SQA)
1st Phase: for one line of products by one particular supplier

EVALUATION: AUDIT
Information regarding QUALITY capabilities
2nd Phase: with respect to a given product of the supplier

INITIATION OF AN INSPECTION SYSTEM FOR
the production process ⟶ approval of the supplier's Quality plan

ACCEPTANCE OF THE INITIAL SAMPLE
standardized product ⟶ authorization for delivery of standardized products

DELEGATION OF INSPECTION
after the trial period ⟶ notification that the product is in SQA

PERFORMANCE EVALUATION: AUDIT
level of supplier quality ⟶ analysis and correction of defects
during acceptance, during assembly, at client sites

- The audit is conducted by the client or by a third party authorized by the client.
- The conclusions are submitted to the authority who requested the audit and to the party audited.
- The audit is used within the framework of the client-supplier relationship and is covered by professional confidentiality unless there is formal agreement by the audited party to release the results. The supplier is free of obligation with respect to the conclusions, unless there is a contractual stipulation to the contrary.

The Auditor's Profile

Apart from the requirement for confidentiality, which applies to the nature and content of the audit as well as to the very fact of its existence, the personal qualities required of an auditor are objectivity, ability to communicate (listening 70 percent of the time), adaptability to circumstances and to the parties audited, capacity for analysis, and good judgment. Auditors are not inquisitors; on the contrary, they should build relationships of trust and cooperation with the parties audited.

Their training should cover quality, audit techniques, and interviewing and communication techniques. They should be familiar with codes, regulations, standards, and, without being experts, should have adequate technical knowledge of the area audited. Auditors can be effective only by maintaining their qualifications through regular practice of their profession after specialized training. They should take courses to update their knowledge and skill.

For an important audit, it is desirable to create a team of auditors (rarely more than three) with a manager, who is the sole supervisor of the audit.

The Phases of an Audit

The *preparatory phase* includes the following activities:

- Collection of documents regarding the situation audited: the reference material.
- Preparation of a carefully worded questionnaire.
- Organization of a preliminary meeting, in which the parties audited will be reminded that the governing philosophy is not to inspect but to cooperate. This meeting should be attended by the manager of the situation audited and the parties audited. Communication should be the rule.
- An official notice citing the date, place, time, and purpose of the audit.
- Preparation of the conduct of the audit itself.

The *conduct of the audit* refers to the following procedure:

- Methodical examination of the situation.
- Documentation of discrepancies, identification of areas of conformance.
- Evaluation of the impact of discrepancies on objectives.
- Investigation of the origin of the discrepancies.
- Meeting at the conclusion of the audit in which the auditor gives a summary of what he has observed and takes note of any comments, suggestions, or rebuttals made by the parties audited. At this stage, the auditor may even

check on points that are not clear or merit reconsidera-
tion, so as to satisfy himself on the accuracy of his observations. He should always give the party audited the
benefit of the doubt.
- Preparation of the audit report.

Since the audit may pertain to small companies or to small areas
of large companies, the term *function* should be used in preference to the term *division*. In a small company, the same staff person may in fact perform several functions without being head of
a division. Often the manager, deputy, or several employees share
a multitude of functions, but that does not mean that the functions do not exist.

The same is true for documents. For example, one cannot say
that quality goods are not produced just because there is no "quality manual."

In an external audit, the results are used in the following
manner:

- The auditing organization transmits its report, its conclusions, and possibly its suggestions. It does not propose
  solutions.
- The organization audited examines the options for corrective action, notifies the auditing organization of the
  measures adopted and time frames for completion.
- The auditing organization evaluates the appropriateness of
  the corrective action measures and may propose a new audit.

In an internal audit, the results are used thus:

- The auditing organization transmits its report, its conclusions, and possibly its suggestions.
- The organization audited determines and carries out corrective actions.

Conclusion

The audit is a valuable tool that enables the supplier to know
its organization better and, in the instance of an internal audit,
holds the organization to preestablished provisions and objectives.

If this tool is used without notice and with coercion, it takes the form of an inspection or investigation. Under such conditions, not only is its effectiveness nil, but a climate of mistrust is established, one that would be difficult to overcome. The notion of a neutral third party is fundamental. A well-trained auditor knows how to create an atmosphere of cooperation, and knows not to provide solutions but possibly to make suggestions (even though he is not obligated to do so). If a uniform audit policy is conducted in this manner throughout a company, it can be a true source of progress. Most difficult for managers and employees is avoiding the temptation to play the role of a police officer. After all, the audited parties are already troubled by the fear that there may be discrepancies. The "assignment of blame" should be left to the audited party.

Since these concepts have been poorly understood for historic reasons, the current situation is such that in Figure 8-1 the term *measurement* could be replaced by the term *audit*. A psychological short-circuit causes these terms to be translated as *inspection*. It is the duty of managers to explain to everyone that only the party who ordered the audit may perform the corrective actions. Everyone should be guaranteed that there will be no judgment nor any communication of the results of the audit to others.

Quality Diagnosis

P. Vandeville, in his book *Quality Management and Control* (*Gestion et contrôle de la qualité,* 1985) gives the following definition of quality diagnosis:

> Quality diagnosis is a methodical examination of the status of a company, an area of a company, or one of a company's activities with respect to quality, which is performed in cooperation with managers for the benefit of the company, for the purpose of evaluating its status, identifying its strong and weak points, and proposing measures for improvement, while taking into account the economic, technical, and human context of the firm.

The *status* of a company includes its activities, resources, operations, earnings, position in the market, and prospects for future development.

The purpose of the *evaluation* is quality management. It entails:

- An approximate assessment of the losses due to lack of quality, expressed as representative ratios
- A complete and systematic examination of the organization and the operations of the company, or of the area of the company being diagnosed, in order to identify the risks or the causes of lack of quality, while taking into account the economic, technical, and human context of the firm.

It can be noted that the principles for audits are retained, but the field of application is much broader, since diagnosis involves the company's performance and a determination of its potential capabilities and weaknesses with respect to quality.

Development of the Quality Function

There is now an accelerating trend toward the elimination of those quality departments and divisions that hold veto rights and supervise a team of technicians assigned to inspection. Under those circumstances there used to be the attitude of "That is not my job; it's quality's job," in the context of the mistrust described in Chapter 4.

A Unit of Experts

The staffing for the unit of experts would obviously be a function of the size of the company and of the field in which it operates. It is the company's internal consulting firm – it brings together traditional quality professionals for the discussion of common problems and obstacles (in the firm) with respect to quality improvement. The unit provides assistance and support, and possibly suggests solutions. Since the quality function is decentralized throughout the company's activities, and each actor is responsible for quality, the role of this consulting firm is essentially advisory.

Responsibility for Quality Policy

Quality policy

Since they have the role of experts, the members of this group participate in the preparation of key documents and procedures for the sole purpose of ensuring the consistency of quality in the company. *Consistency* – in other words, the absence of contradictions – and cohesiveness establish an indispensable interfunctional and interdisciplinary bond that creates a strong rapport with respect to the ideas agreed upon by the various functions and disciplines.

These experts ensure compliance with specifications and legislation and, to this end, are the internal representatives of the client. Their task is therefore to assist top management in defining the quality policy of the company, to set and communicate quality objectives, and to prepare the quality program.

Conformance

This internal consulting firm no longer performs measurement and inspection, but it should furnish inspection systems and programs. Above all, it should provide solutions for problems of nonconformance.

The latter function relates essentially to the analysis of products returned by clients and the checking of internal defects that have been detected. It is not within the experts' authority to correct them. In fact, these *experts* are the clients' spokespersons, who participate in the transmission of data upstream in the process. They have no veto rights but rather the duty to keep the company informed as to the level of quality perceived by clients, particularly on the technological plane. They therefore should review procedures, check their appropriateness, and otherwise monitor company activities.

Their essential role is to provide information on the quality of finished products and key operations. It is their duty not to intervene but rather to suggest, demonstrate, explain, and interpret. They ensure that there is feedback regarding the information they have distributed.

One of their functions is to interface with clients (or their representatives) in dealing with quality problems, and to attend to needs and the resolution of problems. They participate in project reviews as the representatives of clients because they possess the vocabulary to do so.

Their specific tasks are to:

- Prepare or use procedures, methods, and structures in support of quality policy and monitor their implementation with audits, which they may request from an outside organization (even for internal audits) with the approval of top management
- Evaluate components and finished products before production is initiated by ensuring that proof has been furnished as to their appropriateness for the function, conformance with legal requirements, ability to meet safety goals, quality, and reliability
- Prepare and follow up on national and international certifications
- Assist in the establishment of indicators, so that everyone can be aware of their performance as it relates to goals
- Be enthusiastic motivators of quality by promoting progress rather than failure
- Monitor the calibration of measuring equipment and the updating of standards
- Represent the company with national and international organizations in the field of quality
- Participate in the evaluation of suppliers
- Prepare quality agreements with clients and suppliers
- Provide advice during technical disputes among producers, suppliers, and development
- Maintain contacts with after-sales service for feedback of information and the establishment of a service policy
- Provide advice in the event of disputes between production and marketing

Quality training

The principal role of the unit of experts is to participate in quality training for *all* personnel. Its members participate as experts in quality training sessions. The teams provides technical support in quality to both technical and administrative personnel, to both top management and employees. In the future, everyone in the company, from the president to the machine operator, must be trained in simple methods of statistical analysis. Such is the price of quality improvement. It is frequently forgotten that the Japanese spent 10 years training themselves in quality techniques, 10 more years before arriving at quality control circles, and another 10 years after that training each other in quality improvement before touching off the TQC boom of the early 1980s. Their commitment to quality improvement cannot be attributed to cultural differences. Before the Second World War, and even afterward, they produced goods of inferior quality. They subsequently trained their personnel themselves, with the assistance of JUSE.

This training includes, in addition to statistical techniques, product safety, reliability, standardization, and all quality procedures and techniques.

The Key Points of a Quality Function

List of parameters

The quality function supervises the preparation of the evaluation plan. A list of parameters should be drawn up as a summary of the total knowledge of the company with regard to a product or each of its constituent parts, and should take into account legislation, the client's needs, and production requirements. This list should change and evolve in accordance with technical and technological developments, and should be continually updated. Its content should be approved by all the parties participating in development.

Evaluation plan

The evaluation plan contains:

- A description of tests and a list of the documents and equipment necessary to evaluate the product or its components (proofs to be furnished)
- The assignment of responsibilities

- Planning for tests

The plan is prepared jointly with the research and development divisions, which should give their approval. The quality function is the motivator and driving force of the process.

Specifications

Specifications are documents that present the research on, and the final determination of, the value of parameters and their distributions. If these values are set by legislation or standards, the quality function provides technical support in their interpretation. Should that not be the case, the specifications are the result of values negotiated by research and the client for products, or by research and the suppliers for components.

Tests

Tests are opportunities for the company to demonstrate that the product or component conforms to the requested specifications.

Development has responsibility for having the stipulated tests performed by a testing center of its choice, in compliance with mandated time frames. Testing centers should demonstrate that their methods for measurement are valid and that their equipment is properly calibrated.

The methodology for tests mandated by legislation or standards is pre-determined. For functional tests, the metrology, methods of measurement, and tests are determined and approved jointly by the parties participating in development.

Project reviews

Tables 12-8 and 12-9 define a project team and the six points covered by a project review.

A project review enables participants to confirm that all the objectives defined have been attained and are consistent with the project. If the objectives have not been attained, a decision must be made as to the next step.

Table 12-10 summarizes the principal phases involved in the establishment of allocations, preliminary evaluations, assessment of

Table 12-8. Project Review: A Multidisciplinary Team

A Product
A Pilot Study
Appropriateness of the Project for the Objectives Established
Trials
Marketing
After-sales
Production Methods
Purchasing
Product quality

Table 12-9. Design: The Six Points of a Project Review

Suitability for Use	
Maintainability	
Feasibility	Constitute a Whole
Time Frames	
Costs	
Reliability	

prototypes, and feed-back. The quality function is omnipresent as a consultant, but is confined to that role.

Evaluation

Evaluation of the product or component is considered complete if all the points indicated on the evaluation have been accomplished and if the specifications have been met. The quality function performs the evaluation.

Quality plan

After feasibility has been determined, and as the research and development phases are implemented, the quality plan:

- Determines as soon as possible what actions must be taken, what knowledge must be acquired, and what plans must be

**Table 12-10. Between Feasibility and Production:
Methodology and Tools for a Product**

1. Allocations

Require

• Lists of Specifications
• Quantified Goals:
    • Quality during utilization
    • Reliability
    • Maintainability
    • Targets

2. Preliminary Evaluations

Require

• A Project Review
• Value Analysis (VA)
• AMDEC: Product
• Failures Chart
• Supplier Quality Assurance (SQA)

Should Provide

• Preliminary Estimate of Operational Capabilities
• Preliminary Life cycle Estimate

3. Assessments of Prototypes

Require

• Experimentation Plans

Should Provide

• Reliability, Maintainability
• Approval for Use
• Performance Specifications

4. Inspections

Should Provide

• Confirmation of All Allocations through Testing of Pilot Production

5. Feedback

• On products
• On methods

Possible Return to 1, 2, etc.

made with respect to documents, tests, materials, and equipment;

- Informs all interested persons of the parameters involved in achieving a product that is in conformance, is reliable, and is easy to produce;
- Defines responsibility and the contacts to be established, not only with technicians in the company, but also with government agencies and marketing organizations;
- Serves as the collective memory in the event that the list is amplified or modified or that a prior plan is used for a similar product;
- Serves as a line of communication to a manager when a particular development is being monitored.

A sample flowchart for the design of a product is provided in Table 12-11.

Self-inspection

Principles

It has previously been explained that each actor in the company has, for each of his or her activities, at least one input product and at least one output product. Between input and output, the actor adds value by performing tasks, which are categorized as useful value-added, prevention, evaluation, internal failures, and external failures (Chapters 6 and 11).

Self-inspection consists of making all actors in the company responsible for the quality of their individual output products, regardless of their rank in the corporate hierarchy. In other words, they are responsible for the precautions to be taken before undertaking their own work (prevention), and they subsequently check conformance with the needs of their clients (evaluation). The actors must assume individual responsibility for their own internal failures and must cancel out external failures. Thus, they now perform "off the clock" – a function formerly assigned to inspectors.

Zero defects in the value added to the finished product ensures that the product exiting the process will be free of defects,

Table 12-11. Quality Plan

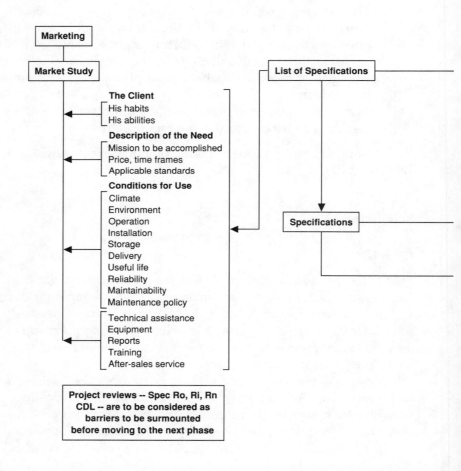

Design of a Product

| The Product |

| Feasibility Study |

Overall Characteristics

Fundamental
Secondary
Functional
Economic

Cost • Production
 • Utilization
 • Service
Time frames
Performance data
Reliability
Maintainability

| Optimization Value Analysis |

Synopsis

Division into functional components
Interfaces, internal, external
Preparation of the quality plan

| Technical Specifications |

Feasibility tests, new techniques
 and technologies
Research and definition of production processes
New components
Use of existing subsystems
Special arrangements, limitations for use

Reproducibility
Reliability
Research trials

Certification of components
Preliminary assessment
 of reliability
Maintenance policy
Safety during use

| R_o |

Analysis of several solutions
Optimization, selection

| Scale Model | → | R_i |

| Prototype | → | R_n |

| Pilot Production | → | CDL |

Comparison of results
 with objectives
Summary
Program of action
Critical points
Analysis of failures
Possible repetition of research

Verification and reproducibility
 of performances
Preliminary reliability
Maintainability
Production documentation

| Release of the documentation for phase J |

providing everyone proceeds in this manner. In the future, actors
will not have to worry about the quality of the entering product,
which comes from upstream. However, it is their job to refuse at
the outset to work on a defective product. This is a true client-supplier relationship in which the negotiated requirements are the rule
for everyone.

If it is assumed, on a purely theoretical plane, that the
amount of time spent at the work station i is t^i at the rate T^i, and
that the material has a price P^i, a preliminary approximation of the
total cost (C) of the product would be:

$$C = \sum_1^n (t^i \times T^i + P^i)$$

The value-added at the work station i is $t^i \times T^i$. On the operational level, this value-added translates into an increase in the
complexity of the transformed product. As indicated in Chapter 6,
the cost of redoing a product increases at an excessive rate when it
is accomplished far downstream in the process. If, as a preliminary
approximation, K^i is designated as the complexity at the work station i, the complexity of the product would be:

$$K = \pi_1^n K^i \quad \text{with } K^i \geq 1$$

A comparison of these two purely theoretical relationships
strongly demonstrates the importance of detecting an error as far
upstream as possible in the production process.

To avoid a duplicative inspection as the product enters work
station i, work station (i-1) must detect the error as the product
exits by using measurements, tests, or checklists. Furthermore, it is
of fundamental importance, particularly in complex processes, to
report as quickly as possible any error or anomaly generated by the
process itself.

In the event of a serious problem, particularly in production,
it becomes imperative to stop the process immediately in order to
detect the cause or causes and provide a solution. The Japanese say
that "It is often only by stopping production that one can be cer-

tain of having nonstop production." In other words, a systematic search for causes, remedies, and prevention is the best way to create a process without faults, and it constitutes active prevention.

The organizational framework must promote this approach, because the critical factor is not the error or defect in itself but rather the guarantee that it is not further duplicated.

Implementation

Implementation of self-inspection should be gradual and can only be firmly established through the "snowball effect" of a total quality program.

It involves the willingness to create an organizational framework that identifies the work stations in which self-inspection is possible and sets forth procedures and methods. It also requires training personnel, who would like nothing better, and having confidence in them. Responsibility creates the need for good faith and trust. Responsibility is not entrusted to the function but to the person responsible for the function.

For the purposes of implementation, the "professionalism" of each employee must include not only competence and ability in performing the work, but also knowledge of the means of measurement to be used. Relevant training includes an understanding of the process in which the employee is participating because he or she may be called upon to take over at various work stations. Knowledge of diagnostic techniques for standard malfunctions will enable the employee to take appropriate action without delay with the most common problems. If the malfunction is serious, he or she would have to participate with others (colleagues, associated functions) in identifying the causes and putting the process back in service. Training in the resolution of problems and knowledge of elementary statistical techniques are indispensable. As indicated in Chapter 4, mechanization, automation, robotization, and computerization are the realities of the future. That means companies need to step up training and self-inspection programs.

Self-inspection is valid for all the company's activities – technical, productive, operational, or administrative – and involves the principles of individual responsibility and the client-supplier relationship. As a result, a new state of mind pervades total quality.

Surveys

Surveys involve searching for and collecting information in a methodical fashion – they are part of the data collection process. The following is a general overview.

Who Should Be Surveyed?

Because of the time and cost involved, surveys rarely cover all personnel, even in large companies. Otherwise, they are called censuses.

Censuses are performed in companies when the number of economic factors is relatively low. Thus, a survey of export firms regarding a given department is often in the form of a census (several dozen or several hundred are involved).

Most surveys are therefore carried out on a fraction or a sample of the persons in the *base population*. The latter term is used to describe any group (of persons or things) that is the subject of statistical studies (of characteristics).

The sample should be *representative* of the base population. In other words, the data collected from the sample should be valid for the base population.

Strictly speaking, representativeness requires determining the degree of confidence that can be accorded to the general conclusions extrapolated from the survey results, or the amount of errors made in converting the data obtained from the sample into data on the base population.

Only one method meets this requirement: the *probability method*, which uses the mathematical laws for computing probabilities. The same term is used for this method and for methods derived from it.

Methods for selecting samples are divided into two categories:

- Probability methods
- Methods that do not entail the use of probability

Probability methods and random methods

The laws for computing probabilities can only be applied if all the economic factors and all the units of the base population have the same chance of being included in the sample. It can then be said that the units were selected at random, that is, each had equal probability of being selected.

A random variable is a variable whose probability is known. To indicate the mathematical and scientific meaning of the term *random*, and to avoid any confusion with other everyday definitions, it is advisable to term these methods *scientifically random*.

Basic probability method: random sampling. To meet the requirement regarding an equal chance for inclusion in the sample, the thinking and attitudes of the person making the selection must not play a role. Tables of random numbers that have been produced by physical or mathematical processes are used. The following are commonly used tables of random numbers:

- Tipett, which includes 41,600 random figures
- Fischer and Yates, which includes 15,000 figures
- Kendall and Babington, which includes 100,000 figures
- Rand Corporation, Smith, which includes 1,000,000 figures

These tables can be used by starting at any point and moving in any direction. Nevertheless, once a direction has been selected, it must be maintained. Random sampling requires numbering the base population. The criterion for ordering should have no relation to the purpose of the survey: for example, alphabetical order or by age. Random sampling also involves extensive travel by field workers when the base population is distributed over a large geographic area. The degree of confidence that can be accorded to the general conclusions drawn is related to

- The size of the sample: it varies as a function of the square root of the sample size (a minimum size of 30 units is required)
- The homogeneity of the base population with respect to the characteristic studied (the greater the homogeneity, the smaller the sample may be).

For all the above reasons, secondary methods have been established.

Secondary probability methods. These methods provide a solution for the problems posed by several sampling methods:

- Numbering requirements: *systematic sampling or sampling by arithmetic progression.* All that is needed is an ordered list (as indicated above) of the base population. The sample is created by selecting the units in accordance with an arithmetic progression. An example would be every 20th name. A selection of $\frac{1}{20}$ of the base population is made, beginning with a unit chosen at random (random table of numbers).
- Travel constraints: *cluster or areolar sampling.* Groups of contiguous units, or clusters (instead of individual units), are selected at random (instead of selecting "individual" units). When the criterion for grouping is geographic, the sampling is areolar. It is advisable to take a larger sample in order to have the same degree of accuracy as in random sampling (the units in the same cluster may in fact present similarities).
- Numbering and travel constraints: *sampling with multiple steps.* A series of random selections are made. For example, in a company with 20 divisions, 1 out of every 4 divisions is selected at random. In the five chosen, one person in 10 is selected; that is:

$$\frac{2,000}{5 \times 10} = 40 \text{ persons}$$

In general, this method has the advantage of concentrating the units in the sample in particular geographic areas.

- Lack of homogeneity in the base population: *sampling in multiple phases.* All members of the sample are queried about the characteristics that involve the greatest differences within the population. A sub-sample is then selected at random from the original sample. The members of the sub-sample are queried about the characteristics that present the smallest differences within the population, and so forth.
- *Stratified sampling.* Statisticians talk about stratification and marketing specialists refer to segmentation. The idea is essentially the same. The population to be studied is divided into strata or layers, that is, segments that are homoge-

neous with respect to the characteristic studied. The study is performed layer by layer. Random selection takes place within each layer, and overall conclusions are extrapolated from the results for each layer.

Empirical methods for selection of samples

Sampling by means of logical selection or by use of quotas. The structure of the sample is determined in advance. This structure must reproduce the percentages (quotas) of characteristics in the base population. It is a scale model of the base population.

This method assumes that when a sample represents the structure of the base population, it also represents the characteristics covered by the survey. Although this has never been proven, sampling by quotas is frequently used, especially in market studies, because it is relatively simple and inexpensive. One significant limitation of this method (apart from the absence of a theoretical foundation) is that it requires the availability of recent statistics on the structure of the base population. The field worker may limit herself to surveying her friends, colleagues, or persons in her immediate environment. She therefore introduces biases, or distortions.

The itinerary method. The purpose of this method is to avoid such biases. The field worker is required to follow a set itinerary (for example, to survey the persons who occupy even-numbered offices). A variant method might require the field worker to interview one person in the company cafeteria every five minutes.

The itinerary method approximates the probability method. It is often used to reinforce the quota method. It is sometimes called the Politz method or the semirandom method.

As a general rule, it is best in performing sampling to use probability methods as guides, and applying them as extensively and as often as possible, within reasonable cost limitations.

The Questionnaire

Choosing a representative sample is not enough to ensure accurate collection of data. The *questionnaire* must have the proper qualities as well. The questionnaire truly is a superior survey instrument.

Quality of preparation

Questions should attract attention and create interest. The questionnaire should in fact stimulate the person surveyed, rather than annoy him. The following guidelines should apply:

- A survey on the results of a quality control circle should show interest in the improvements.
- The question "Do you have a favorite brand of automobile?" is better than "Indicate your favorite brand of automobile" (since the latter does not allow for the possibility that the person surveyed does *not* have a favorite brand).
- The questionnaire should be kept to a reasonable length (as its length is a factor in loss of interest).

The questions should be easy to understand. That means that they should be adapted to the persons surveyed. The temptation is to formulate questions in terms that convey the preoccupations of top management, but that is not always desirable.

The questions should be clear, precise, and unambiguous. For example: the question "Is your car leased or purchased?" would always elicit a response that leaves no room for doubt as to its meaning.

The questions should not elicit inaccurate or imprecise answers. This can occur unwittingly, when a question requires the use of memory. An example would be, "How many times did you go to the photocopying machine during the last month?" The person surveyed can respond only in approximate terms. Innaccuracies also result with questions that involve desires or interests, "Will you go on vacation next winter?" The replies are always overestimations. Such questions can be improved by asking that the "degree of intention" be specified: vague plans? firm decision?.

Also to be avoided are personal questions ("Do you think that . . . ?"), questions that seem prying ("Amount of local taxes?"), or questions that involve image or ego (for example, men always understate the number of women's magazines they read).

Inaccuracies also occur when the "halo effect" comes into play – in other words, when one question affects the response to another questions because of irritation or concern for logical consistency. Questions likely to produce this effect should be dispersed throughout the questionnaire.

Questions should not be worded so as to suggest a response; i.e., they should not be leading questions. Thus, the question "Do you actually smoke one pack of cigarettes a day?" should be reworded as, "How many cigarettes do you smoke a day?"

In any questions that involve personal opinion, an effort should be made to discourage the natural tendency to answer "yes," when the choice is between "yes" and "no". To solve this problem, intermediate responses should be provided ("yes," "probably," "no").

Different types of questions

"Closed" Questions. Possible answers are limited by a mandated list:

- Simple closed questions involve answering "yes", "no", "no opinion" (some authors limit the definition of closed questions to this type).
- More complex closed questions may propose a choice from a certain number of responses. These are multiple-choice questions. For example, a secretary might be asked, "What are your principal activities?" A lot of possible answers would then be supplied: filing, typing, telephone, taking notes, arranging meetings. The proposed replies may be ordered. These are questions with a hierarchical ordering of responses.

Closed questions are easily processed and counted. However, they may be a source of bias, since the survey is limited by the range of replies available.

"Open-ended" Questions. No constraints are imposed on the answers to these questions. The person surveyed therefore has complete freedom to formulate a response. An example is, "What are your principal criticisms of working in a group?"

Open-ended questions may bring a rich harvest of information, but they require a great deal of time to process.

Mixed, semi-closed, semi-open, and cafeteria questions. These are multiple-choice questions that contain the answer or answers, to which open-ended questions may be added. For example, the question "Why do you like to work in a group? might be accompanied by the following possible answers:

- Because your work benefits from the ideas of others?
- To contribute your ideas?
- To resolve problems?
- To be with others, exchange ideas?
- For other reasons?

These are also termed *preformed* questions since the answers in fact create the form of the question.

Structure and presentation of a questionnaire

The effectiveness of the survey depends largely on the questionnaire. Careful attention should thus be given to the questionnaire's format and method of presentation.

For example, it should

- Begin with simple questions that put respondents at ease;
- Group the questions by subject;
- Alternate easy and difficult questions;
- End with identification questions.

An introduction should be provided to explain the purpose of the survey and its relevance for the person surveyed. There may also be material to provide a transition to the questions themselves.

Finally, the questionnaire should be neat, easy to read, and error-free (whether it is intended to be filled out by the person surveyed or the surveyor).

Methods for completing the questionnaires

A questionnaire can be initiated in various ways, each of which presents advantages and disadvantages. It can be distributed by mail; this method is low in cost but tends to elicit a low response rate. It can also be distributed by field workers. There are several ways by which this is done. "Face-to-face" interviews are costly because the field worker must be present. Telephone interviews are less costly but introduce a considerable bias since only persons with telephones are questioned, the questionnaire must be brief, and the respondent's identity is uncertain. Interviews in the work environment are inexpensive but must be brief and have a built-in bias because of the selection of the sample.

In general, the face-to-face interview is the most effective method because the person surveyed is more trusting and a well-qualified field worker will avoid the interference of biases.

In this instance, good qualifications entail objectivity and interpersonal skills.

Different Categories of Surveys

Spot surveys

Individual surveys. These are performed on behalf of a single person or corporate entity. They are the most common type, and are often termed "opinion surveys" or "opinion polls."

Collective surveys. These surveys are performed on behalf of several companies. They can be subscription (or multiclient) surveys, in which case all responses are communicated to each client – that is, each firm – by a market study organization. Alternatively, they can be "omnibus" surveys, in which the sample is defined in advance. Let's say the sample consists of two thousand officials. Each firm that is a client of a market study organization may ask the sample the question of its choice. The advantage is the relatively low cost for each client firm. On the other hand, the questionnaire submitted to the sample runs the risk of being a "catch-all."

Surveys in the business environment. These surveys require in establishing the sample that there be weighting according to the size of the firms involved.

Periodic, panel, or control group surveys

Etymologically, the term *panel* comes from old Provençal, where it meant "length of fabric" and, subsequently, "a board bearing a list of names."

The same questionnaire is submitted periodically (for example, monthly) to the same sample, or *panel* (hence the term *permanent* surveys – in reality, the sample itself is the permanent feature). The panel makes it possible to monitor the evolution of economic factors. The principal problem with this type of survey is that the panelists consciously or unconsciously modify their purchasing habits as a result of awareness that they are being studied. They may either lose interest or become predictable. To resolve this problem, the panelists are periodically re-constituted by third parties – for example, every year.

Often managed by specialized organizations, panels may be composed of consumers or distributors. The latter group is not interested in consumer purchases, but rather in sales to retailers.

Surveys (or studies) of motivations and attitudes

Both spot and periodic surveys use direct questions that require direct answers. These are useful in performing quantitative studies (how much? who? where?) and qualitative studies (how?).

They are less useful when the why? of economic factors is under study. Indeed, a considerable discrepancy has been found between statements elicited from such surveys and actual behavior.

Motivational studies are more effective in determining, for example, the impact of messages. Such studies, which discern the driving forces behind economic factors, can obviously be performed only by specialists trained in psychological analysis.

These studies use various techniques.

Unstructured individual interviews or nondirective individual interviews. The person surveyed speaks freely about a given subject. The interviewer limits himself to follow-up by restating the remarks of the person surveyed or by "echoing" his statements. This technique requires a great deal of time.

Unstructured group interviews or non-directive group interviews. This technique allows a great deal of variety in the interchanges within the group. However, there is the risk that a "leader" will emerge in the group.

Projective interviews or tests. These studies aim to project the personality of the person surveyed on a given subject. The association test is designed to elicit emotional responses through free association. A person may be asked for the associations he or she makes when presented with

- A new product
- A photograph – of stereotypical personalities (businessman, athlete, office employee) for example, or of sailing ships (the person's attitudes about the subject can thus be deduced)
- A word: the word tobacco, for example, is increasingly associated with the words *cancer, cough, pollution*
- A sentence: a sentence is begun, and the person surveyed is asked to complete it – e.g., "Quality of life is . . . ."

The *thematic aperception test* (TAT) might feature a description of persons in various situations. The person surveyed is asked to provide details about these situations.

Attitude scales. Attitude scales permit measurement of psychological attitudes regarding, for example, a brand name: "Where would you place the Peugeot 205 on the following scales?"

Table 12-12. Scales of Attitude

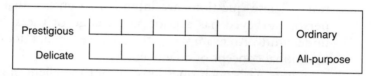

The Summary Report

The summary report details

- The purpose and period of the survey.
- The sources of the data (internal-external).
- The data collection techniques.
- The data processing method. Computers may be useful aids for large samples, but it would be a serious error to believe that a market study *must* be performed with a computer.
- A synopsis of the results.
- Analysis of the results (summary comments). A manager would take this into account in making a decision.

- The degree of reliability accorded to the results. This last point will be discussed in some detail because it is often neglected in the reports of market studies.

The reliability of the results of a market study

Reliability in this instance depends on the techniques applied in detecting and reducing the possible types of errors.

Actions with respect to the questionnaire. The following are several possibilities:

- Launching a pilot survey or preliminary survey to test and, if necessary, improve, the questionnaire. This survey involves only a small number of the persons questioned.
- Inserting a test question in the questionnaire that covers a known characteristic of the base population.
- Improving the structure of the questionnaire. This might be done as follows:

  1. Begin with information questions or "screening" questions. These questions are intended to ensure that the person surveyed has a good knowledge of the subject under study. An example is, "In your view, what does the traditional concept of quality entail?"
  2. Continue with open questions, to put the client at ease. Thus, a question might read, "Are quality improvement groups effective?"
  3. Pose the questions that are the subject of the survey. An example is, "If it were possible, would you like to participate in a quality improvement group?" followed by the answers "Yes," "No," "Don't know."
  4. Conclude with questions that make it possible to assess strength and intensity of convictions. For example, "Are you prepared to participate in a quality improvement group so that you will one day be able to make a presentation to top management?" (followed by "Yes," "No," "Don't know").

Action with respect to the sampling method. In every possible instance, "scientifically random" sampling methods should be given preference. They in fact make it possible to determine and estimate the errors made during extrapolation of the results from the sample into general findings about the base population. Thus, reference can be made to a confidence level of, for example, 68 percent (there are 68 chances in 100 that the actual result is within the range calculated). The closer the confidence level moves toward certainty (99 percent), the greater the range. In practical terms, a confidence level of 95 percent is acceptable. For statisticians, 95 percent involves two standard deviations.

Consider the following example. A company has 2,000 names in its personnel files; these constitute the base population N. The sample n comprises 90 persons. The proportion of persons (P) prepared to participate in a quality improvement group (according to a survey of the sample) equals 30 percent.

The following formula makes it possible to establish a confidence level of 95 percent, a level at which the proportion P corresponds to a proportion of the base population N. A confidence coefficient of 95 percent entails a distribution of $\pm$ 2 standard deviations. The standard deviation is expressed here by:

$$e = s^{1/2} \; ; \quad s = \frac{p\,(1-p)}{n}$$

If $P = p \pm 2e$, then $0.20 \leqslant P \leqslant 0.40$. Between 20 and 40 percent of the persons therefore intend to participate. The range is between 400 and 800 persons with that intention, with a five percent chance of error. With a confidence level of 68 percent, the range would be smaller ($\pm$ 1 standard deviation $P = p \pm e$), so that $0.25 \leqslant P \leqslant 0.35$. Between 500 and 700 persons would therefore be interested. With a confidence level of 99 percent, the range would be larger ($\pm$ 3 standard deviations: $P = p \pm 3e$), so that $0.16 \leqslant P \leqslant 0.44$. Thus between 280 and 880 persons are interested.

Action with respect to field workers. A preliminary meeting or briefing, and monitoring of the progress of the survey are necessary.

Conclusion

Knowledge of the users' needs, ability to satisfy those needs, and acceptance and pursuit of total quality are necessary to the implementation of a total quality program. The application of relatively simple techniques (apart from motivational studies) makes this knowledge available to managers, whose primary trait should be a strong sense of responsibility.

Small and medium-sized companies are often disappointed by the limited services and high cost of a study. Market studies are nonetheless necessary. Determining the approval and acceptance, the involvement of personnel, and the progress of the company is equally important, and can be accomplished through the use of simple methods such as surveys.

Summary

This chapter has given a broad overview of a vast subject. Table 12-13 contains a brief summary of this chapter, which, though itself far from being exhaustive, lists the methods and tools necessary for building and improving Quality.

Table 12-13. Methods and Tools

Necessary for Creating Quality

Written specifications for finished products
Written procedures
Exhaustive follow-up on client complaints (investigation of causes)
Written specifications for procurements
Monthly report on quality
Written specification for process phases
Systematic reviews of products that are not in conformance,
  beginning with their detection
Written quality policy
Statistical controls
Internal audit plan

Indispensable for Improving Quality:

Quality training program
Quality improvement program (QIP)
Quality control circles (QCC), progress groups, etc.
Quality objectives by: unit, department, division
Quality improvement groups (QIG)
Posting of quality indicators
Quality instrument panels
"Public" presentations of results achieved
Evaluation of suppliers (external audits)
Monitoring of costs, quality
Quality manual
Project reviews

Part 4

Implementation Strategies

*The art of being daring at times, and prudent at others,
is the art of being successful.*

– Napoleon I

Part 4

Implementation Strategies

13

The Beginnings

Reason's protests are in vain – imagination has endowed
Man with a second nature.

– B.Pascal, *Pensées*

Sample Strategies

The current situation of French firms requires a strategy for *Victory*, that is, a set of coordinated actions, as well as a *Method*, a sequence in which these actions should be carried out.

In 1983, Juran proposed a 13-point strategy, which is set forth in Table 13-1. Crosby later provided a 14-step strategy (Table 13-2). The second strategy is not strictly chronological, and is divided into three parts. Steps 1 through 6 are actions to be taken by the corporate hierarchy, 7 through 9 concern the involvement of all personnel, and 10 through 13 require the interaction between the two previous courses of action. Step 14 means "go to step 1."

Juran's strategy is chronological, although step 13 is carried out concurrently with the other 12 steps.

These methods have been adapted for internal use within private firms (for reasons to be indicated later). The methods used by the IBM Company in France and the Philips France organization are provided as examples in Tables 13-3 and 13-4.

IBM based its 9-step program on Crosby's strategy, but eliminated, for example, the step for "zero defects day." It was found that this step was not always appropriate to French culture, even if it met with great success in the United States.

The Philips France organization justifiably attached great importance to the first step. This step involves convening a meeting of top managers and assisting them to reach a consensus as to the meaning of quality in their company. This entails a discussion of the

Table 13-1. Juran's Method for Implementing an Annual Improvement Plan

1. Formulate a Quality Policy

The quality bonus — There should be progress every year — Everyone must participate — The quality policy should influence performance criteria

2. Assess the Most Important Aspects of Quality

Quality is an essential component of competitiveness — Cost of quality deficiencies — Effectiveness in launching new products — Profitability of prior improvements

3. Determine the Organization for and Establish a Project System

Encouraging and attracting volunteers — Making a selection — Choosing projects — Setting up project teams

4. Assign Responsibility for the Successful Completion of Projects

Establish the team's organization — Assign responsibility for selecting and assigning facilitators, team members, and team leaders

5. Identify Training Needs

The methodology for improvement in quality — Problem solving — Forming a tightly knit team — Group work — Participation

6. Identify Those Who Should Be Trained

Facilitators — Leaders — Members

7. Schedule Training

Content — Organization into individual courses — Providing resource materials — Recruitment of instructors and lecturers — Budget — Planning

8. Determine the Support Required by the Teams

Time to work on projects — Field diagnostics — Diagnosis of the organizational framework — Facilities for trials — Testing facilities — Assistance in overcoming obstacles

9. Provide Coordination

Meeting of facilitators — Meeting of leaders — Project progress reports — Constructive reviews for better team organization

10. Initiate New Measures

Promoting improvement — Product performance — Performance by top managers

11. Review Performance Criteria

The quality of operations — Improvements in the field of quality

12. Design a Publicity Plan

Awards ceremony for those who have successfully completed a project, and for those who have served as facilitators — Use of media: company newspaper, local press, TV, radio — Presentation of the final report to top management

13. Actions Recommended for Top Management

Examine and approve the policy — Authorize the organizational infrastructure: quality committees, project system, roles, responsibilities, training schedule, assistance to teams, coordination plan, publicity plan — Examine and approve modifications in improvement charts, in the performance criteria system — Examine progress reports — Participate in projects — Participate in training

Table 13-2. Crosby's 14-Step Quality Improvement Program

1. Commitment by Top Management
2. Quality Improvement Team
3. Measurement of Quality
4. The Cost of Quality
5. Awareness of Quality
6. Corrective Action
7. Zero-defect Planning
8. Training
9. "Zero-defect" Day
10. Drawing up Objectives
11. Elimination of the Causes of Errors
12. Giving Recognition
13. Quality Committee
14. Ongoing and Permanent Implementation of the Program of Action

Table 13-3. IBM's 9-Step Quality Program

1. **Commitment by Top Management**
   - Policy statement
   - Education of managers
   - A change in attitude
2. **Quality Committees**
3. **Cost of Quality**
   (COQ)
4. **Creating Awareness among Employees**
   - Initiated during the preceding phases
   - Training in methodology
5. **Measurement of Quality**
   - Client-supplier relationship
   - System of measurement
6. **Zero Defects**
   - Setting of objectives
   - Start-up date
7. **Improvement in Quality**
   - Analysis of errors
   - Analysis of causes
   - Elimination of causes (Quality improvement groups or quality control circles)
8. **Recognition of Merit**
9. **Rewards**

Table 13-4. 12 Steps for Implementing an Overall
Quality Policy (Philips France)

1. **Determine the Direction for the Quality Policy**

2. **Personal Commitment by the Unit Manager**

3. **Prepare a Plan for the Unit** (or Update It)

4. **Express a Collective Commitment**

5. **Initiate Training** (or Develop It)

6. **"X-ray" the Current Situation** (All Functions, Activities)

7. **Set Objectives**

8. **Decide on Projects and Priorities**

9. **Take Action for Improvement**

10. **Conduct Project Reviews, Evaluate the Results**

11. **Provide Recognition for Merit**

12. **Begin Again at Step 2**

company's values, meaning, content, and means of expression, as well as the direction it wishes to adopt with respect to quality.

These are a few fairly clear examples, whose common points should be noted: the involvement and commitment of top management, setting a good example, the determination to use measurement to achieve progress, and the participation of everyone, both individually and collectively.

Total Quality: Management of the Two Flows

During one of my trips to Japan to investigate the subject of TQC (July 1-15, 1985), I brought back a rich store of examples, anecdotes, and documents.

The owner of one small company, M. Kawaibe (Hamada Juko Co.: approximately 300 employees), who works as a subcontractor of the Nippon Steel Company, showed me a Plexiglas model that had been designed to explain what was involved in managing the two flows that make up total quality.

As indicated in Figure 13-1, the model is a pyramid with a triangular base, on which there is a descending flow that the Americans have christened *top-down* and an ascending flow termed *bottom-up*.

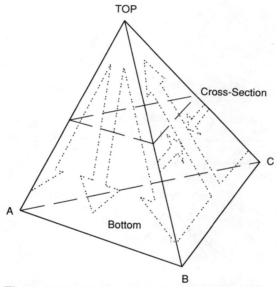

Figure 13-1. The Pyramid: Top-down and Bottom-up Flow

Figure 13-2 shows the arrows representing the top-down flow regarding quality policy, the various levels, and the setting of priorities, from the voluntary perspective. Figure 13-3 shows the bottom-up aspect, in which quality control circle activities (as well as those of other groups) send out information in an ascending direction. Doing so requires effective support, represented by the two horizontal arrows, including that provided by the organization and by corporate management in particular.

The organizational aspect in Figure 13-4 shows that, at the top, middle, and bottom levels, individual efforts are organized in working groups for quality improvement, thereby providing a solid organizational structure that is capable of managing this beehive of activity.

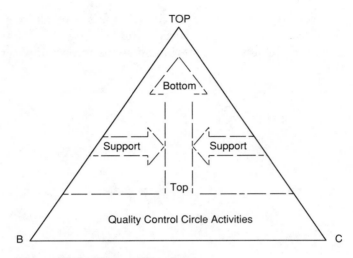

Figure 13-3. Bottom-Top Aspect

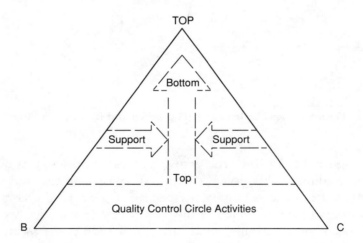

Figure 13-3. Bottom-Top Aspect

Figure 13-1 shows that this pyramid, which has a triangular base, may at any level be cross-sectioned on a plane parallel to its base, producing the cross-section diagram shown in Figure 13-5. In the middle is the inevitable Deming wheel, which was described

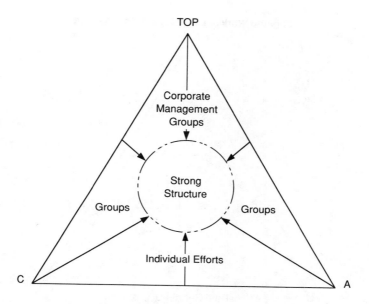

Figure 13-4. Organizational Aspect

in Chapter 10. *Personal and reciprocal commitment* is apparent at every level. *Creative manifestations of interchange and joint action* should also occur at every level, and *expanded use of quality tools* should be everyone's concern. It is therefore a multilayered structure in which there is ease of communication within each layer of every company, and each person can help turn the wheel to achieve improvement in quality.

The multilayered structure is of good quality because all the layers are nurtured by a descending stream of communication. Moreover, because of the ascending flow and its results, there is ease of communication between every layer, which is kept current by the action of the wheel.

This image clearly illustrates what constitutes total quality in a company, and specifically how total quality operates. It can be noted that some flows are functional (Figure 11-1, see pg. 205), but, in every layer, the process that drives the wheel upward toward quality improvement is interfunctional. It is this direction that leads to success.

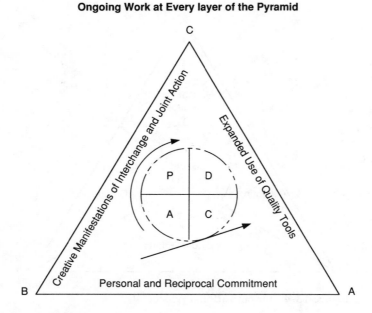

Ongoing Work at Every layer of the Pyramid

Figure 13-5. Cross-Section Diagram

A Quick Look at Those Who Have Been Successful

Honor to Whom Honor Is Due: Japan

The Japanese today are pressing forward with total quality. After more than 30 years of unremitting effort, they have decided to hit the accelerator. Westerners have termed this the TQC boom. The following is a summary status report regarding total quality control.

Current status of total quality control

First of all, the "crisis" has not spared a single company, not even Japanese firms, and for many total quality has been a means of survival.

New life had to be breathed into quality and quality control circles. In many cases, total quality has been the organizational banner under which participatory activities (*e.g.*, QCCs) and quality requirements can be categorized, organized, and coordinated.

It was also necessary to involve subcontractors as closely as possible in quality improvement, to turn away from the notion of intracompany quality and to move toward the concept of intercompany quality, and to achieve customer satisfaction by all possible means, including helping subcontractors to do better work.

Finally, it has become necessary to extend quality improvement methods to every sector of activity and to new products. When I asked Professor Ishikawa what the difference was between total quality in 1960 and total quality in 1985, he replied that the new developments involved essentially three new directions.

First, the range of areas in which it is applied has expanded. Formerly, only a portion of industrial sectors were involved in total quality. Today, all sectors are involved, including service industries, construction, civil engineering, and even small and medium-sized companies. There have also been some experiments in government – for example, some local organizations in the provinces (town government, police) – but these have not yet reached a national level. Some experiments have also been made in telecommunications, in the private sector.

Second, the emphasis today in companies involved in total quality is on research and development of new products. There is now an interest in developing total quality in the upstream portion of the production process, not solely in manufacturing.

Finally, total quality is now being developed in foreign subsidiaries of multinational firms. In addition, there are "joint venture" agreements with American firms for the introduction of total quality: for example, the agreement between Toyota and GM. Total quality has also been presented on American television.

Five additional points were also cited by the people I spoke with in Japan.

An expanded definition of quality. Quality is not only the satisfaction of clients, but has become a *philosophy of action for each person in a company* (the switchboard operator can make sales!). Not only the client, but also the environment, the persons affected by the product (repair and maintenance personnel), and subcontractors are concerned with quality. Likewise, every person in the company is a client or supplier of the work station upstream or downstream.

In addition, the notion of quality deficiency should now be replaced by the concept of *positive quality*, which is measured by client satisfaction and an increase in sales or market share.

A different philosophy regarding control. A number of mistranslations have plagued the concept of total quality control. In France, for example, TQC has been translated as the *inspection of total quality*. Professor Ishikawa, in speaking of the problems encountered with Americans, shared this short analysis with me.

> The term TQC, or total quality control is an imperfect translation of the Japanese concept. In Japan, we increasingly tend to use the word kanri, which is not correctly translated by the English word control. Kanri encompasses several concepts that cannot be translated by a single word: administration, management, and improvement. When Americans translate it as improvement, the meaning is not adequately conveyed. An improvement is a one-time action, while we mean by this term permanent and ongoing improvement. In the United States, we often use the word kaizen instead of improvement. This has even been accepted by American labor unions. In French, the word contrôle (inspection) is very different from our concept: it would be better to use the word amélioration (improvement).

This relatively clear explanation is a very good exposition of the total quality philosophy.

In addition to involving all divisions and functions of a company, this approach gives priority to prevention and training all personnel in quality methods and tools.

Assumption of responsibility by management at the highest level. "If top management believes in total quality, the battle is won." "Total quality is first and foremost a matter of management." "The first thing to do is to mobilize, and therefore to train, top management." These statements are a clear indication of the tremendous movement toward assumption of responsibility for quality by the highest level of management – and of the desire of promoters of this movement to mobilize top managers in the total quality effort. Furthermore, these are not quality or total quality managers who are talking about quality: they are managers with the rank of "general manager," or "managing director." Professors S. Mizuno and K. Ishikawa acknowledge the wisdom of Feigenbaum and Crosby in insisting that the entire organizational structure be mobilized for total quality. However, they think that this approach is incomplete, a point that will be covered elsewhere. Mizuno even told me that total quality is the use of quality control circles at every level of a company, beginning with top management. However, all of them insist on the necessity of mobilizing and creating awareness in all professional employees.

Mobilization of all personnel. This point is what most differentiates certain Western approaches (Feigenbaum and Crosby, in particular) from the Japanese approach. Total quality means the active participation of all actors (organized in circles, quality improvement groups, and *ad hoc* groups). Total quality is implemented first and foremost by establishing quality control circles, and it is impossible to conceive of total quality without them, according to Mizuno. However, it should be emphasized that total quality also involves middle management, professionals at every level, and all administrative and operational services.

A constant balance between the top-down and bottom-up flows. This approach, or at least its expression as a precise system, is relatively new. All the companies contacted placed considerable emphasis on what some of them termed management by objective. First of all, there should be a company plan, which serves as a general framework for everyone's actions. Next, there should be improvement objectives (for example, to reduce quality deficiencies by one-half every year, attain zero accidents and zero returns). These objectives are subsequently apportioned throughout the entire corporate chain of command and serve as targets for quality control circles. In the field and inside companies themselves, 80 percent of the subjects are chosen by quality control circles, and 20 percent are initiated by quality improvement plans. For some, the principal skill required for total quality is coherent management of the ascending flow and descending objectives: there is no black box. It appears that this development is the result of economic constraints and the need to revitalize or to give better focus to quality control circles. In any case, dissemination of information and extensive training of all managers, professionals, and operators in total quality are definitely the most effective means for achieving this balance.

In Search of Excellence

In 1985, T. Peters and R. Waterman (of the MacKinsey consulting firm) authored a book that has gained an international reputation: *In Search of Excellence*. The thesis of these authors is that high-performing companies have always observed eight basic principles, which are striking in their simplicity. Though conceptually uncomplicated, these principles are difficult to put into practice. They can be outlined as follows:

"Action" rather than "study":

- Selection and training of personnel.
- Setting objectives.
- Rapid setting up and disbanding of small *ad hoc* teams for problem solving (a maximum of 10 members).
- Insistence on experimentation.
- Seeking a rapid solution rather than an ideal solution.
- Excellence in small things.

Streamlined organizational structures and simple procedures:

- A lean central organizational structure.
- A commonly agreed upon organization into divisions, with a limited number of personnel categories (five or six).
- In a number of instances, few general procedures.
- A few simple objectives (five maximum) at every level: if possible, they should be expressed in concrete terms, rather than as purely financial goals.
- A limited amount of paperwork.
- An insistence on informal relationships: "an open-door policy," arranging office and dining facilities so as to promote contacts.

The client is king:

- Innovations are achieved jointly with the client.
- Priority is given to follow-up and quality instead of short-term profitability.
- Management control observes the priorities of service and quality.

Personnel is the essential factor:

- Competitiveness is based on motivating personnel.
- Objectives are demanding but attainable.
- The incentive system uses rewards rather than sanctions.
- The information system compares performance data with objectives.
- The management system is based on trust.
- The working environment promotes informal relationships.

Promote company morale and innovation by providing maximum autonomy:

- Heavy decentralization.
- Neglecting "economies of scale" to a certain extent, and seeking the ideal.
- The development of "champions."
- An insistence on team work and team spirit.

Insist on basic values:

- Maintain a credo of simple ideas that distinguishes the company from its competitors.
- These basic beliefs are almost always expressed in terms such as: "we are the best," "clients are the priority," "details matter," "the right to make mistakes," "the best relationships are informal relationships," "growth," and "profit."
- These beliefs are repeated often and applied unfailingly.
- Strategies and objectives may change, but beliefs are immutable once the company begins to perform well.

- These beliefs are nurtured by myths and anecdotes that answer the question, "What are we proud of?"
- A strong personality, backed by a close-knit top management team, has often played a major role in creating this corporate culture.

Stick to your area of expertise. Confine your efforts to what you know how to do:

- The failure of conglomerates and overly sophisticated diversification is manifestly obvious.
- Companies that perform best diversify their activities only to a very limited degree.
- A recent trend: acquiring minority interests in joint ventures in areas where there is rapid technological development.

Make flexibility and discipline coexist:

- Decisions are made in the field: decentralization and flexibility.
- Each year, management control sets several priorities. Achievement of goals is a sacred obligation.
- Corporate culture is pervasive, but is initiated from the top down.

In high-performing American companies, these eight principles are fanatically applied. On the whole, these principles fall well within the framework of the concepts set forth in the preceding chapters; they therefore constitute an introduction to strategy.

The Dialectic between Improvement and Innovation

Definitions

To avoid confusion among terms such as *creativity*, *invention*, and *innovation*, it should be considered that *an invention is the result of a person's creativity*. An invention may or may not be patented, but may also be a law of physics, a trademark, or a new concept. In every field of endeavor, there are countless inventions that have gone years, sometimes centuries, before being noticed by a company. Of course, the number of inventions that have no future is much greater. For purposes of the following discussion an *innovation* is *an invention that has been accepted by a company.*

In French, the word *invent* has an extensive semantic field that encompasses connotations and denotations ranging from *imagination* to *progress.*

Invention, imagination, and innovation concern both the concrete (objects, forms, tools, techniques), and the abstract (mental activities such as theories, ideas, fantasies, ethics). In every instance, they involve knowledge and actions by human beings.

Innovation may be welcomed or feared. Society's inertia in the face of innovation may be due to a fear of the unknown. Innovation produces change and, inevitably, resistance to change: the desire for novelty conflicts with the desire to preserve past achievements.

In contrast, *improvement* invokes only positive associations. It is the action of making something better, making a change for the better. In this respect, improvement is akin to progress.

Since *invention* is the result of an idea, it is personal, and therefore generally suspect. It is thus difficult to transform an invention into an innovation. Inventors tend to be solitary people. In Western society, innovation has aspects of nobility because it suggests a form of elitism based on education. We are fond of it and prefer it to improvements. The Oriental point of view is that improvements are the first priority and that, since they are the result of working in groups, they can only serve to promote innovation. Furthermore, their positive nature can only help the group to progress.

Improvements as Opposed to Innovations

Table 13-5 (borrowed from my friend Professor Maasaki Imai) compares and contrasts the characteristics of improvements and innovations.

Table 13-5. Improvements versus Innovations

Characteristics	Improvements	Innovations
Impact:	Visible over the long term, permanent, not dramatic	Immediately visible but may be dramatic
Rhythm:	Small steps	Very noticeable steps
Frequency:	Continuous	Discontinuous, unique
Changes:	Gradual	Abrupt
Participation:	Everyone	Selective
Approach:	Joint, group efforts, systematic approach	Individual ideas and efforts
Operating Method:	Improvements to the existing system	Replacement with something new
Knowledge Required:	Simple and conventional	New theories and technologies
Level of Effort:	Minor initial investment, but sustained effort	Very significant initial investment
Assessment Criteria:	The functioning of the process the efforts made	Earnings and profits

Innovations Without Improvements

Innovations lead to great leaps forward. They are introduced on a periodic basis and therefore entail discontinuity. The theoretical progress curve is a staircase with steps that are unequal in both height and length. According to Imai, if there is no policy for improvements, the actual curve, drawn with an unbroken line on the left side of Figure 13-6, shows that the progress achieved deteriorates because the total effort has not been sustained. There is consequently a loss of the progress made possible by innovations and, in addition, discontinuities are accentuated because there is no prior understanding of how to preserve past achievements (see Chapter 10), in other words, how to keep the Deming wheel turning.

Innovations With Improvements

It has been previously indicated that, since improvements are permanent, they create linear progress in both quality and productivity. If the same upward trend is sustained after the onset of innovations, the actual curve, on the right side of Figure 13-6, indicates that discontinuities have been reduced. The difference between these two actual curves demonstrates the effect of the implementation of total quality in a company. It can be seen that, all things being otherwise equal, the company that applies this management policy can be certain of achieving very significant gains in productivity over time, regardless of the nature of the innovations involved, which, in this instance, are considered to be identical. This is the true meaning of kaizen.

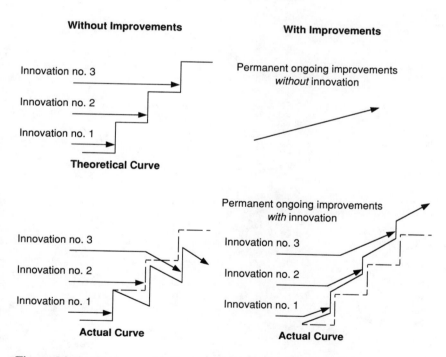

Figure 13-6. Progress with Improvements and/or Innovations

14

A French Strategy for Transformation

Success breeds success, just as money makes money.

– Chamfort

Corporate Culture

The concept of corporate culture appeared in the United States during the late 1970s. It was a response to a fundamental concern for companies: how to mobilize all personnel, and, in particular, create an organizational framework based on a unique "identity" to which each person could relate. In other words, *construct an ideal image with which everyone could easily identify*, then mobilize the entire company on the basis of new values.

Every company, and every geographic unit within the same company, has a culture of its own – a set of values, beliefs, myths, symbols, rituals, and images that are described by employees in their own unique terminology. The company's past, its habitual behavior, its personnel policy, and often its product, each exert an influence. Likewise, logos, the aesthetic characteristics of the product, its "nobility," the decor, advertising messages, the speeches of top managers, internal memoranda, booklets, introductory brochures, and annual reports are all symbols that create an "atmosphere," a "tone."

W.G. Ouchi and A.L. Wikins (1983) go so far as to believe that "a company not only has a culture, it is a culture." The term *culture* is considered to mean the governing processes, the processes for relationships and interactions, and the other transactions between the members of a particular organization. J.L. Vachette (1984) defined corporate culture as being a coherent set of attitudes common to all salaried employees within a working environment. It is therefore the sum of all the "constants" that are accepted by everyone. These constants may be values, beliefs, or rituals.

Table 14-1. Three Approaches to Understanding Corporate Identity

Culture	One Component	Symbols	Processes
Origin	Corporate culture: Creating a corporate identity	Institutional image: Building a coherent image	Ethnographic approach: The organization as culture — a set of transactional processes
What to Measure?	Values, myths symbols, rites images	Communication media: logo, design, image	Individual behavior Transactions between individuals and groups
How to Measure?	Internal surveys, observations Study of internal and external communication documents	Documentary analysis Semiotic analysis Group meetings by top management	Long term observation by becoming part of the organization
Limitations of each Approach	Unwieldy implementation Difficult to find a unique rationale Difficult to validate	Analysis must be limited to outward symbols Distortions in relation to current reality	Research project

Vachette proposes using the term *values* to describe these shared elements. He cites three approaches to corporate culture, which are summarized in Table 14-1. Corporate culture should be studied in a manner that includes the following steps:

- Base the study on the experience of salaried employees.
- Eliminate the influence of external constraints.
- Take into account the history of the company.
- Convey the reality rather than intentions or desires.
- Obtain top management's encouragement.
- Obtain acceptance by salaried employees.

The purpose of the study may be to select avenues of communication that are consistent with overall policy and respond to expectations of personnel.

However, one must bear in mind that, in an organizational entity and living system as complex as a company, a process for improvements must be put in place, just as it must be when innovations are initiated (Chapter 13). A new logo, a new decor in offices or factories, a new aesthetic design for products, an internal publicity campaign – each of these occurrences demonstrates to salaried employees that top management intends to change and develop the company. However, if there is no alteration in behavior – particularly in management style – apart from developing new symbols, the operational reality of work life quickly becomes inconsistent with the image desired by top management. Even more seriously, salaried employees feel deceived and consider this "cultural" initiative an extravagance on the part of a top management, which simply wishes to improve its image with the general public (see Chapter 9 on mistrust).

A change in culture can only come by *example* and through *action* by top management and managerial staff.

The Company Plan

Figure 9-1 (see pg. 127) demonstrates that a company evolves over time. In growing, an organization forgets its initial mission and that of its founder. The history of IBM is typical in this regard. In 1914, Thomas J. Watson (1874-1956) took over the management of Computing Tabulating Recording (CTR), which was the result of the merger of three companies: the Tabulating Machine Company (adding machines), International Time Recording Company (time clocks), and the Computing Scale Company of America (weight scales). Watson, foreseeing the future importance of mechanical accounting systems in business management, changed the name of CTR to International Business Machines (IBM) in 1917. Three phrases appear in the founding charter: *excellence, client service, respect for the individual.* When IBM initiated a total quality program at the beginning of the 1980s, it was easy to provide a name for the project: it was christened Excellence. Such is not always the case.

In many cases, the founding owner is succeeded by managing directors; the original first employees, who had ties to the owner, are succeeded by technocratic professionals; colleagues are replaced by anonymous salaried employees. The company is no longer aware of its "calling." Its novelty disappears. Given the constraints of today's marketplace, however, companywide awareness of the company's reason for being is a *requirement for survival.*

It is not important what particular approach is adopted, but considerable prudence should be exercised with "plan salesmen." The company plan is *a summary of its financial and corporate priorities.* It is drawn up in the form of a *charter* which may be a few words to one page in length. "That which is well conceived is clearly stated, and the words to express it come easily," wrote Nicholas E. Boileau in *L'Art poétique.*

The purpose of the plan is to obtain approval and compliance by the greatest possible number of people. More important, its preparation can serve as an occasion for creating a dynamic process, a mobilizing force for the entire company.

The plan should have an ethical aspect so that everyone can identify with common values. It becomes a frame of reference for questions such as "What purpose do we serve?" and "For whom are we here?" It should be *clearly written* so that it can respond to the company's growing, compelling, and unpredictable complexity. Its *consistency* should prevail over the inevitable contradictions that exist in any company. Consistency requires a clear, positive orientation toward the *future.* The basic aspiration of employees, and managers in particular, is *involvement* in the company and a sense of belonging. Finally, the plan should enable personnel to mobilize themselves, to varying degrees, in order to become personally involved in a *challenge.*

These characteristics dictate that the plan be specific to a particular company, and that it therefore be:

- *Simple*: serve to reduce the complexity and seeming inconsistency of the company
- *Ambitious*: constitute a challenge
- *Collective and meaningful*: give persons at all levels a concrete idea of their contributions to the preparation and implementation of the plan and what they will receive from it in return

- *Permanent*: serve as a frame of reference
- *Personally relevant*: be accessible to each member of the company

It would be even better if the plan were drawn up by the company itself with the participation of the greatest possible number of employees. In France, many consulting firms "sell plans," but the four experts are still J.C. Fauvet and J.Y. Koch of the Bossard Institut, B. Malcor of the Eurequip group, and M. Godet of CNAM. The bibliography provides a basic document prepared by "Entreprise et Progrès."

Fauvet and Koch, who are long-standing practitioners in the field, describe both the general characteristics of, and the method for formulating, the company plan and the plans for units, departments, divisions, and subsidiaries. This process involves the issue of corporate culture.

The Five-Phase AFCERQ Strategy

The goal to be achieved is the *success* of the company in its conversion to total quality. This process involves:

- The balance sheet and performance data
- Competitive standing
- Assets and investments
- Resources
- The general atmosphere
- The management system
- The corporate culture

The challenge is to change all of these elements in a way that improves performance but preserves positive accomplishments. This strategy involves the entire company. In this undertaking, management is 80 percent responsible for the movement toward total quality.

Table 14-2 summarizes, in an intentionally succinct fashion, the five phases.

This strategy is based on experiences in France, using data compiled during a research project lasting several years.

**Table 14-2. The 5-Step (AFCERQ) Strategy for
Corporate Transformation in France**

1. Create Awareness
   Get a Commitment from Top Management

2. Analyze the Current Situation
   Prepare a Summary Statement of the Company's Status

3. Organize and Finalize
   Strategy, Prepare the Quality Improvement Plan (QIP)

4. Implement the QIP

5. Evaluate
   Begin Again

The five major phases are divided into secondary stages, using prudent step-by-step management. The company must invent and perfect its own strategy. I propose an exhaustive approach to this process, that can be adapted to any context and any situation. It is a checklist whose points are of unequal weight and importance but deserve to be considered. The cycle is *reflect, understand, organize, act, adapt, reflect.*

During the first three phases example and actions count. The last two phases are for action and adaptation.

First Phase: Creating Awareness and Commitment by Top Management

Creating awareness inspires action and provides information about the profound changes necessary in a company to clarify the direction to be taken. A top management that has understood this is aware of the direction the company must follow in order to better its performance. The term *performance* means achievement and success. Success itself is defined in terms of profitability and earnings. For a company with a sales volume of one billion, profits are not "10 to 30 percent", but "100 to 300 million dollars." This is clear and precise language. To make oneself understood, it is better to use a unit of measurement with which everyone, and particularly every general manager, is familiar – the franc.

One might then be able to say to a general manager: "Yes, the cost of quality in our company is currently $50 million per year. If you implement total quality, we can save half that! It depends on you!"

Simple, direct language is always conducive to thought and serious reflection. Do not accept statements such as: "That's impossible, we know what quality is; we produce only quality products." You must explain that the highest performing companies, with the highest profits, have already started down this road.

Other companies mean competition, and competition means internationalization of markets. It is conceivable that, in the future, protected enterprises and organizations will face competition by either domestic or foreign private firms. In any case, the need to change is not only an economic fact of life, but above all a corporate fact of life: employees demand improvements, changes, modifications, progress, and participation in every area.

The words of R. Drouin summarize these points: *"Quality begins with top management."* The same thought is expressed in Figure 14-1, whose caption is a Rumanian proverb.

Figure 14-1. Stairs Must Be Swept from the Top Down!

Evaluation of the Company

Top managers should assess the company's principal motivations and, in doing so, evaluate its status. This is not a diagnosis, but an assessment of the company's strengths and weaknesses in financial, economic, and corporate areas.

Financial evaluation

The financial evaluation should be based on the results from several fiscal years. Value-added is the preferable indicator, since sales volume is too vulnerable to parasites such as changes in prices or changes in the amount of subcontracting. Value-added is the only aggregate figure that indicates the relative significance of a company's activities.

J. F. Daigne, in *Dynamique du redressement d'entreprise (The dynamics of re-organizing a company)*, provides a detailed method for in-depth diagnosis, but the process described here requires only a general overview.

For example, in the financial area, the question could be asked: "Would we loan money to the company?" A simple response is provided by the "credit men" method, an assessment of banking risks which involves three aspects:

- Financial status   40 percent
- Ability and reputation of top managers   40 percent
- Analysis of the company's sector of activity   20 percent

Assessment of the first point involves using five weighted ratios based on a ratio for each type of activity. These ratios are determined by specialized organizations:

- R_1 = liquidity: (liquid assets and cash on hand)/(short-term debt)
- R_2 = indebtedness: (company assets)/(total indebtedness)
- R_3 = client receivables: (sales volume including all taxes)/(clients + notes receivable + discounted notes that are not yet due)
- R_4 = inventory rotation: (cost price of sales)/(average inventory at the cost price)

- R_5 = coverage of capital spending: (internal capital)/(value of net fixed assets)

The following formula is used:

$$R = 25.R_1 + 25.R_2 + 20.R_3 + 20.R_4 + 10.R_5$$
if R = 100: a normal situation

R > 100: a good situation

R < 100: a troubling situation

Economic evaluation

The economic evaluation is concerned with marketing operations and production facilities.

Environment. Since a company is a living microcosm of modern society, its president should stay informed regarding the following contexts:

- Institutional: relations with government agencies
- Political and union: industry practices
- Technological: monitoring of new patents
- Consumer: consumer protection
- Cyclical: on the domestic level and with respect to major economic decisions

Demand. A particular effort should be made to assess potential demand, its future trends, and the needs that must be satisfied, so that products may be appropriately adapted. Analysis of the sector/market/client segment and the portfolio of company activities should focus on the following points:

- Sector: characteristics and directions
- Market: qualitative and quantitative developments with respect to needs; the company's standing in the market:
  1. Brand name image
  2. The sensitivity of prices
  3. Market segmentation
- Clients: distribution of sales volume in relation to the number of clients, analysis of risks, and quality of clientele: loyalty, development, and diversification.

Marketing. Attention should be focused on:

- The distribution network
- The motivation of the sales force
- The motivation of sellers
- Control
- Promotion, advertising
- Adaptation to change
- Information and compensation systems
- The match between products and marketing system
- Marketing competitiveness and aggressiveness

Competition. Aspects to be inventoried include:

- The market
- Human resources
- Production facilities
- The marketing network
- The financial structure
- Policy: overall, product, price, distribution, communication
- Developments in the field: strategic orientation

Products. Evaluation focuses on:

- Analysis by activity or product: the age balance for products
- Product profile: adaptation to demand, competition
- Profitability
- Homogeneity of the product line with respect to technology, marketing, and price
- Market penetration for each product
- Research and development: capabilities, cost, results, future prospects

Subcontractors and suppliers. To be analyzed are their:

- Appropriateness to company needs
- Developments with respect to risks

Production. Particular attention is given to:

- Resources, policy, measurement criteria
- Production capacity and rate of use
- Production control (planning and inventory)

- Control of procurements and shipments
- Production costs

Other. This economic evaluation should include:

- Geographic location of assets; age of the company
- Decision-making authority
- Self-diagnosis of the management team: ability to manage
- Credibility vis-a-vis its operating environment
- Written/official/operational organization chart

Company Evaluation. Relate these to the corporate atmosphere:

- Dominant union: activity, nature of past demands
- Labor-management committee: level of activity, influence
- Analysis of company conflicts during recent years: the sensitivity of personnel, strikes, settlement of conflicts
- Labor market in the sector
- Participation and miscellaneous advantages
- Motivation
- Comparison with competing companies: staffing, salaries, work hours
- Career planning

Organization. This includes:

- Functions
- Responsibilities
- Staffing
- Production/marketing/administration: operational and functional organization
- Age pyramid

Managerial staff. The measurement criteria are effectiveness and ability.

Summary

Table 14-3 recapitulates the principal points of this summary evaluation. A rating of 1 to 5 should be assigned to each heading, where:

1 = far from an ideal situation: *radical and urgent improvement* is required

2 = *significant improvement* must be made without delay

3 = *moderate improvement* should be planned

4 = *slight improvement* is possible

5 = a desirable situation: *no improvement is necessary*

This method is not a diagnostic tool and does not serve to measure the effectiveness of the company or the person leading it. It makes it possible to discern various problems and functions as a complement to other sources of information. Evaluation of the subject headings is marked on a summary card by placing an *x* under each rating. These points are then joined by straight lines, thereby providing an overview of the situation at a glance. The lines toward the right are the strengths, and those toward the left are the weaknesses. This is an excellent group project for top managers of a company.

Understanding

Total quality management must be learned and understood. Remember that one of the gravest errors is to "believe you know." Learning is therefore a necessity in order to acquire the knowledge and methodology required to practice total quality on a daily basis.

Understanding is having a clear idea of the factors that cause the company to lose profits and the reasons the implementation of total quality is irreversible. For example, top management must begin training itself at the outset, and thereby serve as a driving force for change. Otherwise, those who are subsequently trained wonder why those above them in the organization are *not* trained in this method. The implication is that managers were unwilling to make the necessary commitment.

Perform a Preliminary Diagnosis

Choose an area or function in the company as the subject for a quick preliminary diagnosis. It is preferable to select an administrative sector or function. With the assistance of the principal interested parties, and working as a group, an approximate COQ can

Table 14-3.

Principal Headings	1	2	3	4	5
1. Financial Status • Level of activity • Profitability • Operating liquidity • Financial structure					
2. Economic Status *General Policy:* • Area of activity • Area of specialization • Objectives *The Company in Relation to its Markets* • Markets in which it operates • Brand name image • Competition *Business Methods* • Product policy • Pricing policy • Distribution policy • Sales policy • Communication policy • After-sales service policy • Information policy *Production Resources* • Production capacity • Technological level • Cost methodology • Production organization • Inventory management • Production staff					
3. Personnel and Organization • Top management team • Operational staff • Staff for specific functions • Organizational chart for operations • Organizational relationships • Delegation of responsibilities • Social atmosphere					
4. Constraints • External • Internal					

be estimated. This approximation should be reasonable and should include all the items set forth in Chapter 11. The important thing is to create awareness on the part of managerial staff by providing concrete examples. This process will obviously be more successful if the managers and assistant managers in the sector concerned are willing participants in it.

This phase is useful as a trial – a means of creating awareness and gauging approval and compliance.

The Quality Committee

Set up a quality committee and make it aware of total quality. The quality committee is made up of the top managers of the company, who should in no case send deputies. The leader of this committee, which should have no more than eight members (for reasons of efficiency), is the general manager himself. Another top manager should be named head of the total quality project. The members' tasks are to:

- Plan the quality improvement program
- Provide representation for their particular sector on the committee
- Represent the committee within their own sector
- Ensure that the decisions of the committee are implemented within their sectors
- Contribute to the creativity of improvement measures
- Meet frequently to discuss the total quality program, not product quality

The committee's role is not to resolve quality problems, but to ensure that the entire company initiates a total quality program. It is an organization for deliberation and for leadership of the total quality project.

The meetings should be brief. For example, a half-hour should be devoted exclusively to the program at each weekly, bimonthly, or monthly meeting. Subsequently, it is possible to make provisions for duplicating this quality committee at each plant and in each unit.

The Charter

Determine an initial direction and provide the basis for a total quality plan for the company. As was discussed previously, the company plan is a synthesis of the financial and corporate priorities of a company. The charter should set forth a challenge and demonstrate that the company has decided to change. The decision to initiate a total quality program and a formal commitment by top management are prerequisites for its preparation: it is a *total quality charter*. It is the medium for demonstrating the genuine and unswerving commitment made by top management, not only to personnel, but also to clients, suppliers, and the environment. It should include the *what* (the plan), the *why* (the policy), and the *how* (the values).

Some Advice

- Having an idea of what is being lost is necessary, but this knowledge should be used to achieve an appreciation of what the company actually has. Everyone should learn to think in a positive manner. Stop assigning blame.
- The use of existing data requires that it be evaluated.
- Put more emphasis on pertinent "critical" points than on completeness.
- Speedy action is necessary at the beginning.
- An initial approach must be made to the client regarding the total quality program. Though it is the client who pays, the client follows the advice of users, who in effect make the decisions.
- "Remember that the winning company manager never brandishes his weapons better than in a period of crisis." (E. Véron)
- Peter Drucker believes that managers should devote 90 percent of their time to diagnosis.

The following major instructions have been taken from an article by J. de Rosnay:

1. Organize yourself simply, but rationally.

2. Organize your time according to priorities.
3. Classify and plan actions to be taken as follows:
   • Urgent and important;
   • Urgent but not important;
   • Important but not urgent;
   • Neither urgent nor important.
4. Almost always delegate, always check
5. Criticize or compliment the actions of your employees, but never the persons themselves.
6. Do not confuse effectiveness with efficiency, activity with results, feverish effort with accomplishment.
7. Set realistic deadlines.
8. Never react in the heat of the moment, because 40 percent of what is troubling you never happens, 30 percent has already happened, 12 percent concerns health, ten percent miscellaneous worries, and 8 percent truly merits your attention: this is your personal Pareto analysis.
9. Think about the validity of certain laws:
   • *Pareto*: the 80/20 rule applies to documentation to be processed.
   • *Murphy*: nothing is as simple as it seems. Anything that can go wrong will go wrong.
   • *Douglass*: the more orderliness there is, the more documentation piles up.
10. Acquire a new corporate attitude:
    • Have solid management ideas
    • Have the ability to forge a team and "team" spirit
    • Know how to do well what you know how to do
11. Be aware that "nothing will be as it was before." Figure 14-2 provides Itoh's diagram, which was cited by Juran and which shows that, once a total quality program is initiated, time is no longer allocated as it was before.
12. The number of people who complain that they don't have time is on the increase. (The time lost in *saying* that time is being lost is considerable in itself.) Indeed, lack of time is a crucial problem for some of today's top managers. Professional performance is the result of rational organization, which includes setting aside intervals for reflection and one's personal life. Here are several rules for saving time:

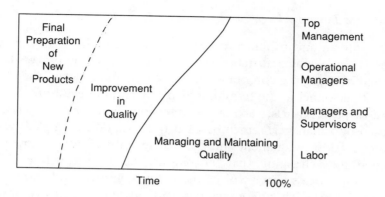

Figure 14-2. Allocation of Time: ITOH Diagram

- Set clear priorities
- Concentrate on the essential
- Know what you want
- Plan your ideas and actions
- Do not forget anything
- Manage and control unforeseeable circumstances
- Know how to be available
- Be punctual
- Improve team work
- Relax and eliminate stress
- Set aside calm moments for reflection
- Respect other people's time

Second Phase: Analyze the Current Situation and Prepare a Summary Statement of the Company's Status

Train the Quality Committee

All members of top management's quality committee, and of the quality committees for plants, units, and so on, must be trained in total quality. This can be an opportunity for making use of turnaround training, subdividing this effort internally in the case of large companies.

Mobilize Personnel

Inform and mobilize personnel: How should this be done? The entire managerial staff should be trained and the process continued by using the corporate chain of command to adapt the training of personnel to the terminology of the corporate culture. In the case of professionals, each training session should be opened and closed by a manager: remember that to set a good example is what counts. Top management and the managerial staff must show that something is changing, that "nothing will be as it was before." This is a long process that involves the entire company and should be carried out with perseverance and, above all, enthusiasm. Enthusiasm can be communicated. The charter is there to indicate the general direction. Top management and the managerial staff should be totally committed. Progress will be made by means of behaviors that are developed and demonstrated.

The aim here is to "whet appetites," calm initial misgivings, provide a preliminary idea of what total quality is, and prepare personnel to measure COQ.

Identify the Actors

The actors could be divisions, functions, departments, units, and so on. During training of the managerial staff, it should be possible to note instances of good will and appeal for voluntary cooperation. At the beginning, there may be incredulous and even hostile individuals. Do not try too hard to convince them, and do not coerce them. Take advantage of the training period to seek out examples of successful improvements – put all the trump cards on the table.

The aim of total quality is evolution, not revolution. Nevertheless, it can be explained in terms of a Leninist strategy, later simplified by Trotsky, based on the simple metaphor of a freight train. In a company as a whole, approximately:

8 to 12 percent of the staff are *locomotives*   (+ +)
20 to 30 percent of the staff are *tenders*   (+)
50 to 70 percent of the staff are the *silent mass* of railroad cars (0)

2 to 3 percent of the staff are *brakes* $(-)$
1 percent of the staff are *stars* $(--)$

To carry out a successful revolution, the theory goes, it is best to take several locomotives, organized in small teams, that will create epiphenomena by means of small individual actions that are illicit but successful. This is a challenge to established authority. The persistence of "brilliant feats," supported and supplied by tenders that provide covert publicity, is termed "poisoning." The railroad cars maintain their silence. Doubt is created and they ask each other: who is right? Who is in power? Who is issuing the challenge? The silent mass increases if the phenomenon persists; it is even prepared to support a new source of authority and new rights. In a revolution, it is at this stage that subversion occurs, and power is assumed by someone from the outside. If the phenomenon becomes more widespread and no one has assumed power, there is the risk that a charismatic figure will take power.

In the case of total quality, however, gradual progress – not revolution – is desirable, but power remains the same.

Use the locomotives, hitch up the tenders to them, and give them the opportunity to achieve brilliant feats on the journey toward total quality. The silent mass will grow in this case as well, but it will be trained and informed of top management's satisfaction in seeing these measures succeed. There is a good chance that this mass not only will follow, but even will advance at a rapid pace. The brakes will no doubt continue to exert pressure, but they will be drawn along anyway: such is human nature. As for the stars, they are individualists and will remain so.

This discussion demonstrates not only the importance of the involvement of top management in directing and channeling the move toward total quality, but also the importance of actions and example. There will be no revolution, but rather a successful evolution.

In summary, identifying the actors is accomplished by seeking out the locomotives and tenders, ignoring the brakes and stars, and making a serious effort to inform the railroad cars of the success achieved. In short, volunteers must be sought out, helped to succeed, and publicized.

Measurement System

Finalize the system for measuring quality and the cost of quality. Two concepts are involved under this heading: indicators (Chapter 8) and COQ (Chapters 6 and 11). Bear in mind that initially simplicity is preferable to exhaustive completeness. What counts is being able to show that plans have been implemented.

Measurement of COQ

Inform and prepare the principal actors for diagnosis based on measurement of COQ. There must be teams whose task it is to "weed out" problems in order to arrive at a gross approximation of the company's COQ. This task is more complex than is generally thought, because only the broad general parameters – which will be used as a reference in future years – should be established. This may be accomplished by function or by process, but with a single idea in mind: setting priorities rather than achieving a precise assessment. At this stage, the number of assessment team leaders to be trained, or the number of managers to conduct the assessment, should be determined.

Assess the Company's Status

Conduct an analysis of the situation and assess the status of the firm. Since the preceding phase covers strategy, the training of assessment teams, and the training of team leaders, in this phase a "consolidation" of costs should be performed. First, agreement should be reached regarding weighting, deficits, minimization, the information to be provided regarding the assessment, and other factors.

Since the consolidated COQ is not indispensable, emphasis should be placed on approximating it and using it to detect hidden potential. This is an important step in mobilization – one that requires time to do correctly.

Measure Priorities

Determine priorities by using Pareto analyses by plant, unit, function, and division. Pareto analyses are like policemen: they come in twos. In this case the two are conformance and noncon-formance. In addition, the indicators must be chosen. Their num-ber and dissemination should be determined: a maximum of two to three per division, function, department, and unit.

The priorities may be corporate (personnel, interfunctional problems), technological (equipment, materials, procedures), or competitive, but they always involve comparisons under each COQ heading.

Determine Corrective Action

Not everything can be achieved immediately. A choice must be made as to the corrective actions to be carried out. The most important factor is the number of groups that can deal with prob-lems. These groups will be informed as to priorities and deadlines (for example, three months) and it will be up to them to set realis-tic objectives (see Chapter 10). At this stage, the number of lead-ers and quality improvement groups to be initially trained is determined.

These initial corrective actions are the froth – the outward and spectacular manifestations. Everyone begins to see more clearly and to feel impelled to act. The implementation of measurement will enable the effort to begin and make it possible to record the progress of each person in his or her own unit, division, or sphere of influence.

Third Phase: Organize and Finalize Strategy and the Quality Improvement Plan

The first two phases involved a commitment by top manage-ment and the management staff. This commitment must now be extended to the entire company.

Completion of the Charter

Detail and explain the Total Quality Plan for the company. The charter has evolved, and a final, definitive version of it should be prepared and addressed to all employees, in accor-dance with company procedures. The training of management staff is practically complete, and each of them has had the opportunity to express an opinion regarding the charter, in which they will all participate. Their role is to explain to all employees the management's priorities, intentions, and desires with respect to the plan, values, and chosen policy. It is also their role to explain what will happen and how it will happen.

The Quality Improvement Organization

Set up an organizational structure for quality improvement, then allocate and commit the necessary resources. Quality should become everyone's business. This requires a streamlined organizational structure based on

- Leadership by internal groups that, function by function, can report to the quality committee and serve as the quality committees for their own sectors
- Coordination of actions under the direction of a project manager, who is assisted by facilitators from the quality control circles
- Problem-solving teams with trained leaders (a breeding ground for leaders within the company is an excellent undertaking)
- Teams that, in implementing the solutions recommended, may become involved in (active) prevention, as well as teams for failure mode and critical effect analysis, value analysis (all areas), and the like

Table 14-4 summarizes the characteristics of the principal work groups.

The motto for the quality improvement organization should be the words of Plato: "We cannot know truth if we are unaware of causes."

The preceding steps should be carried out slowly, with the effort distributed so as to make the best use of internal capabilities and the resources at hand.

The development of quality control circles has led companies to create a new position: quality control circle facilitator. This position is a full-time assignment when the number of circles exceeds 10.

Table 14-4. Work Groups

	Extraordinary Work Groups	Quality Improvement Groups (QIG)	Quality Control Circles (QCCs)
Purpose	Immediate correction of a problem	Subsequent prevention of problems	Permanent and ongoing improvements
Useful life	Limited	Long-term	Permanent
Timetable	Dictated by corporate management	Controlled by corporate management	Controlled by the circle
Participants and Leaders	Persons appointed on the basis of subject matter	Persons appointed and/or volunteers on the basis of subject matter	Volunteers who have a common interest
Decisions	Leader/ Consensus	Leader/ Consensus	Consensus
Method/ Tools	Unrestricted	Available	To be taught to them systematically
Implementation	By others, to be designated	According to priority, as a function of affiliation	By the members

The tasks of a facilitator are to:

- Inform the entire company about the quality control circle program
- Provide and ensure compliance with the rules of the game (the facilitator is the guardian of the quality control circle charter)
- Monitor and coordinate the work of the quality control circles
- Train members in working in a group setting, which entails introducing them to appropriate behaviors and communication skills
- Assist members in using quality tools (see Chapter 11) (correct use of these tools is the key to effectiveness in dealing with 95 percent of all problems)
- Advise the members and leaders of new quality control circles

- Maintain an open-door policy for providing information, meeting with experts, and other communication needs.

Total quality broadens this function to include coordination of all of the groups' activities. The facilitator may be trained in statistics and inspection. In addition to the above tasks, he or she should provide technical assistance to functional divisions.

The facilitator therefore needs to have experience with the company, experience in human relations, diplomacy, knowledge of tools and methods, and the acceptance of everyone at every level of the corporate pyramid.

The organizational structure for quality improvement therefore includes:

- One or several quality committees
- A project manager
- A facilitator
- Trained leaders at every level

Training

Organize and finalize quality training for all levels and implement the training plan. Table 14-5 summarizes the various types of training in terms of the actors and the various purposes:

- Information: know
- Training: understand, practice, master
- Training the trainers: encourage, train

In this fashion, training is disseminated throughout the internal structure of the company.

Training for persons in the company who are not quality professionals should follow this sequence:

- Training in total quality:
  - Priorities
  - Concepts
  - Requirements
  - The various phases of the method

This training should be performed at two levels that have the same content but different terminology.

Table 14-5. Total Quality: Information, Training, Action

	Top management	Senior Executives	Management Staff	Supervisors	Operator	Project manager, facilitator
Components of Policy and Strategy	+ + +	+ + +	+ +	+	+	+ + +
General Concepts	+ + +	+ + +	+ +	+	+	+ + +
Overall QIP	+ + +	+ + +	+ +	+	+	+ + +
QIP for Individual Units	+	+ +	+ + +	+ + +	+ +	+ + +
Measurement and COQ	+ +	+ +	+ + +	+ +	+ +	+ + +
Quality Measures and Tools	+ +	+ +	+ +	+ + +	+ +	+ + +

+ Know
+ + Understand, practice, master
+ + + Encourage, train

1. Training in leadership of quality improvement groups:
   - Methodology for problem solving
   - Anticipatory and active prevention
   - Tools and indicators
   - Leadership with respect to methods and tools
   - The training of others in tools and methods
2. Training of quality control circles:
   - The quality control circle concept and charter
   - The organizational structure: orientation committee, facilitators, experts, management staff, leaders, members, nonmembers
   - Problem-solving methodology
   - Tools
   - Publication of information, promotion, support
   - Follow-up, preparation of the final report, implementation of solutions
   - Presentation to top management

3. Training for leadership of corrective action teams:
   • Problem-solving methodology
   • Tools
   • Tangible and intangible COQ
   • Processes
   • Indicators
   • Surveys
4. Training in quality audits:
   • Total quality within the company
   • Audit principles
   • The various types of audits
   • Preparation by the audited party
   • Preparation by the auditor
   • Rating of suppliers

Table 14-5 above shows that not only are top managers, project managers, facilitators, leaders, and management staff all directly involved, but that, in addition, all personnel gradually become involved.

Figure 14-3 demonstrates that, if training plays a preponderant role, the attitude of the corporate hierarchy and the behavior of facilitators are equally significant causes of the termination of quality circles.

Initial Corrective Actions

Perform the first corrective actions. It is imperative to initiate the first corrective actions as soon as possible in order to use the results achieved not only for purposes of recognition, but also for training purposes. These are the most vivid and striking examples of what has been achieved, and should be publicized and explained. This is even more true when, under normal conditions, the cost of quality deficiency follows the curve shown in Figure 14-4. This figure shows three areas: people, management, and money. The spectacular improvement achieved at the outset is an indicator of the project's effectiveness. If this improvement does not occur, the involvement of top management and management staff should be reviewed and it should be determined whether the

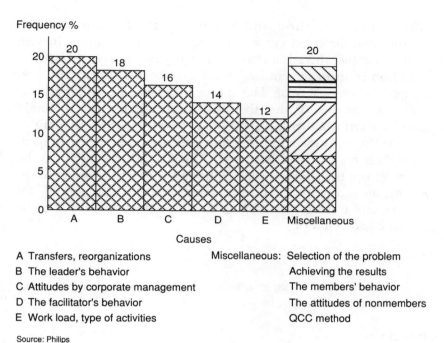

A Transfers, reorganizations

B The leader's behavior

C Attitudes by corporate management

D The facilitator's behavior

E Work load, type of activities

Miscellaneous: Selection of the problem

Achieving the results

The members' behavior

The attitudes of nonmembers

QCC method

Source: Philips

Figure 14-3. Causes for the Termination of Quality Control Circles

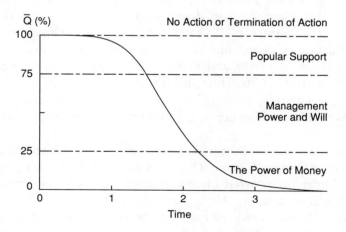

Figure 14-4. Power, Will, and Improvement in Quality

total quality method and requirements are understood. Throughout the entire curve, no progress is permanently achieved. If, for example, there is a change in management style or a demobilization of management staff there may be a return to 100 percent of the original total. This means that there are no longer any corrective actions, or that they have been interrupted. It should then be asked whether it is appropriate to continue the program.

At the third stage investment is necessary, but savings in quality deficiency can still be made. The necessary funds may be derived from the savings realized during the two preceding phases. Finally, the second phase shows that management is responsible for success, and it is up to management to maintain "pressure" by its example and behavior.

Recognition

Prepare a system for evaluating the results and giving personal recognition to participants.

Principles

Every result achieved, however minimal, should be evaluated. There are no small results. What counts is action and achievement. Quality deficiency must not remain like a rock that no one can budge: "Incessantly falling drops wear out rocks" (Choerilos de Samos, fifth century B.C.). Falling rain is nothing more than an accumulation of drops, just as "the rock" is nothing more than an accumulation of errors and failures. It will disappear if everyone contributes to its destruction. Each person inspires the next person to do even better, until the process becomes irreversible. The actions of group effort are not always immediately visible, but they are certainly effective.

To preserve this dynamic, companies should learn to *assign values* to accomplishments. This does not involve prices or money, but rather defining what makes an individual or group worthy of respect and admiration. *Merit* is an equivalent notion.

Recognition tends to reinforce behavior. "Winners" want to win more; losers also wish to "win" more, if they are considered "winners" by association.

"Recognition is a duty that must be fulfilled, but not a right that can be demanded" (Jean Jacques Rousseau). To put it another way, recognition is the expression of indebtedness one feels toward a benefactor – it is *gratitude*.

Everyone is sensitive to recognition, regardless of their rank or status.

Methods

Giving recognition and rewards presupposes knowledge (do not offer luxury cigars to a nonsmoker!). Top management and management staff must therefore make a distinct effort to become acquainted with people in the company. Recognition also requires that the initiator be capable of gestures that convey gratitude. Gestures and acts of recognition further demand that the initiator know how to play down his own status without losing his identity. Recognition is a dynamic process:

- Singling out and identifying
- Rewarding
- Remunerating

Recognition should be rendered at the appropriate moment, in appropriate circumstances, often, with small acts, not with important but infrequent actions. It can be accorded by peers, but an award should not be given by a manager outside the chain of command. It can be in the form of long-term benefits or gifts, rather than monetary awards. The recognition process requires a search for criteria that create a concrete model that is attainable by everyone, though with the awareness that any competition produces losers. It should be targeted and individualized, and should be an enjoyable event. Imagination and creativity should be exercised so that recognition and its outward manifestations may continue to evolve – it is a new operational aspect of the evaluation system. Thinking about recognition is indeed an act of prevention.

If recognition is commensurate with achievement, it accentuates differences and will produce significant results in functional areas (because practically nothing has been done there up to now), and much less noticeable results in operational areas (because they have been working on the problem for a long time). Poorly designed displays of information may create competition based on indicators. Care should therefore be taken that the slopes on graphs appear similar or that the indicators provide meaningful comparison.

Information systems for the results might be publications, awards ceremonies, gifts, work-related but prestigious training, advancement, prizes, bonuses, profit-sharing, or subtler means such as:

- Introductions to important persons inside or outside the company
- Social attentions (for example, an invitation to have coffee)
- Promotion
- Assigning the person to receive distinguished visitors
- Conveying compliments from clients or important people
- Giving recognition in front of peers
- Putting your initials or comments on a graph, diagram, or report addressed to the interested party
- Permitting the individual to present his achievements to top management
- Asking the advice of an individual with respect to a change in procedures or policy – taking him or her into your confidence
- Giving the individual more significant responsibilities
- Allowing the individual to make decisions regarding his work, organization, strategy, or projects
- Giving the individual a special assignment
- Granting prestige items such as title or special furniture
- Giving the person the opportunity to attend important conferences
- A letter of congratulations from the manager who is the individual's immediate supervisor, from the section manager, or from the manager of the activity
- Asking the person for his advice and opinion regarding the management of a project or the manner in which work should be done
- A verbal compliment
- A smile, a nod, a handshake, etc.
- Offering your assistance

- Placing the person's photograph on the bulletin board or in the company newspaper
- Placing an article regarding the individual in the company newspaper or in the local newspaper

This list, which is far from exhaustive, provides items often considered to be positive incentives. When used in the work environment, they reinforce desirable behavior. Find out in advance whether they will actually be appreciated – get to know the person better.

The discovery of the "presentation to top management" as a tool for quality control circles has indicated a direction that should be pursued. In mid-June of 1985, the first national convention of quality control circles at the Porte de Versailles in Paris brought together nearly six thousand people. No one who attended, from presidents to machine operators, has forgotten those two days of celebration. Many companies that have grasped the importance of recognition have quality award meetings at their own facilities.

Table 14-6 (provided by G. Stora of IBM) summarizes the sequence of indispensable criteria to be met by a quality improvement group before presenting its results to top management. M. Nemoto (1985) indicates three levels and the pertinent criteria for the presentation of projects by quality control circles in Japan. These will not be reproduced here, but they serve as a source for the following discussion.

Table 14-6. Elements of Presentation to Top Management (G. Stora, IBM)

- Plan
- Start-up Date
- Ending Date
- Principal (Group Leader)
- Functions of the Participants
- Analysis of the Problem (Pareto)
- Measurement of Quality
- Objectives
- Actions Taken
- Results
- Comments

In Japan, recognition is given not only through presentations to top management, but also through trips, shows, profit sharing, a display of all suggestions (good or bad), or other means.

The top management should be thinking now in terms of the following cycle: growth in personal effectiveness, increase in quality, increase in profits. If the company has nothing in particular to celebrate that is no reason to put off discussions with labor representatives regarding profit sharing. Such discussions are also a form of prevention.

The most difficult aspect of recognition is providing rewards for the creation of preventive measures, which constitute venture capital (Chapter 10). Recognition must nevertheless be given; moreover, there should be regular monitoring of their conversion into permanent improvements. The required risks should be taken, provided there is no threat to the safety of persons or property. In the latter eventuality, there is a legitimate need for further study.

Communications

Finalize the communication and information strategy for the quality improvement plan (QIP). The annual QIP should subdivide company priorities into priorities for each plant, unit, department, division, and even for each individual.

These priorities are negotiated through management of the two-way flow (bottom-up/top-down). Mutual commitments should be made on the basis of these directions and orientations. These priorities are not goals to be attained, but rather guiding elements of the quality improvement plan. To ensure that objectives are realistic, groups, teams, and individuals should themselves set concrete, quantified goals and, after having described their problems and constraints, set their own objectives. Only the size of objectives should be set, but in a realistic manner – in other words, everyone must be given the opportunity to win. *Total quality is based on success as the sole incentive.*

Measurement

Finalize the measurement system for quality improvement. The ideal is to arrive at individual indicators, which are consolidated in accordance with a consensus agreement reached by the persons involved. Remember that indicators pertain only to the reduction of quality deficiency. The true indicator is the dollar. Strictly speaking, percentages may be used, but it is better to use the number of errors or defects (Chapter 8). Basing indicators on causes rather than on effects is essential but difficult to achieve; it requires a great deal of creativity and, therefore, group work. Indicators for the prevention of causes of errors or defects should avoid mistaking effects for causes.

Control charts should be designed to monitor the reduction in quality deficiencies, and should serve as communications media. It should not be forgotten that indicators cover (internal and external) client satisfaction, personnel satisfaction, and mobilization (number of teams, quality improvement, or prevention work groups, month by month).

Fourth Phase: Implementing the Quality Improvement Plan (QIP)

The official launching of the QIP is an "event." It is an appropriate occasion for a congress, a convention, an "excellence" day, a poster campaign, or the adoption of a specific total quality logo.

Everyone should take part in a combination of mobilization, participation, and training (Figure 14-5). The company should express its own originality in an event that will subsequently become part of its corporate culture. How? This can only be determined on a case-by-case basis. Training may have made it possible for everyone to express how they would prefer to live at work. A team could be set up as a microcosm of the various functions of the company at different levels. The event must be shared and attended by the greatest possible number. The message is serious: for once, not only production is involved, but also research, development, purchasing, marketing, the personnel department – and why not several clients and suppliers, the press, and the media, too? The entire community should know that "things will not be as before." A collective decision like this strengthens commitment.

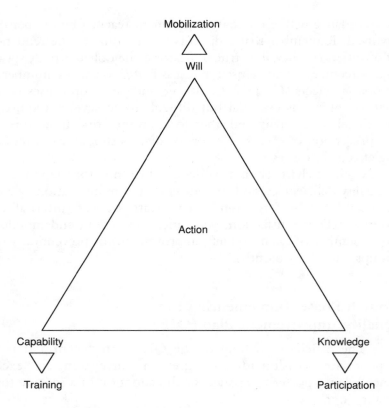

Mobilization

Will

Action

Capability

Training

Knowledge

Participation

Figure 14-5. Implementing QIP

Figure 14-6 indicates two different approaches: In the traditional approach everyone closely guarded what he considered to be his sphere of authority and delegated what he deemed to be within the capacities of his subordinates. Only one person in this diagram "has nothing else to do but" perform work. In the proposed approach, there is a desire to establish a system in which everyone has the right and duty to handle the problems at his own level. In doing so, he may be assisted by others who have the same interests (quality control circles) or by those who have complementary interests (interdisciplinary groups). In the traditional approach, a pile of problems accumulates at every level, so that each pile has another above and below it. In the proposed approach, there is a permanent and ongoing pursuit of problems in order to avoid such accumulations.

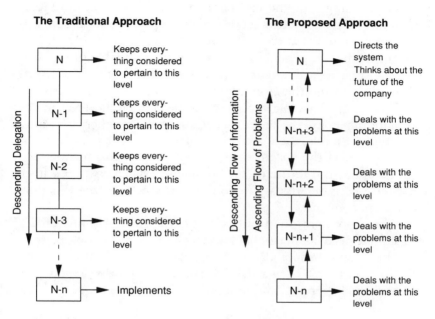

Figure 14-6. Two Approaches to QIP (E. Le Gouvello)

It is well known that when faced with an accumulation of problems, people usually deal with them in the following order: (1) those which interest us most and which we know how to deal with; (2) those which we know how to deal with; (3) the easiest, which must nonetheless be dealt with; (4) the most annoying, which we know how to deal with and which must be dealt with; and finally, (5) those which we do not know how to deal with.

Since there is never enough time in the day to do everything, we most often stop when we reach the most annoying problems – after the top part of the pile has been dealt with. The next day, the process begins again, and the problems on the bottom of the pile increase in number, some never to be dealt with. Indeed, it can be said that all chronic defects accumulate (Chapter 10).

With the new approach, several people set out to deal with one and only one problem at a time. Is their time wasted? No, because with one-hour meetings each week, for example, there is no risk of falling into the bad habit of ineffective "meeting-itis." One hour per week is less than 3 percent of our working hours. It has been demonstrated that we have been spending nearly 65 percent of our time in generating failures. Who is capable of organizing their time to account for every 3 percent of the total time? This method would therefore represent a gain rather than a loss.

When this principle is followed, the higher the level in the corporate hierarchy, the fewer ascending problems there are, until at the highest levels, there are no problems. All that remains to be done is to direct the system so that it operates in this manner and to think about the future of the company. Managers, freed from short-term considerations, can concentrate on their true function: leading the company.

The aforementioned publicity of the quality improvement plan should make all personnel aware of the change taking place in both the organization and in top management – it is the kick-off. It is an occasion to reward, give special emphasis, recognize, express formal approval, and mobilize.

Training For Everyone

The training of personnel is a massive effort that, over time, should make everyone aware of total quality and capable of employing the elementary tools of quality. The Japanese, who spent 25 years achieving total quality, proceeded no differently. Westerners should be able to move faster since we know what errors to avoid. For example, France spent less than four years creating 10,000 quality control circles, while Japan required 16 years to achieve the same number (Chapter 1).

Goals for Improvement

Figure 14-7 shows a cycle involving the two flows: The plan is an example of top-down, whereas mobilization is an example of bottom-up. This cycle dictates that challenges be given to the actors who have been assigned responsibility, who in turn respond with goals for improvement. These challenges are issued by top management, and the goals for improvement come from groups, teams, and individual persons. The management staff performs an essential role: it functions like a gearshift for the process, and must be adept in the art of compromise. This well-focused management system has internal improvement objectives that are determined by interfunctional processes. The skepticism and notions of good and evil inherited from the past have been eliminated.

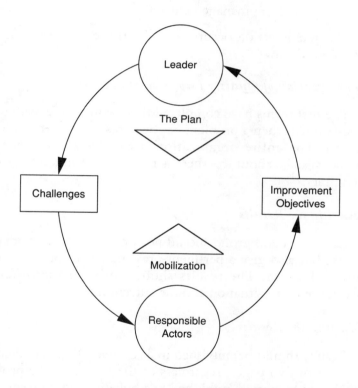

Figure 14-7. Interaction Between Planning and Mobilization within the Company

The management staff will imitate top management's style, as it did in the past. If top management demonstrates by its actions that it has changed, the management staff will follow suit. Indeed, personnel in general will imitate the behavior of the professional staff. This means that top management and the professional staff should have their own improvement objectives. The organization is like a fuel injection motor for which the fuel is:

- Commitment by top management
- Prevention
- Improvements
- Investment in training
- Pressure from management staff

This fuel injection occurs in a uniform sequence that is valid for every company.

Implementation of Quality Improvement Actions

The first teams have completed their work. Others are set up and disbanded when a problem has been resolved or the objective achieved. The entire organization resembles a beehive, but – make no mistake about it – there is no loss in productivity – quite the contrary.

Measuring the Results

Each team and group should not only prepare a summary of its work, but also give a pertinent presentation to peers, management, and so on. The results should indicate the difference between the initial situation and the current one.

Publishing the Results

Results should be published in a summary that is limited to a maximum of two pages, regardless of the nature of the problem. They should be posted, published in a bulletin, and, in some cases, formally presented to top management. In the latter event, they should conform with the criteria set forth in Table 14-6. The most outstanding results should be rewarded. Quality committees should have been trained in judging results so that they can identify the best. They may be assisted by an opinion poll conducted after publication of the results. The process should be expedited so that those who deserve a reward are not disappointed by delays. Remember that *all* results should receive recognition, but only the best should be rewarded.

Recognizing and Rewarding Individuals

This phase involves the implementation of the system previously established with respect to all of the results achieved. Remember that it is essential to make a success of this phase, which is both collective and individual: results must be tangible, visible, and appreciated by those who implement the solutions involved. For recognition to be effective, it must be serious, meaningful, and gratifying, not a cliché: "The world most often rewards the appearance of merit rather than merit itself" (La Rochefoucauld). True merit with respect to quality improvement and prevention should be rewarded.

Fifth Phase: Evaluating and Beginning Again

Making a Balance Sheet for the Annual Projects Completed

The term *balance sheet* is used here in a figurative sense: *preparing a final statement, and determining final results*. The final results are improvements made, gains achieved, the number of groups and teams in operation, suggestions, and proposed prevention measures. Certain results may be consolidated. The important thing is that everyone share in success. Remember that one of the principles of total quality is the *dynamics of success*. Successes should be identified and presented to peers so that they can adapt the results achieved to their own particular situations – ideas are shared. The balance sheet should be published, but without any excuses for "failures." The latter are often due to poor definition of objectives. Instead of praising employees for a job well (but not perfectly) done, managers must learn to be positive. Only in physics does positive repel positive. In human nature, *positive attracts positive*.

Extending the Quality Improvement Plan

The quality improvement plan should be reviewed for the following year, and all of the phases set forth earlier in this chapter should be repeated as per the Deming wheel. If the entire company was not involved in the initial phase because of lack of time, budget, or strategy, this is the occasion to finalize a strategy for extending the quality improvement plan to the other functions and units.

It is now possible to establish new directions – this is the second quality spiral (see Figure 4-9, pg. 57). While acknowledging that the first column of the Pareto graphs for nonconformance has sufficiently decreased (Fig 10-6, pg.171), the second column should be addressed, after there has been an investment in prevention, as evidenced in the Pareto graphs for conformance (Fig 10-7, pg.172). Since this phase also involves the inauguration of the program in new sectors, which should be trained if necessary, priorities should again be disseminated throughout the company so that each group and team may set its objectives.

Disseminate the Company's "New" Quality Culture through Networking

Networking was defined in Chapter 4. Presentations of results and internal events are part of the company's internal networking. Clients, suppliers, and subcontractors need to benefit from such experience. Since total quality must become a national movement that stimulates all of our business organizations, accomplishments and methods should be published externally, and others will do likewise. Stockholders, banks, and external credit institutions have everything to gain by this process, as do the external and internal brand name images. Other companies, whether competitors or not, need to know what is happening, and each company has everything to gain by this interchange. This does not mean that there can be any breach in confidentiality. Any company involved, since it understands that confidentiality is a commitment, will be discreet as it demonstrates its ability to achieve progress. Others contribute their comments, ideas, suggestions, and questions. Such networking can be extended to reports, courses, conferences, congresses, and symposiums. All these ele-ments contribute to recognition of the company and therefore promote its interests. Much can be learned by making a tour of France, as business representatives in former times did, but even more can be learned by taking a trip around the world. First-hand observation is best. One will acquire that much more information in an organized interchange. Networking should be both internal and external. In both cases, it is both horizontal and vertical. For example, external to the company, *vertical* means everything dis-seminated in the field of activity involved, whether upstream or downstream (field organizations, trade associations, distribution networks, distributors, buyers, etc.). *Horizontal* means any com-munication made by individuals (clubs for top managers, project directors, facilitators, group leaders, quality control circles, man-agers and facilitators who talk to quality control circles, managers, facilitators, and so on). On the regional or national level, net-working is a corporate function in which the AFCERQ can play a major role.

Setting New Improvement Objectives and Reinitiating the Quality Improvement Plan

The setting of new objectives, which each year will become more ambitious and more difficult to achieve, returns the company to the beginning of the total quality process. *Total quality is an endless series of beginnings.* It is a constant process of renewal, from the first phase to the last. Obviously, some points should not be repeated, but rather replaced by others. Little by little the process allows everyone to achieve *professionalism.*

How to Begin

An initial assessment must be made: what is the maturity of the company with respect to participatory structures and product quality? Service companies generally have no product quality inspection procedures, and, obviously, none will be instigated. On the other hand, there is no reason to believe that an industrial com-pany that has no experience with product quality can suddenly embrace total quality and use it as a remedy for all of its ills. The 1950s' touting of large computers as a panacea should not be duplicated. Corporate culture must inspire the will, not solely to improve product quality, but *to achieve progress through total quality*.

In every instance, whether service or industrial firms are involved, there must be a desire to set up participatory structures that suit the nature of the company. In addition to these structures, a certain rigor in the use of tools and methods must be accepted, without any false pretenses. Finally, there must be the will to push onward to *prevention*, which is the final systematic phase for the method.

Within the same company, it is not necessary that all facilities, units, or functions meet the prerequisites. The correct approach can be expressed through various strategies that are better understood by referring to Figure 14-8.

The best strategies, in descending order, are the following:

1. Formal agreements by top management and local management, and initiation of a total quality program in a sector in which there are quality control circles already in existence (1 + 3).
2. Formal agreement by top management, establishment of quality control circles, and initiation of a total quality program throughout the company (1).
3. Formal agreement by local management, support from top management, and initiation of a total quality program in a sector in which there are quality control circles already in existence (3).
4. Formal agreement by top management and local management, and initiation of a total quality program in a sector that has been specially prepared (1 + 2).
5. Formal agreement by local management, support from top management, and initiation of a total quality program in a sector that has been specially prepared.
6. Formal agreement by top management and local management, and initiation of a total quality program in two sectors, one of which has quality control circles (1 + 2 + 3).

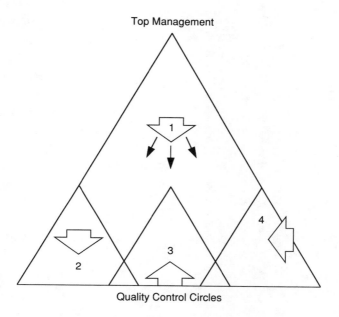

Figure 14-8. Possible Strategies — How to Begin

7. Formal agreement by top and local management, external constraints in one sector (competition, reorganization, plant renovation, a new product, etc.), and initiation of a total quality program after preparation (1 + 4).

8. Formal agreement by top and local management, external constraints in one sector, and initiation of a total quality program after preparation (4).

Selection of a strategy should be made on the basis of an assessment of the company sector by sector, as was explained in the first phase.

Bibliography

Argyris, C. *Participation et organisation* (Participation and organization). Paris: Dunod. 1974.

Archier, G. *Le soleil se lève à l'ouest* (The sun is rising in the West). Paris: Sodefir. 1981.

Archier, G., and H. Serieyx. *L'entreprise du 3 type* (The type three company). Paris: Seuil. 1984.

_____. *Les pilotes du 3 type* (The type three managers). Paris: Seuil. 1986.

Association Française pour les Cercles et de la Qualité Totale (AFCERQ). *Le livre blanc des faciliteurs* (The white book of facilitators). Paris: AFCERQ. 1984.

_____. *Les Battants de la qualité* (The doors of quality). Paris: AFCERQ. 1985.

Basile, J. *La formation culturelle des cadres et des dirigeants* (The cultural conditioning and background of top managers and management staff). Paris: Marabout Service. 1965.

_____. *Face a l'imprevisible, la renaissance du livre* (The rebirth of Pound Sterling in the face of unpredictability). Brussels: Editions Université de Bruxelles. 1968.

Bazin, R. *Développement personnel et entraînement mental* (Personal development and mental training). Paris: Entreprise Modern d'Editions. 1981.

Bernard, Y., and J. C. Colli. *Vocabulaire économique et financier* (Economic and financial terminology). Paris: Seuil. 1976.

Von Bertalanffy, L. *Théorie générale des systemes* (General systems theory). Paris: Dunod. 1973.

Blanchard, M. *Connaître et appliquer le Grafcet* (Knowing and applying Grafcet). Paris: Cépadues Editions. 1979.

Blanchard, K., and S. Johnson. *The one minute manager*. New York: Morrow. 1982.

Boeri, D. *Reduire les frais généraux* (Reducing general expenditures). Paris: Les Editions d'Organisation. 1974.

Boston Consulting Group. *Les mecanismes fondamentaux de la compétitivité* (The basic tools for competitiveness). Boulogne: Editions Hommes et Techniques. 1980.

Bouquerel, F. *L'étude des marchés au service des entreprises* (Market studies performed for corporations). 2 vols. Paris: P.U.F. 1975.

365

Cathelat, B. *Styles de vie: cartes et portraits—Styles de vie: courants et scenarios* (Lifestyles: Sketches and portraits). Paris: Les Editions d'Organisation. 1985.

Cegos. *Pratique des cercles de qualité* (Implementation of quality control circles). Paris: Editions Hommes et Techniques. 1982.

Chalvin, D. *L'entreprise négociatrice* (The company as negotiator). Paris: Dunod. 1984.

_____. *Autodiagnostic des styles de management* (Self-diagnosis of management style). Paris: Editions E.S.F. Entreprise Moderne d'Editions. 1985.

Chalvin, D., in association with Cegos. *Analyse transactionnelle et relation de travail* (Transactional analysis and labor relations). Paris: Editions E.S.F. Entreprise Moderne d'Editions. 1985.

Chalvin, D., et al. *Utiliser tout son cerveau—De nouvelles voies pout accroître son potentiel de réussite* (Using all of your mind). Paris: Editions E.S.F. Entreprise Moderne d'Editions. 1982.

_____. *L'expression des salaries, conduire, animer les reunions et y participer* (Performing as an employee: Conducting, leading, and participating in meetings). Paris: Editions E.S.F. Entreprise Moderne d'Editions. 1983.

Changeux, J. P. *Neuronal man: The biology of the mind*. New York: Pantheon. 1983.

Collignon, E., and M. Wissier. *Qualité et compétitivité des entreprises* (Quality and competitiveness in business firms). Paris: Economica. 1984.

Cremer, M., and B. Monteil. *Principes de management* (Principles of management). Montreal: Presses de l'Université de Quebec. 1975.

Crosby, P. B. *Quality is free*. New York: McGraw-Hill. 1979.

_____. *Quality without tears*. New York: McGraw-Hill. 1984.

Crozier, M. *La sociéte bloquée* (The blockaded society). Paris: Seuil. 1965.

_____. *The bureaucratic phenomenon.* Chicago: University of Chicago Press. 1967.

_____. *The world of office employees.* Chicago: University of Chicago Press. 1971.

Daigne, J. F. *Dynamique due redressement d'entreprise* (The dynamics of reorganizing a company). Paris: Les Editions d'Organisations. 1984.

Darbelet, M., and J. M. Langinie. *Economie d'entreprise* (Corporate economics). 2 vols. Paris: Editions Foucher. 1976.

Deming, W. E. *Quality, productivity and competitive position*. Center for Advanced Engineering Study. Cambridge: MIT. 1982.

Dossiers du savoir-faire (Information on know-how). *Comment lancer et animer des cercles de qualité* (How to launch and lead quality control circles). Strasbourg: Edition de l'Entreprise. 1983.

Douchy, J. M. *Vers le "zero-defaut" dans l'entreprise* (Toward "zero defects" in a company). Paris: Dunod. 1986.

Drucker, P. F. *The effective executive*. New York: Harper and Row. 1967.

_____. *New corporate management practices*. Paris: Editions d'Organisation. 1975.

_____. *L'entreprise face à la crise mondiale* (The implications of the international crisis for business firms). Paris: Inter Editions. 1976.

Dubreuil, H. *Le travail et la civilisation* (Work and civilization). 1953.

_____. *Promotion*. 1963.

_____. *Si tu aimes la liberté* (If you like freedom). 1965.

_____. *J'ai fini ma journee* (I've finished my day's work). 1969.

_____. Publications of the Hyacinthe Dubreuil Committee for the Development of Independent Corporate Teams, Paris.

Entreprise et Progres (Paris). *Le projet d'entreprise* (Company plan). July 1984.

Fauvet, J. C. *Traiter les tensions et les conflits sociaux* (Dealing with corporate tensions and conflicts). Paris: Les Editions d'Organisation. 1975.

Fauvet, J. C. and X. Stefani. *La socio-dynamique* (Corporate dynamics). Paris: Les Editions d'Organisation. 1983.

Favrod, C. J. *L'economie* (Economics). Paris: Edma. 1976.

_____. *Les evenements du XX siecle* (The events of the twentieth century). Paris: Edma. 1978.

_____. *Les idees du XX siecle* (The ideas of the twentieth century). Paris: Edma. 1978.

Fayol, M. *General industrial management*. Belmont: D. S. Lake. 1987.

Feigenbaum, A. V. *Total quality control*. New York: McGraw-Hill. 1983.

_____. *Total quality control*. 3d ed. New York: McGraw-Hill. 1961.

_____. *Comment appliquer le controle total de la qualité* (How to implement total quality control). Paris: Editions de l'Entreprise, S.A. 1985.

Fey, R., and J. M. Gogue. *La maitrise de la qualité* (Quality management). Paris: Les Editions d'Organisation. 1981.

Fourastie, J. *Les trente glorieuses* (The thirty glorious years). Paris: Fayard. 1979.

Fourastie, J., and B. Bazil. *Pourquoi les prix baissent* (Why prices decrease). Paris: Hachette. 1984.

Gaudin, T. *L'ecoute des silences* (Listening to silences). Collection 10/18. Paris: Christian Bourgois Editeur. 1978.

_____. *Les dieux interieurs* (Internal gods). Paris: Editions Cohérences. 1985.

Gelinier, O. *Nouvelle direction de l'entreprise* (The new corporate management). Paris: Editions Hommes et Techniques. 1979.

_____. *Morale de la compétitivité* (The ethics of competitiveness). Paris: Editions Hommes et Techniques. 1981.

_____. *Strategie d'entreprise et motivation des hommes* (Corporate strategy and personnel motivation). Paris: Editions Hommes et Techniques. 1982.

Germa, P. *Depuis quand?* (Since when?). Paris: France Loisirs. 1982.

Godet, M., and J. Desourne. *La fin des habitudes* (The purpose of habits). Paris: Seghers. 1985.

Gruere, J. P., et al. *Optimisation des ressources humaines dans l'entreprise* (Making optimal use of human resources within a company). Paris: Editions ESF, Entreprise Moderne d'Editions. 1984.

Hertzberg, F., et al. *The motivation to work*. New York: John Wiley & Sons Inc. 1959.

Hertzberg, F. *Le travail et la nature de l'homme* (Work and the nature of man). Paris: Entreprise Moderne d'Editions. 1974.

Hougron, T. *L'analyse de la valeur* (Value analysis). Paris: Eyrolles. 1978.

IAE. *La qualité dans l'entreprise* (Quality within a company). Paris: Les Editions d'Organisation. 1985.

Ifrah, G. *From one to zero: A universal theory of numbers.* New York: Penguin. 1987.

Ishikawa, K. *Le T.Q.C. ou la qualité Japonaise* (TQC or Japanese quality). Paris: AFNOR-Gestion. 1981.

_____. *La gestion de la qualité (Outils et applications pratiques)* (Quality management [tools and practical applications]). Collection "Dunod Entreprise." Paris: Bordas. 1984.

_____. *What is total quality control? The Japanese Way.* New York: Prentice-Hall. 1985.

_____. *Manuel practique de gestion de la qualité* (A practical manual for quality management). Paris: AFNOR-Gestion. 1986.

Javeau, C. *L'enquête par questionanaire* (Surveys using questionaires). Brussels: Editions de l'Université de Bruxelles. 1972.

Joannis, M. H. and G. Dehove. *De l'etude de motivation à la creation publicitaire et a la promotion des ventes* (A study of motivation in the creation of advertising and sales promotion). Paris: Dunod. 1973.

Joineau, C. *L'analyse de la valeur* (Value analysis). Paris: Entreprise Modern d'Editions. 1976.

Juran, J. M., and F. M. Gryna. *Quality planning and analysis.* 2d ed. New York: McGraw-Hill. 1979.

_____. *Quality control handbook.* 3d ed. New York: McGraw-Hill. 1984.

Juran, J. M. *Juran on planning for quality.* New York: Free Press. 1987.

Kaufmann, A., et al. *L'inventique.* Paris: Entreprise Moderne d'Editions. 1970.

Koestler, A. *Les somnambules* (The sleepwalkers). Paris: Calmann-Levy. 1960.

_____. *Le cri d'Archimède* (The cry of Archimedes). Paris: Calmann-Levy. 1965.

_____. *Le cheval dans la locomotive* (The horse in the locomotive). Paris: Calmann-Levy. 1968.

_____. *Janus.* Paris: Calmann-Levy. 1978.

Laborit, H. *Les comportements* (Behavior). Paris: Masson. 1973.

_____. *L'homme imaginant* (Human imagination). Coll. 10/18. Paris: Christian Bourgois Editeur. 1974.

_____. *L'inhibition de l'action* (Inhibition of action). Paris: Masson. 1979.

Langevin, J. L., et al. *La direction participative par objectif* (Participatory management by objective). Quebec: Les Presses de l'Université de Laval. 1979.

Le Boeuf, H. *Techniques de commercialisation* (Marketing techniques). 4 vol. Paris: Foucher. 1974.

Lemaitre, P., and J. F. Begouën-Demeaux. *Pratique d'organisation des services administratifs* (Organizations practices in administrative departments). Paris: Les Editions d'Organisation. 1982.

Lesourne, J. *L'entreprise et ses futurs* (The company and its future). Paris: Masson. 1985.

De Ligny, G. *Maitriser vos frais généraux et tous vos coûts indirects* (Managing your general expenditures and all your indirect costs). Paris: Editions Hommes et Techniques. 1981.

Likert, R. *The human organization: Its management and value.* New York: McGraw-Hill. 1967.

_____. *Le gouvernement participatif de l'entreprise* (Participatory company management). Paris: Gauthier Villars. 1974.

Limbos, E. *Les barrages personnels dans les rapports humains* (Personal obstacles in human relationships). Paris: E.S.F., Entreprise Moderne d'Editions. 1984.

Litaudon, M. *Memento de l'analyse de la valeur* (Value analysis handbook). Paris: Les Editions d'Organisation. 1980.

MacGregor, D. *The human side of enterprise.* New York: McGraw-Hill. 1960.

Maier, N. R. F. *Prise collective de decision et direction des groupes* (Collective decision-making and group management). Paris: Editions Hommes et Techniques. 1964.

Marrow, A. J., et al. *Management by participation.* New York: Harper & Row. 1965.

Maslow, A. H. *Motivation and personality.* New York: Harper & Brothers. 1954.

Merese, J. *Approche systemique des organisations* (A systems approach to organizations). Paris: Editions Hommes et Techniques. 1979.

Monteil, B., et al. *Les cercles de qualité et de progrès* (Quality control circles and progress). Paris: Les Editions d'Organisation. 1983.

Monteil, B., et al. *Les outils des cercles et de l'amélioration de la qualité* (Tools for quality improvement circles). Paris: Les Editions d'Organisation. 1985.

Moreau, R. *Ainsi naquit l'informatique* (How data processing began). Paris: Dunod. 1982.

Morin, P. *Le developpement des organisations* (The development of organizations). Paris: Dunod. 1982.

Mucchielli, A. *Psychologie de la relation d'autorite* (The psychology of the authority relationship). Paris: Edition E.S.F., Entreprise Moderne d'Editions. 1977.

Nemoto, M. *Total quality control for management.* New York: Prentice-Hall. 1987.

Nicolas, P., and J. Mortemard de Boisse. *La gestion du temps* (Time management). Paris: Les Editions d'Organisation. 1984.

Nicollet, J. L., and J. Celier. *La fiabilité humaine dans l'entreprise* (Human reliability in a company). Paris: Masson. 1985.

Ortsman, O. *Changer le travail* (Changing work). Paris: Dunod Entreprise. 1974.

Osborn, A. F. *L'imagination constructive* (Constructive imagination). Paris: Dunod Entreprise. 1974.

Ouchi, W. G. *La theorie Z* (Theory Z). Paris: Interéditions. 1982.

Papin, R. *Le directionnaire* (Management dictionary). Paris: Dunod. 1985.

Parkinson, C. N. *Les lois de Parkinson* (Parkinson's laws). Paris: Robert Lafont. 1979.

Pearson, E. S., and H. O. Hartely. *Biometrika, Tables for Statisticians.* 2d ed. Vol. 1. New York: Cambridge University Press. 1958.

Perigord, M. *Un outil de pilotage pour l'amelioration de la qualité totale* (A management tool for improvement in total quality). AFCERQ technical handbook. no. 2. Paris: AFCERQ. 1985.

Peters, T., and R. Watermann. *In search of excellence.* New York: Harper & Row. 1982.

Peters, T., and N. Austin. *The passion for excellence.* New York: Random House. 1985.

Petitdemange, C. *La maitrise de la valeur* (Value management). Paris: AFNOR-Gestion. 1985.

Raveleau, G. *Les cercles de qualité français* (French quality control circles). Paris: Entreprise Moderne d'Editions. 1985.

Roustang, G. *Le travail autrement* (How work can be different). Paris: Bordas. 1982.

Sauvy, A. *La machine et le chômage* (The machine and unemployment). Paris: Dunod. 1980.

Schonberger, R., and Ch. Moisy. *Japanese manufacturing techniques: Nine little lessons in simplicity.* New York: Free Press. 1980.

Serieyx, H. *Mobiliser l'intelligence de l'entreprise* (Mobilizing the company's brainpower). Paris: Entreprise Moderne d'Editions. 1982.

Shewhart, A. W. *The economic control of quality of manufacturing product.* New York: Van Nostrand. 1931.

Shingo, S. *Maîtrise de la production et methode Kanban* (Production management and the kanban method). Paris: Les Editions d'Organisation. 1983.

Stora, G., and J. Montaigne. *La qualité totale dans l'entreprise* (Total quality in a company). Paris: Les Editions d'Organisation. 1986.

Tardieu H., et al. *La méthode Merise* (The Merise method). 2 vols. Paris: Les Editions d'Organisation. 1985.

Tassinari, R. *Le rapport qualité/prix* (The quality/price ratio). Paris: Les Editions d'Organisation. 1985.

Taylor, F. W. *Principles of scientific management.* New York: Norton. 1967.

Thelliez, S., and J. M. Toulotte. *Grafcet et logique industrielle programmée* (Grafcet and industrial programmed logic). Paris: Eyrolles. 1982.

Vandeville, P. *Gestion de controle de la qualité* (Management of quality control). Paris: AFNOR-Gestion. 1985.

Veron, E. *Pour s'en sortir* (How to overcome difficulties). Paris: Editions Albin Michel. 1984.

Vigier, M. *Methodes d'assurance qualité—fiabilité et d'expérimentation* (Quality assurance methods—Reliability and experimentation). Collection "Université de Compiègne." Paris: Maloine. 1981.

Vogel, E. F. *Japan as number one: Lessons for America.* Cambridge: Harvard University Press. 1979.

Volle, J. *Comment les Japonais qui produisaient mal produisent-ils maintenant trop bien?* (How do the Japanese, who used to produce such bad products, now produce such good products?). Paris: Editions Hommes et Techniques. 1982.

Weiss, D., and P. Morin. *Pratique de la fonction personnel, le management des ressources humaines* (Personnel practices and human resources management). Paris: Les Editions d'Organisation. 1982.

Index

Total quality *(cont.)*
  and human relationships, 154,
    157
  and measurement, 117
  current status in, 310-14
  goal of, 69
  movement toward, 37-57
  tools for achieving, 249-99
  two flows of, 306-9
Total quality control (TQC), 4, 6
Total quality management (TQM),
    3-8, 161-98
Toyota Motor Company, 311
Training, 48, 51, 112, 148-49, 276-
    77, 285, 344-46, 356
Transformation, geopolitical, 39-40
Truman, Harry, 4
Trust, and authority, 131

United States, 3-4
  quality control circles in, 6, 37
United States Army, 177, 179
United States Department of
    Defense (DOD), 261
User, 19, 61

Vachette, J. L., 321-22
Value, definition of, 20
Value-added, 211, 328
Value analysis, 257-66
Vandeville, P., 273
Veblen, Thorstein, 63
Verification. *See* Evaluation
Veron, E., 335
Vertical external control, 99

Waste, 67, 69
Waterman, R., 314
Watson, Thomas J., 323
Wikins, A. L., 321
Work-in-process (WIP) inventory,
    182-83

Zarouk, Claude, 29
Zero, 105-7
Zero-defect philosophy, 166, 182

OTHER BOOKS ON QUALITY

Productivity Press publishes and distributes materials on continuous improvement in productivity, quality, customer service, and the creative involvement of all employees. Many of our products are direct source materials from Japan that have been translated into English for the first time and are available exclusively from Productivity. Supplemental products and services include newsletters, conferences, seminars, in-house training and consulting, audio-visual training programs, and industrial study missions. Call 1-800-274-9911 for our free book catalog.

Quality Function Deployment
Integrating Customer Requirements into Product Design
Yoji Akao (ed.)

This casebook introduces the concept of quality deployment as it has been applied in a variety of industries in Japan. The materials include numerous case studies illustrating QFD applications. Through methodology and case studies the book offers insight into how Japanese companies identify customer requirements and describes how to translate customer requirements into qualified quality characteristics, and how to build them into products and services.
ISBN 0-915299-41-0 / 400 pages / $ 75.00 / Order code QFD-BK

Handbook of Quality Tools
The Japanese Approach
Tetsuichi Asaka and Kazuo Ozeki (eds.)

The Japanese have stunned the world by their ability to produce top quality products at competitive prices. This comprehensive teaching manual, which includes the 7 traditional and 5 newer QC tools, explains each tool, why it's useful, and how to construct and use it. Information is presented in easy-to-grasp language, with step-by-step instructions, illustrations, and examples of each tool. A perfect training aid, as well as a hands-on reference book, for supervisors, foremen, and/or team leaders.
ISBN 0-915299-45-3 / 336 pages / $59.95 / Order code HQT-BK

Zero Quality Control
Source Inspection and the Poka-yoke System
Shigeo Shingo, translated by Andrew P. Dillon

A remarkable combination of source inspection (to detect errors before they become defects) and mistake-proofing devices (to weed out defects before they can be passed down theproduction line) eliminates the need for statistical quality control. Shingo shows how this proven system for reducing defects to zero turns out the highest quality products in the shortest period of time. With over 100 specific examples illustrated. (Audio-visual training program also available.)
ISBN 0-915299-07-0 / 328 pages / $70.00 / Order code ZQC-BK

Productivity Press, Inc., Dept. BK, P.O. Box 3007, Cambridge, MA 02140 1-800-274-9911

TQC Solutions
A 14-Step Process

JUSE Problem Solving Research Group (ed.)

Foreword by Dr. H. James Harrington

Here's a clear-cut, thoroughly explained process for putting the tools of quality control to work in your company. With a strong emphasis on the use of quality control in problem solving, this book was originally written as a handbook for the Union of Japanese Scientists and Engineers' (JUSE) renowned Quality Control seminar. Filled with practical, highly useful information, it shows you not only *how* to use the 7 QC tools, the 7 "new" QC tools, and basic statistical tools, but also suggests *when* to use them.
ISBN 0-915299-79-8 / 448 pages, 2 volumes / $120.00 / Order TQCS-BK

TQM for Technical Groups
Applying the Principles of Total Quality to
Product Development

Bunteru Kurahara, Kiyoshi Uchimaru, and Susumu Okamoto

This practical book provides a new perspective especially for technical groups working to achieve total quality in product development. Written in two parts, it first details the application of TQM methods to product design at NEC IC Microcomputer Systems, winner of the 1987 Deming Prize. It then addresses the process of TQM implementation in technical groups with emphasis on the role of corporate management and policy deployment (hoshin kanri). The case study provides an inside look at the trials, errors, and ultimate success of NEC's TQM program.
ISBN 1-56327-005-6 / 224 pages / $59.95 / Order code TQMTQ-BK

Management for Quality Improvement
The 7 New QC Tools

Shigeru Mizuno (ed.)

Building on the traditional seven QC tools, these new tools were developed specifically for managers. They help in planning, troubleshooting, and communicating with maximum effectiveness at every stage of a quality improvement program. Just recently made available in the U.S., they are certain to advance quality improvement efforts for anyone involved in project management, quality assurance, MIS, or TQC.
ISBN 0-915299-29-1 / 324 pages / $59.95 / Order code 7QC-BK

Productivity Press, Inc., Dept. BK, P.O. Box 3007, Cambridge, MA 02140 1-800-274-9911

COMPLETE LIST OF TITLES FROM PRODUCTIVITY PRESS

Productivity Press, Inc., Dept. BK, P.O. Box 3007, Cambridge, MA 02140 1-800-274-9911

Japan Human Relations Association (ed.). **The Idea Book: Improvement Through TEI (Total Employee Involvement)**
ISBN 0-915299-22-4 / 1988 / 232 pages / $49.95 / order code IDEA

Japan Human Relations Association (ed.). **The Service Industry Idea Book: Employee Involvement in Retail and Office Improvement**
ISBN 0-915299-65-8 / 1991 / 294 pages / $49.95 / order code SIDEA

Japan Management Association (ed.). **Kanban and Just-In-Time at Toyota: Management Begins at the Workplace** (rev.), Translated by David J. Lu
ISBN 0-915299-48-8 / 1989 / 224 pages / $36.50 / order code KAN

Japan Management Association and Constance E. Dyer. **The Canon Production System: Creative Involvement of the Total Workforce**
ISBN 0-915299-06-2 / 1987 / 251 pages / $36.95 / order code CAN

Jones, Karen (ed.). **The Best of TEI: Current Perspectives on Total Employee Involvement**
ISBN 0-915299-63-1 / 1989 / 502 pages / $175.00 / order code TEI

JUSE. **TQC Solutions: The 14-Step Process**
ISBN 0-915299-79-8 / 1991 / 416 pages / 2 volumes / $120.00 / order code TQCS

Kanatsu, Takashi. **TQC for Accounting: A New Role in Companywide Improvement**
ISBN 0-915299-73-9 / 1991 / 244 pages / $45.00 / order code TQCA

Karatsu, Hajime. **Tough Words For American Industry**
ISBN 0-915299-25-9 / 1988 / 178 pages / $24.95 / order code TOUGH

Karatsu, Hajime. **TQC Wisdom of Japan: Managing for Total Quality Control**, Translated by David J. Lu
ISBN 0-915299-18-6 / 1988 / 136 pages / $34.95 / order code WISD

Kato, Kenichiro. **I.E. for the Shop Floor: Productivity Through Motion Study**
ISBN 1-56327-000-5 / 1991 / 224 pages / $39.95 / order code SHOPF2

Kaydos, Will. **Measuring, Managing, and Maximizing Performance**
ISBN 0-915299- 98-4 / 1991 / 304 pages / $34.95 / order code MMMP

Kobayashi, Iwao. **20 Keys to Workplace Improvement**
ISBN 0-915299-61-5 / 1990 / 264 pages / $34.95 / order code 20KEYS

Lu, David J. **Inside Corporate Japan: The Art of Fumble-Free Management**
ISBN 0-915299-16-X / 1987 / 278 pages / $24.95 / order code ICJ

Maskell, Brian H. **Performance Measurement for World Class Manufacturing: A Model for American Companies**
ISBN 0-915299-99-2 / 1991 / 448 pages / $49.95 / order code PERFM

Merli, Giorgio. **Co-makership: The New Supply Strategy for Manufacturers**
ISBN 0915299-84-4 / 1991 / 224 pages / $39.95 / order code COMAKE

Merli, Giorgio. **Total Manufacturing Management: Production Organization for the 1990s**
ISBN 0-915299-58-5 / 1990 / 224 pages / $39.95 / order code TMM

Mizuno, Shigeru (ed.). **Management for Quality Improvement: The 7 New QC Tools**
ISBN 0-915299-29-1 / 1988 / 324 pages / $59.95 / order code 7QC

Monden, Yasuhiro and Michiharu Sakurai (eds.). **Japanese Management Accounting: A World Class Approach to Profit Management**
ISBN 0-915299-50-X / 1990 / 568 pages / $59.95 / order code JMACT

Productivity Press, Inc., Dept. BK, P.O. Box 3007, Cambridge, MA 02140 1-800-274-9911

Nachi-Fujikoshi (ed.). **Training for TPM: A Manufacturing Success Story**
ISBN 0-915299-34-8 / 1990 / 272 pages / $59.95 / order code CTPM

Nakajima, Seiichi. **Introduction to TPM: Total Productive Maintenance**
ISBN 0-915299-23-2 / 1988 / 149 pages / $45.00 / order code ITPM

Nakajima, Seiichi. **TPM Development Program: Implementing Total Productive Maintenance**
ISBN 0-915299-37-2 / 1989 / 428 pages / $85.00 / order code DTPM

Nikkan Kogyo Shimbun, Ltd./Factory Magazine (ed.). **Poka-yoke: Improving Product Quality by Preventing Defects**
ISBN 0-915299-31-3 / 1989 / 288 pages / $59.95 / order code IPOKA

Nikkan Kogyo Shimbun/Esme McTighe (ed.). **Factory Management Notebook Series: Mixed Model Production**
ISBN 0-915299-97-6 / 1991 / 184 / $125.00 / order code N1-MM

Nikkan Kogyo Shimbun/Esme McTighe (ed.). **Factory Management Notebook Series: Visual Control Systems**
ISBN 0-915299-54-2 / 1991 / 194 pages / $125.00 / order code N1-VCS

Nikkan Kogyo Shimbun/Esme McTighe (ed.). **Factory Management Notebook Series: Autonomation/Automation**
ISBN 0-0-56327-002-1 / 1991 / 200 pages / $125.00 / order code N1-AA

Ohno, Taiichi. **Toyota Production System: Beyond Large-Scale Production**
ISBN 0-915299-14-3 / 1988 / 162 pages / $39.95 / order code OTPS

Ohno, Taiichi. **Workplace Management**
ISBN 0-915299-19-4 / 1988 / 165 pages / $34.95 / order code WPM

Ohno, Taiichi and Setsuo Mito. **Just-In-Time for Today and Tomorrow**
ISBN 0-915299-20-8 / 1988 / 208 pages / $34.95 / order code OMJIT

Perigord, Michel. **Achieving Total Quality Management: A Program for Action**
ISBN 0-915299-60-7 / 1991 / 384 pages / $45.00 / order code ACHTQM

Psarouthakis, John. **Better Makes Us Best**
ISBN 0-915299-56-9 / 1989 / 112 pages / $16.95 / order code BMUB

Robinson, Alan. **Continuous Improvement in Operations: A Systematic Approach to Waste Reduction**
ISBN 0-915299-51-8 / 1991 / 416 pages / $34.95 / order code ROB2-C

Robson, Ross (ed.). **The Quality and Productivity Equation: American Corporate Strategies for the 1990s**
ISBN 0-915299-71-2 / 1990 / 558 pages / $29.95 / order code QPE

Shetty, Y.K and Vernon M. Buehler (eds.). **Competing Through Productivity and Quality**
ISBN 0-915299-43-7 / 1989 / 576 pages / $39.95 / order code COMP

Shingo, Shigeo. **Non-Stock Production: The Shingo System for Continuous Improvement**
ISBN 0-915299-30-5 / 1988 / 480 pages / $75.00 / order code NON

Shingo, Shigeo. **A Revolution In Manufacturing: The SMED System**, Translated by Andrew P. Dillon
ISBN 0-915299-03-8 / 1985 / 383 pages / $70.00 / order code SMED

Shingo, Shigeo. **The Sayings of Shigeo Shingo: Key Strategies for Plant Improvement**, Translated by Andrew P. Dillon
ISBN 0-915299-15-1 / 1987 / 208 pages / $39.95 / order code SAY

Shingo, Shigeo. **A Study of the Toyota Production System from an Industrial Engineering Viewpoint**
ISBN 0-915299-17-8 / 1989 / 293 pages / $39.95 / order code STREV

Shingo, Shigeo. **Zero Quality Control: Source Inspection and the Poka-yoke System,**Translated by Andrew P. Dillon
ISBN 0-915299-07-0 / 1986 / 328 pages / $70.00 / order code ZQC

Shinohara, Isao (ed.). **New Production System: JIT Crossing Industry Boundaries**
ISBN 0-915299-21-6 / 1988 / 224 pages / $34.95 / order code NPS

Sugiyama, Tomo. **The Improvement Book: Creating the Problem-Free Workplace**
ISBN 0-915299-47-X / 1989 / 236 pages / $49.95 / order code IB

Suzue, Toshio and Akira Kohdate. **Variety Reduction Program (VRP): A Production Strategy for Product Diversification**
ISBN 0-915299-32-1 / 1990 / 164 pages / $59.95 / order code VRP

Tateisi, Kazuma. **The Eternal Venture Spirit: An Executive's Practical Philosophy**
ISBN 0-915299-55-0 / 1989 / 208 pages/ $19.95 / order code EVS

Yasuda, Yuzo. **40 Years, 20 Million Ideas: The Toyota Suggestion System**
ISBN 0-915299-74-7 / 1991 / 210 pages / $39.95 / order code 4020

Audio-Visual Programs

Japan Management Association. **Total Productive Maintenance: Maximizing Productivity and Quality**
ISBN 0-915299-46-1 / 167 slides / 1989 / $749.00 / order code STPM
ISBN 0-915299-49-6 / 2 videos / 1989 / $749.00 / order code VTPM

Shingo, Shigeo. **The SMED System,** Translated by Andrew P. Dillon
ISBN 0-915299-11-9 / 181 slides / 1986 / $749.00 / order code S5
ISBN 0-915299-27-5 / 2 videos / 1987 / $749.00 / order code V5

Shingo, Shigeo. **The Poka-yoke System,** Translated by Andrew P. Dillon
ISBN 0-915299-13-5 / 235 slides / 1987 / $749.00 / order code S6
ISBN 0-915299-28-3 / 2 videos / 1987 / $749.00 / order code V6

Returns of AV programs willl be accepted for incorrect or damaged shipments only.

TO ORDER: Write, phone, or fax Productivity Press, Dept. BK, P.O. Box 3007, Cambridge, MA 02140, phone 1-800-274-9911, fax 617-864-6286. Send check or charge to your credit card (American Express, Visa, MasterCard accepted).

U.S. ORDERS: Add $5 shipping for first book, $2 each additional for UPS surface delivery. CT residents add 8% and MA residents 5% sales tax. For each AV program that you order, add $5 for programs with 1 or 2 tapes, and $12 for programs with 3 or more tapes.

INTERNATIONAL ORDERS: Write, phone, or fax for quote and indicate shipping method desired. Pre-payment in U.S. dollars must accompany your order (checks must be drawn on U.S. banks). When quote is returned with payment, your order will be shipped promptly by the method requested.

NOTE: Prices subject to change without notice.

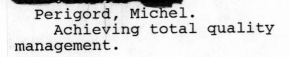

Perigord, Michel.
    Achieving total quality
management.